S0-DUT-751

# Talcott Parsons on economy and society

# Talcott Parsons on economy and society

Robert J. Holton
and
Bryan S. Turner

**R**

ROUTLEDGE
London and New York

First published in 1986
by Routledge & Kegan Paul plc

Reprinted 1988 by Routledge
11 New Fetter Lane, London EC4P 4EE
29 West 35th Street, New York, NY 10001

Set in Linotype Palatino
by Input Typesetting Ltd
and printed in Great Britain
by St Edmundsbury Press Ltd
Bury St Edmunds, Suffolk

© Robert J. Holton and Bryan S. Turner 1986
© Chapter 3 Roy Fitzhenry 1986

No part of this book may be reproduced in
any form without permission from the publisher,
except for the quotation of brief passages
in criticism

Library of Congress Cataloging in Publication Data

Holton, R.J.
    Talcott Parsons on economy and society.
    Bibliography: p.
    Includes index.
    1. Parsons, Talcott, 1902–        —Criticism and
interpretation.    2. Sociology—United States.
I. Turner, Bryan S.    II. Title.
HM22.U6P3747    1986    301'.092'4        86—629

British Library Cataloguing in Publication Data

Holton, R.J. (Robert John), 1946–
    Talcott Parsons on economy and society.
    1. Society. Theories of Parsons, Talcott,
    1902–1979
    I. Title    II. Turner, Bryan S. (Bryan
    Stanley), 1945–
    301'.092'4

ISBN: 0-415-03192-3

# Contents

**Nostalgia**
'A form of melancholia caused by prolonged absence from one's home or country.'
**Melancholia**
'A functional mental disease characterised by gloomy thought-fulness, ill-grounded fears and general depression of mind.'
(Oxford English Dictionary)

# Acknowledgments

This study of Talcott Parsons grew out of a series of public seminars from the Thursday workshop in sociology at the Flinders University of South Australia. We are grateful to the participants for the quality of their critical response which provided an important stimulus for this book. In particular, we wish to thank Dr Anna Yeatman who was one of the principal organisers and discussants in the sessions on Parsons. Her forceful presentation of Parsons' identification of the 'social' proved to be a major determinant of our conceptualisation of this project. Professor Bruce Kapferer also contributed a valuable paper on Parsons' analysis of the social system which influenced the course of this study. We are also grateful to Dr Roy Fitzhenry who has contributed a chapter on the debate between Parsons and Alfred Schutz.

We are particularly grateful to Kevin White who read the original manuscript and warned us against over-enthusiastic commitments. Ina Cooper and Susan Manser converted handwritten manuscripts into a readable text.

# Reading Parsons: Introductory Remarks

*Robert J. Holton and Bryan S. Turner*

# Introduction

It is an unfortunate feature of academic life that the death of an author is typically the occasion for a revival of his influence. Since the death of Talcott Parsons in Munich in 1979, it has become clear that a significant re-appraisal of Parsons' sociology and his impact on modern sociology is well underway (Münch, 1981; Holmwood, 1983a; 1983b; Alexander, 1984). Although few commentators would question Parsons' influence, there is massive doubt as to the value of Parsonian sociology. As Richard Münch has recently observed, while Parsons cannot be generally ignored, 'the conventional attitude toward his theory is one of critical aloofness' (1981, p. 710). Despite the abundance of texts on Parsons' sociology a comprehensive evaluation of his sociology sufficient to dissipate this stance, has yet to appear.

This volume on Parsons and the sociological paradigm may be appropriately regarded as part of this new wave of re-evaluation. At the same time, our aim is somewhat wider than to provide an exposition of Parsons' sociology. One of our underlying assumptions is that to provide an adequate justification and appreciation of Parsons' sociology is simultaneously to offer a defence of sociology itself. The importance of Parsons' work is that it attempted to outline in an unambiguous manner a map of the 'social'. This comprised both the defining of boundaries between 'society' and organic life, and the internal exploration of social relations between culture, personality, and social structure. Parsons' sociology can thus be seen as a quest for the sociological paradigm.

This study is not then yet another textual exegesis of Parsons's major works; it is not even an attempt to develop a uniform interpretation of the corpus of Parsons' sociology. There already exists a number of useful interpretations of Parsons (Black, 1971; Rocher, 1974; Adriaansens, 1980; Bourricaud, 1981; Savage, 1981; Hamilton, 1983). Interpretation and re-interpretation clearly have a place in the development of sociological theory, but they are not the overriding exercise or endeavour. As Alexander (1984) has recently implied in his important assessment of Parsons, the aim of theorising is ultimately with matters of application, extension, elaboration and comparison. The present study is offered in this spirit. The chapter on Parsons' economic sociology (chapter 1) is a particularly apposite example of this perspective. Here the argument is not primarily concerned to offer an exegesis of Parsons – although that clearly has to play a part – but to explore a range of areas for research where Parsons' approach to the boundary between society and economy has not been fully appreciated and followed up through empirical work. Similarly, the complexity of Parsons' medical sociology has not been adequately grasped. Parsons' contribution has been understood almost exclusively in terms of the concept of the 'sick role' (Parsons, 1951a). In this presentation of his medical sociology, the aim is to consider Parsons' complete analysis of medicine in relation to society, but also to use a Parsonian perspective to suggest further lines of research (chapter 2).

While this analysis of Parsons has sought to avoid a repetitious exegesis of key texts, it does not attempt to redress the present lack of an intellectual biography of his development. There have been attempts to locate Parsons' sociology in the context of American capitalism and intellectual life, but such studies so far lack authority because they are too general and unbalanced to command respect (Gouldner, 1971; Mills, 1959). An intellectual history of Parsons of the stature of Reinhard Bendix's classic work on Max Weber (Bendix, 1969) or Steven Lukes' study of Emile Durkheim (Lukes, 1973), has not as yet been forthcoming, although Jeffrey Alexander's recent work (1984) offers many pertinent comments in this area. Parsons himself has of course offered a useful autobiographical essay 'On building social system theory; a personal history' in *Daedalus* in 1974 which is reprinted in *Social Systems and the Evolution of Action Theory* (Parsons, 1977b). There are, in addition, a number of other reflexive articles by Parsons which are valuable in understanding the growth of his ideas (Parsons, 1964a; 1973a; 1981b). Since our own objective is to re-affirm the value and scope of Parsons sociology, we have not sought to locate Parsons in the context of an intellectual history.

This study also seeks to avoid the usual extremities of critical reaction to Parsons. In some sociological circles the term 'structural functionalism' is often an epithet of abuse, being associated with ideological conservativism, political naivety and bourgeois values. This critical epistrophe is widely adhered to amongst so-called radical sociologists. Since Parsons is held to be a central figure in the development of structural functionalism, he is held to be conservative, bourgeois and old fashioned.

Many of these attitudes can be traced back to C. Wright Mills' critique of Parsons in the 1950s. Given the authority of C. Wright Mills among radical sociologists, it is hardly surprising that Parsons' later sociology has often been ignored or neglected. There is a taken-for-granted assumption that Parsons did not advance beyond *The Social System* of 1951 and that C. Wright Mills' critique of the early Parsons applies to the whole. This critical treatment of Parsons is thus hardly judicious or scholarly. It is rather like giving a student Eugen von Bohm-Bawerk's *Karl Marx and the Close of his System* as an introduction to Marx and then telling the student not to read beyond *The 18th Brumaire of Louis Bonaparte* since Marx's subsequent work was wholly a reproduction of his earliest notes on class exploitation. It would be generally agreed that such a student would have a somewhat peculiar appreciation of Marx's sociology as a whole. Yet in the case of writers like Parsons such lop-sided interpretations appear to have very wide currency. It is generally held that an adequate reading of an author requires considerable sophistication, because texts have many levels and layers. Although writers like Karl Marx have been afforded the luxury of such elaborate inquiry (Althusser and Balibar, 1970), writers like Max Weber (Turner, 1977) and Talcott Parsons have often been interpreted in the most one-sided and superficial manner. It is, however, interesting that in recent years a more comprehensive interpretation of the complete works of Parsons is beginning to replace the conventional critique. For example, recent re-appraisals of Parsons' contribution to the sociology of religion (Robertson, 1982b) are hopefully indicative of a more balanced and systematic reading of his sociology.

## A critical defence of Parsons

It is now almost obligatory that most reviews or assessments of Parsons commence with the question 'Who now reads Parsons?' (Bryant, 1983) which reflects on the opening passages of *The Structure of Social Action* where Parsons, quoting from Crane Brinton's *English Political Thought in the Nineteenth Century*, suggested that nobody now reads Herbert Spencer. The problem with any book on Parsons, at least outside the American context, is that we are dealing with an author who is both massively influential and also heavily criticised and rejected.

It is important to emphasise at the outset that a defence of Parsons need not be apologetic. While this study is founded on the presupposition that Parsons' work represents the major twentieth-century restatement of the sociological paradigm, it is not our intention to present an exclusively positive or uncritical evaluation. At various points in the text – as in the discussion of power in Parsons' economic sociology (chapter 1) or of the state and professions in his sociology of medicine (chapter 2) – problematic or inadequate features of his work are located. The predominant emphasis of the study is nonetheless sympathetic in the broadest sense both to Parsons' theoretical ambition and to much of the substance of his social theory. Given the widespread condescension and vulgar opposition that Parsons' sociology has generated, even a critical defence of this kind requires justification.

One simple but important defence of Parsons is to recognize that in almost every area of modern sociology he made some important and lasting contribution. It is, therefore, almost impossible to work in modern sociology without confronting and coming to terms with the Parsons legacy. There are a number of key examples which will serve to validate this claim. In the sociology of religion, Parsons wrote a number of essays which defined the scope of the sub-discipline and determined the contours along which it would develop. In particular, Parsons recognized better than most why the sociology of religion was important to the analytical development of sociology as such (Parsons, 1944; 1958h; 1960a; 1962k; 1963c; 1966e; 1967g; 1973a; 1974i). For Parsons, religion was one of those theoretical problem areas which are especially sensitive to the issue of reductionism and positivism. In the course of following this issue in the sociology of religion, Parsons was also able to focus attention on the significance of the anthropological contribution of writers like Bronislaw Malinowski and Emile Durkheim (Parsons, 1938a; 1981a).

There is also the prominent example of medical sociology where Parsons' concept of the 'sick role' played a crucial part in the development of a specifically sociological perspective on sickness. Other substantive areas of sociological inquiry where Parsons' influence has been significant would include the sociology of the professions (Parsons, 1939a, 1951d; 1952c; 1960a; 1969a; 1975c), the sociology of the family (Parsons, 1943; 1951a; 1953d; 1954d; 1955a; 1965c; 1971b; 1971d), the sociology of education (Parsons, 1959h; 1968h; 1968n; 1970i; 1972a; 1972b; 1973b; 1974a; 1976a) and the analysis of social stratification (Parsons 1940a; 1949c; 1953a; 1970g). While he has thus made a major contribution to the development of certain substantive fields in sociology, Parsons has been more commonly perceived in terms of his development of certain theoretical themes and problems in sociology.

Parsons' contributions to theoretical sociology can be considered under a number of headings. First it is important to remember that Parsons played a crucial role between the 1930s and 1960s in maintaining and promoting a commitment to classical sociological theory in an often unsympathetic American environment. It would be an exaggeration to claim that the American sociology Parsons first encountered was entirely confined to social journalism or descriptive survey research (Hinkle, 1980). It is the case, nonetheless, that Parsons' first major study *The Structure of Social Action* was launched in 1936 within a sociological context which was neither sympathetic to the idea of a general theory of action nor closely integrated with the European tradition of sociology.

Parsons was important in keeping alive a movement of analytical sociological theory and for providing a framework for the interpretation of early sociology (in the convergence thesis) which remains highly original and seminal. While this convergence thesis has been challenged in the recent move to 'de-Parsonise' the interpretation of the history of sociology it remains a powerful interpretation of the impact of residual problems on the transformation of theoretical paradigms. Parsons' interpretation of the early European sociological legacy has yet to be fully explored and completely assimilated by American sociology (Alexander, 1982).

Secondly, we obviously have to take note of the fact that Parsons' major contribution to modern sociology was to have identified and addressed the central analytical issues which face any general theory of social action. At this stage, we can simply list and comment on these major issues of analytical sociology. For example, much of Parsons' sociology centres on the question of agency and structure in sociological theory. Parsons has been accused of abandoning his action perspective in the *Structure of Social Action* for a deterministic systems perspective in *The Social System* (Scott, 1963), but it is clear that the issues of human agency and social action remained central to Parsons' sociology throughout his career (Holmwood, 1983b).

One of the abiding philosophical issues in Parsonian sociology is the Kantian problem of moral responsibility and the capacity for human choice (Münch, 1981). Indeed, the questions raised by Parsons' action schema have profound implications outside sociology, not only for philosophy, but for theology (Robertson, 1982b). In chapter 1, we attempt to show that Parsons' sociology does not imply the dominance of a coherent ideology or cultural system and his work is not premised on an 'oversocialized conception of man' (Parsons, 1962c). As Parsons pointed out neatly but simply, no human being is ever socialised into the whole social system and therefore deviance and 'strains' are endemic.

The general relevance of Parsons' treatment of the problem of action has often been neglected and Parsons' ongoing interest in the philosophical questions of *verstehende soziologie* has not received adequate attention. In chapter 3, we pay special interest to the exchange between Alfred Schutz and Talcott Parsons on matters relating to the importance of *verstehende soziologie*, that is to the role of interpretative procedures in sociological investigations. Premature and inaccurate characterization of Parsons as a 'grand theorist' of macro-societal processes tends to suppress Parsons' continuous interest in debates within the philosophy of social science relating to the problem of the 'meaning' of social action. While Parsons retained a long-term interest in Durkheim's contribution to the integration of social systems in terms of common values, he also maintained an active interest in Weber's contribution to the nature of social action – an interest which is illustrated by the exchange with Schutz over the role of ideal types, meaning and hermeneutic interpretations. The idea that Parsons suppressed the agency/ structure dilemma in his 'mature' work on social systems is wide of the mark.

One defence of Parsons is that his work represents one of the most sustained inquiries into the relationship between agency and structural constraint which we possess in modern social thought – an inquiry which is to be located within the Kantian problematic of phenomenal and noumenal worlds. In this collection of essays, we attempt to show the relevance of that debate with reference to the so-called 'sick role' perspective on illness. Parsons' conceptualisation of sickness raises in an acute form the question 'Do people choose to be sick?' and therefore offers a major critique of the medical model which seeks the origins of human illness in biology.

Although Parsons made a major contribution to the sociological understanding of action through his voluntaristic theory, he is probably more identified in contemporary theory with the analysis of social systems. In particular, Parsons is associated with solutions to what he called the Hobbesian problem of order. For Parsons, the nature of social order in human societies could not be explained by reference to the utilitarian interests of rational actors, because a rational actor would always resort to fraud and force to achieve their individual goals. Social order is only possible on the basis of some shared values. It was on the basis of this assumption that Parsons sought to challenge the presuppositions of classical economics and conventional

Marxism – a challenge which is discussed at some length in chapter 1.

Parsons' analysis of value consensus in society has been widely criticised in modern sociology. It has been argued that modern societies do not in fact possess such extensive agreements around values and that Parsons' sociology systematically neglects the centrality of force, coercion and constraint to social order (Dahrendorf, 1968). Empirical studies of the working classes in the advanced capitalist societies suggest that capitalist cultures contain a diversity of belief systems, many of which are oppositional and radical (Mann, 1970; Parkin, 1972). It has also been argued that it is important to make an analytical distinction between social cohesion, value consensus and system integration, and that these distinctions are not clearly worked out in Parsons' social system theory (Lockwood, 1956; Giddens, 1979).

These criticisms of the theory of social order were in fact part of a wider and more general attack on Parsonian functionalism. The functionalist paradigm came to be rejected on a variety of grounds: it could not adequately explain social change; it was tied to unacceptable values which were broadly conservative; it was circular and tautological as a theory, since the continuity of an institution was automatically evidence of its functional usefulness. The influence of functionalism was thus held to be pernicious, especially as an explanation of, for example, social stratification (Tumin, 1970). These criticisms passed eventually into the folklore of sociology and have become part of the taken-for-granted baggage of assumptions of modern sociologists.

In large measure, these criticisms of Parsons do not provide a valid or coherent attack on Parsonian sociology. In chapter 4 we examine a wide range of critical perspectives on Parsons, arguing that Parsonian sociology more than adequately survives most existing lines of criticism. In general, there are very strong reasons for reading and re-reading Parsons without the blinkered prejudices of the critique of functionalism. Briefly, we need to note that Parsons' account of the nature of social order in the analysis of the unit-act is not incompatible with his subsequent formulation of system integration; in fact Parsons' analysis of the action framework is a necessary stepping-stone to the later formulation of systems theory. There is no theoretical gap or

epistemological rupture in Parsonian sociology separating the
early 'humanistic' interest in action from the subsequent
'scientific' inquiries into social systems. With respect to criticisms of 'structural functionalism', there is a cogent argument
to suggest that it is difficult to conceive of a social science which
did not contain some version of structural functionalism (Davis,
1959). The concept of 'structure' indicates some degree of
pattern over time between elements or parts of a social system
and 'function' refers to the contribution or otherwise of some
patterned element to the continuity and maintenance of such a
social system (Lazarsfeld, 1973). In this simplistic definition, the
perspective suggests that the most basic question in social
science should be 'How does this society work?'

Formulated in this manner, it is clear that structural functionalism has no conservative or ideological presuppositions.
Marxism – at least in its 'scientific' manifestation – can be
regarded as a form of structural functionalism which asks questions like 'What is the function of individualism as an ideology
in capitalism?' and 'How is class inequality maintained?' That
Marxism perceives capitalism in terms of various dialectical and
contradictory processes and structures is simply to say that the
equilibrium of the capitalist social system is regarded as highly
unstable. In short, a functionalist perspective does not preclude
an analysis of conflict, contradiction and coercion, as 'Parsonian'
writers such as Williams (1965) and Bellah (1970, 1980) have
demonstrated. Thus the notion of conflict functionalism is
perfectly compatible with the underlying assumptions of
Parsonian structural functionalism.

This type of defence may ultimately be unproductive with
respect to the development of sociological theory. Its rehearsal
is nonetheless necessary since, without a proper understanding
of the history of functionalist theory, it would be impossible to
achieve any perspective on more recent developments in major
paradigms in social theory. It is, for example, difficult to see
how much of the work of Louis Althusser and Nicos Poulantzas
could be regarded as original in view of pre-existing formulations of systems theory in Parsonian sociology. There is, for
example, a direct parallel between the Althusserian notion of
'necessary conditions of existence' of a mode of production and
the 'functional prerequisites' of a social system. Both of these

notions are perfectly legitimate and important questions for understanding the continuity of social systems. Our argument here is that a mature appreciation of Althusserian Marxism would not see it as a major departure from conventional social theory, but primarily an elaboration of structural functionalism. The same argument would apply elsewhere. For example, it would be impossible to make sense of the debate between Niklas Luhmann and Jürgen Habermas (Bleicher, 1982) without an appreciation of Parsons' contribution to general systems theory. This is to state the defence of Parsons in a rather indirect fashion. More forcefully, it is often the case that what appears as a fundamental contribution to modern social thought is highly parasitic on Parsonian sociology. Typically the parasitism is covert.

Parsons is thus characteristically associated with the theory of action, the Hobbesian problem of order and the structural-functionalist perspective on social systems. These three dimensions to his sociology offer some indication of the scope of his theoretical contribution to modern sociology. We have already acknowledged, however, that these three facets of his work have been the subject of extensive criticism. Although different aspects of Parsons are held up for critical evaluation, his work is also often rejected, not so much for its content, but for its 'style'. Parsonian sociology is typically regarded as too abstract, general and abstruse to be of value in sociological research. The abstract character of Parsonian sociology means that the empirical referent for his concepts is often unclear and hence many of the propositions of his theories are not open to empirical inspection and evaluation in social research. C. Wright Mills' critique of Grand Theory is thus taken as the definitive statement on Parsonian abstraction. Other sociologists were equally critical of Parsons' alleged 'formalism' (Rex, 1961).

There are three preliminary arguments in support of Parsons' style of abstract theory. In the first place, social theory relies to a considerable extent on non-empirical or unobserved presuppositions of a philosophical kind about 'society', 'the individual', 'history' and so on. The failure to produce an adequate defence of empirical verification or falsification procedures within the philosophy of science is testimony to the weaknesses of empiricist objections to theoretical abstraction. Secondly, sociological theorising is inconceivable without the use of such formal concepts as 'action', 'system', 'role' or 'value'. Such formal terms represent an important component of empirically-oriented research. In this situation, the clarity of the formal connection between concepts on which Parsons insists is a virtue rather than a vice, provided a distinction between conceptual elaboration and empirical discourse is maintained. Thirdly, it is perfectly appropriate for sociology to make a contribution to social philosophy. The place of values in sociology is not restricted to questions concerning the methodological procedures necessary to test certain sociological assumptions in a scientific manner. Issues of value and morality lie at the heart of sociological enquiry both in the sense of shaping the cultural-relevance of sociological research, and in terms of the implications of research for social policy and the realisation of the good life.

Of course, there is an alternative position which would say the critique of empiricism, the development of a meta-theoretical language of social relations and the evaluation of moral and philosophical matters could have been achieved without the high level of abstraction which is thought to typify Parsonian sociology. To some extent, this was the position taken by writers like R. K. Merton in the notion of theories of the middle range and by T. H. Marshall in the idea of 'stepping-stones in the middle distance' (Marshall, 1977). One problem here is how exactly to make a valid distinction between Grand Theory and Middle-range Theory.

This collection of essays makes a rather different evaluation of Parsons. In the first place we claim that Parsons' work – while not without internal shifts and changing emphasis – represents a more powerful contribution to sociological theory than that of Marx, Weber, Durkheim or any of their contemporary followers. In this respect his theories have much of insight to contribute to recent developments like the impasse of Marxist theory around the dilemma of structure and agency, or the attempt by feminist theorists to integrate 'personality' into the study of social structure. Parsons' contribution is not best seen through Alexander's (1984) somewhat flaccid notion of theoretical 'multidimensionality', but rather through the determinate lines of causal relations and interchange that he posits between the various social sub-systems.

Secondly, we claim that Parsonian sociology represents a research programme the full empirical richness and implications of which have yet to be appreciated and explored. It would be foolish to deny the existence of the broadly Parsonian school of sociological enquiry represented in the work of Smelser (1959, 1962), Bellah (1970, 1980), Barber (1957) and so on. Nonetheless there remain huge areas such as the study of professional ethics, the continuing development of social differentiation in modern society and in the normative basis of economic institutions, which have yet to be brought in a systematic manner within this programme. Modern sociology has far too readily accepted that the apparently abstract nature of Parsons' sociological theory precludes meaningful empirical research.

Thirdly, we would point out that many of Parsons' important contributions to sociology were not abstract (in the 'Grand Theory' sense) at all. Parsons produced a great variety of essays and occasional papers (often relating to 'social problems' in American life) which are clearly 'empirical' with strong implications for social policy. This neglected feature of Parsonian sociology ought to be taken far more seriously, because these 'empirical' essays show how Parsons' abstract sociological theory could be operationalised or at least how his sociological theory is highly relevant to understanding empirical issues.

For example, a number of articles collected in *Essays in Sociological Theory* clearly illustrated Parsons' profound concern to demonstrate the relevance of Parsonian sociology to the explanation of the modern social structures of such societies as Germany, Japan and America. In part these essays were addressed to the problem of how ascriptive values and institutions survived during a process of industrialisation. Parsons saw clearly that any isolation of Japan within the post-war world system would have the consequence of re-asserting the traditional authoritarianism and hierarchy of the Japanese social structure and this situation would inhibit the development of more democratic institutions. It is interesting that the pattern variables are, despite criticism, highly relevant to the analysis of Japanese values and institutions (Dore, 1967; Nakane, 1973).

Similarly, Parsons' discussion of the unstable mixture of pre-modern ascriptive hierarchies with an industrial economy in German society has proved particularly insightful. More importantly, these essays demonstrate that Parsons did not adhere to any teleological view of history and did not view societies as smoothly functioning systems. Although Parsons has been accused of taking 'social statics' for granted (Moore, 1967, p. 486), Parsons did appear to recognise clearly the problem of how certain social structures and values may survive massive changes in the economy and in the polity. For Parsons it was the very uneven quality of German 'feudal' structures in relation to the rapid development of a capitalist economic base which provided at least one ingredient for the emergence of fascist politics.

Parsons on domesticity and sociality

From the perspective of the 1980s much of the sociology of the first half of the century looks distinctively out of date and backward on one major issue, namely its neglect of the nature of the family, gender relations and the position of women in society. Another feature of this absence is the failure of conventional sociology to come to terms with the nature of sexuality and the legacy of Freud's psycho-analysis. There are some obvious exceptions to this rule and among these exceptions one would include the critical theory tradition of Germany and especially the work of Herbert Marcuse. With the development of the women's movement and the emergence of a powerful feminist critique, sociology has subsequently responded to this gap in its view of the social structure and considerable work has been done as a consequence on such topics as women and the labour force, the domestic role of women, the impact of women on the nature of social stratification, and the problem of women in relation to the expansion of civil rights. The debate about women and sexuality has become one of the main items on the agenda of late twentieth-century sociology. In addition, there have been a variety of interpretations and appreciations of the work of Freud. Freud's impact on, for example, the Frankfurt School has been widely discussed in the secondary

literature (Jay, 1973; Held, 1980; Bottomore, 1984). Much of the
weakness of early sociology with respect to the analysis of
women, reproduction and the family have been identified and
many of the lacunae have been rectified in subsequent analysis.

Although traditional sociology can be justifiably criticised for
its neglect of these issues it is interesting to note that Parsons
had debated in detail and in depth most of the major issues
which have subsequently been elaborated in the 1970s and
1980s. Parsons has made major and valuable contributions to
the analysis of kinship systems (Parsons, 1943), the oedipus
problem (Parsons, 1953b), the incest taboo (Parsons, 1954d),
the socialisation process (Parsons et al., 1955b), psycho-analysis
(Parsons, 1961d), the family system (Parsons, 1943; 1951a; 1971c;
1971d) and we may note that Parsons had an enduring and
specific interest in the work of Freud (Parsons, 1974d). These
rather diverse interests came together around a number of key
issues such as the centrality of the family, the significance of
the processes of socialisation and internalisation, the personality
system and the significance of affectual relationships within
domestic space. As a result of these interests it is possible to
suggest that Parsons within the context of a sociological paradigm was groping towards a more complete and elaborate
theory of domesticity and sociality. The argument is that
Parsons anticipated many subsequent developments in
sociology but more importantly his contribution to those later
developments has neither been fully recognised nor wholly
appreciated.

While some sociologists would be ready to admit Parsons'
long-term interest in the family and in the socialisation process
they would argue, presumably, that Parsons' functionalism
prevented the development of an adequate theory of family and
that Parsons retained an over-socialised view of human beings
(Wrang, 1961). Parsons is typically criticised for overstating the
functional relationship between the isolated nuclear urban
family and the requirements of an industrial system which
depends upon not only the replacement of labour but on its
geographical mobility. Parsons' view that the role of the nuclear
family is to provide mobile, educated and disciplined labour
for the capitalist system has become highly unfashionable in
contemporary sociology especially where sociology has been

exposed to a feminist critique. Parsons' argument that the incest taboo (Parsons, 1954d) had the consequence of driving offspring from the household with the consequence of forming new households which strengthened the integration of societies no longer commands much support in the relevant literature (Fox, 1967).

In defence of Parsons' view of the family we might note first that Parsons did at least see the family as playing a crucial role in the general functions of public society. While many sociologists typically ignore the family or neglect the family's contribution to public life, Parsons clearly saw the necessary inter-relationship between the private and the public in social life. For Parsons, the family is essential for the creation of individual subjects who subsequently contribute to the reproduction of public relationships. The much vaunted recent discovery of the notion of interpellation (Therborn, 1980) had already been amply debated in Parsons' notion of internalisation and socialisation. It would be relatively easy to re-interpret or re-describe Parsons' account of the role of the family and other institutions such as the school in terms of a structuralist account of interpellation as the process whereby persons are hailed from the private into the public. Our second defence of Parsons would be that Parsons does not see the nuclear family wholly in terms of its positive functional relationship to the wider society. Quite simply, Parsons was well aware of the negative and more problematic features of private life especially with respect to the mental health of its inmates. He noted, for example, that the isolation of the nuclear family and its precarious relationship with a wider set of kin created particular strains on inter-personal relations within the family where individuals were exclusively dependent upon each other for emotional gratification and affectual stimulation. The emphasis on love and devotion within the family (namely the romantic complex) placed high expectations on social relations within the family and, in particular, placed high demands upon the mother. Accordingly Parsons noted that women in contemporary society faced a series of contradictory expectations and demands, so that mothers were expected to be simultaneously sexually attractive, domestically competent and able to provide intellectual companionship for other members of the family. Parsons thus argued that women were especially likely to succumb to what he called the 'neurotic illness of compulsive domesticity'. Parsons went on to argue that

> in all of these and other fields there are conspicuous signs
> of insecurity and ambivalence. Hence it may be concluded
> that the feminine role is a conspicuous focus of the strains
> inherent in our social structure, and not the least of these
> sources of these strains is to be found in the functional
> difficulties in the integration of our kinship system with
> the rest of the social structure (Parsons, 1954b, p. 194).

In his writing on the 'sick role' (Parsons, 1951a; Parsons and Fox, 1953d) we can also observe Parsons' argument that, given their dependency and isolation in the nuclear family, women will be especially prone to mental illness and that women will be forced in the direction of adopting the 'sick role' as a permanent occupation. In this respect, Parsons anticipated much of the subsequent discussion in medical sociology of the special problems of women and social isolation in the epidemiology of mental illness (Gove, 1973).

A similar account of Parsons' views on socialisation and internalisation could be offered as a defence of Parsons against the charge that he over-states the stability and eufunctional consequences of family life and the training of children. One interesting illustration of Parsons' more complex view of socialisation could be presented from his important essay 'Propaganda and social control' from 1942 where in a footnote Parsons argues that socialisation can never be entirely functional for the social system because training in one stage of the life cycle may well produce persons who are not equipped to fulfil activities and obligations in later stages of their life cycle. Thus Parsons argued that one source of deviant behaviour or institutional strain in society will derive from the fact that 'socialization at one stage of the life cycle probably sometimes positively unfits the person for the roles he must assume in a later stage' (Parsons, 1954b, p. 148). In any case, it was a favourite argument of Parsons that no individual could ever be totally or simultaneously socialised into all features and aspects of the social system. The very fact of socialisation thereby produces inevitably a variety of forms of deviance because socialisation can never produce the entirely integrated individual. Furthermore, Parsons retained enough of Freud's original pessimism to assume that there would always be various contradictions between individual needs and social control. The coherence and stability of the social system would always at least in part be dependent on a variety of historical and contingent features of the socialisation process and ultimately upon the nature of socialising institutions such as the family, the school and the church. As we argue subsequently, it is wholly wrong to view Parsons' analysis of the social system as an analysis which is completely committed to the view of society as a stable, smoothly functioning, integrated whole.

In contemporary sociology there is much criticism of the neglect of the problem of women in the labour force; for example it is argued that sociology has traditionally neglected the significance of female employment and unemployment (Marshall, G., 1984). Although it was traditionally assumed that women would remain within the domestic domain as providers of emotional support and services, women now constitute a significant proportion of the labour force; for example, in Britain in the 1970s women represented about 40 per cent of the British labour force. Traditional definitions of class ignored the problem of locating women within a system of social stratification and it was conventionally assumed that the social class position of women could be determined by that of their husbands or fathers. These views of class and analyses of employment which neglected the place of women are now regarded as wholly unsatisfactory. In this area, the work of Parsons, while much criticised, was in fact very modern in its perspective. Although the so-called functionalist theory of social stratification has numerous shortcomings, at least Parsons was clearly aware of the need to develop a theory which would combine one's location in a kinship system with one's location in a system of social stratification based upon an occupational division within the economy. While Parsons in the article 'Analytical Approach to the Theory of Social Stratification' (Parsons, 1940a) approached class in terms of individuals via the pattern variables of universalism and achievement he nevertheless defined class in terms of a system of kinship units organised hierarchically by virtue of their status differentials. Thus, in the article 'Social Classes and Class Conflict in the light of recent sociological theory' (Parsons, 1954b) Parsons defined class as 'a plurality of kinship units which, in those respects where status in a hierarchical context is shared by their members, have approximately equal status. The class status of an individual, therefore, is that which he shares with other members in an effective kinship unit' (p. 328). This definition of class by modern theoretical standards can be regarded as confused in some respects because it conflates a debate about economic class positions with status hierarchies. Modern sociological approaches to class would probably follow either a Marxist or a Weberian perspective which would more sharply differentiate social status from class membership. While these criticisms may be valid, at least Parsons should be given credit for developing a theory of social stratification which systematically and consciously sought to combine an analysis of kinship with an analysis of class. In this as in other respects, Parsons is strikingly modern.

In these studies of personality, Freudianism, the status of women and the nature of gender relationships we can suggest that Parsons was attempting to formulate an analysis of the relationship between public sociality and domestic sociality which would transform existing conceptualisation of the social as wholly and simply about the public institutional space. That is, while most sociological theories conventionally relegated the family and personal life to a sub-social level, Parsons brought the family into the very centre of sociological inquiry by arguing that the family had a crucial role to play in the development of personality. We can suggest that contemporary sociology still lacks an adequate conceptualisation of the relationship between the public, the private and the domestic but Parsons at least should be recognised as a precursor of an appropriate analysis of the sociology of domestic spaces.

Although these essays on post-war social structures in the industrial societies are notable examples of Parsons' capacity to provide theoretically informed commentaries on empirical issues, there are many other illustrations. In this volume, we will consider Parsons' medical sociology and it is important to note that Parsons' concept of the 'sick role' (Parsons, 1951a) gave rise to a long debate which informed empirical research for many decades into the social nature of sickness. This research had important policy implications for the doctor–patient relationship. Parsons also made important contributions to the development of research into youth (Parsons, 1964j), into race relations (Parsons, 1965b; 1966c), into the sociology of death (Parsons, 1967d) and into education (Parsons, 1970b; 1970c; 1972a; 1972b; 1973b; 1974a). A more comprehensive evaluation of Parsons' sociology may well come to the conclusion that Parsons was in fact an important commentator on American society rather than simply the author of abstract Grand Theory. Whether or not mature reflection on Parsons' sociology comes to that conclusion, it cannot be denied that Parsons contributed empirically grounded analyses of actual societies or that Parsonian sociology gave rise to an empirical research tradition or that Parsons' sociological theory can be successfully operationalised in a number of areas to make it, at least potentially, exposed to empirical discourse.

## Parsons and American society: the sociology of optimism

Like economics, modern sociology may often be regarded as a dismal science. Sociologists at the turn of the century typically sounded like prophets of doom. Max Weber's sociology of the iron cage of capitalism is probably the best example of this inclination towards fatalism (Turner, 1981), but similar moods of despair underlined the work of Simmel, on the one hand, and critical theory, on the other. Sociologists are often most powerful when they adopt this fin-de-siècle mentality. Pessimism is often easier to sustain as a moral perspective because it appears less naive than optimism; furthermore, as a pessimist it is usually much better to be proved wrong. Much of the opposition to Parsons appears to be based on the fact that Parsons, almost alone among modern sociologists, was essentially optimistic about the nature of modernity and certainly optimistic about the long-term future of American society. While C. Wright Mills went about preaching the inevitability of a third world war (Wright Mills, 1960), Parsons saw the future of human societies in a more positive light. Whereas Weber saw modern society in terms of symbolism drawn from the Old Testament – Fallen Man and the Tree of Knowledge – Parsons

saw modern societies (at least modern, industrial, western societies) as embodiments of Christian culture, especially individualism, the separation of religion and politics, and tolerance for
intellectual values. It is also well known that Parsons regarded
professional values as an important alternative to egoistic utilitarianism in the market. In general, Parsons argued that
complex, differentiated and integrated societies like America
represented the leading edge of the historical movement of
societies towards universalistic, achievement-oriented cultures.
While Parsons thought that modern industrial societies would
have to face many serious and long-term problems – such as
ageing populations, youth problems, moral dilemmas of genetic
engineering – he did not believe that these crises would turn
out to be fatal. It was Parsons' optimistic view of the development potential of modern societies, which separated him from
more pessimistic brands of modern sociology, and it was this
optimism with respect to American culture which provided the
covert point of much criticism.

   From the vantage point of Parsons' theory of social change,
it is plausible to argue that we might think of Parsons as a
moral theorist as much as a sociologist. Whereas Marxists and
Weberians emphasised the limiting effect of modern society on
the individual (via the concepts of alienation and rationalisation), Parsons saw the evolutionary development of western
society as enhancing the freedom of the individual from
tradition, the narrow constraints of kinship and the dominance
of hierarchical structures based on ascribed, particularistic
criteria. In this respect, we might usefully conceive Parsons'
analysis of modern societies as an extension and application of
Marshall's analysis of citizenship. Parsons' studies of the
problem of equality and inequality in modern societies were
focused on political problems which arose out of Marshall's
discussion of the contradictory relationship between citizenship
and class (Parsons, 1970f). Parsons' reflections on the problem
of the social rights of American blacks were also strongly
influenced by Marshall (Parsons, 1965b; Lockwood, 1974).
Marshall's argument that social equality expanded as a consequence of the political organisation of the working class can be
seen as a particular case of Parsons' pattern variables, namely
that ascriptive criteria of political participation are incompatible

with the process of modernisation. Our argument is that while
the pattern variables are at one level descriptive of broad
changes in western society away from the ascriptive arrangements of traditionalism, they are also moral categories, speci-
fying how we *ought* to behave. The implication for political
policy is that societies which seek to maximise their adaptive
capacity ought to promote universalistic citizenship and
achievement motivation. The notion of 'modernisation' is not
just a descriptive statement about global social change, but also
contains a moral evaluation of desirable future goals.

While some sociologists might think that this moral under-
tone to Parsons' sociology is a sign of its theoretical limitations,
we would argue that its moral quality is a positive advantage.
Parsons is unusual among contemporary sociologists in being
unambiguously modern; there is no element of backward-
looking, romantic nostalgia about Parsonian sociology. There is
no hankering for a world we have lost, characterized by small
communities, warm social relations, ritual and close kinship
ties. Sociologists who are deeply critical of modern societies
often, even when they are explicitly socialist about their critique,
imply or explicitly adopt a romanticism about the past which is
in fact unwarranted and, to quote Weber, lacking in serious-
ness. In Parsonian sociology, all nostalgic conceptualisation of
*gemeinschaft* is completely liquidated in favour of a sociology
which advocates the modern world, warts and all. One indicator
of this modernism is that for Parsons the fact of secularisation
was never a moral problem. By contrast, for sociologists of
religion like Peter L. Berger and Thomas Luckmann, the event
which Nietzsche proclaimed as the Death-of-God raises massive
problems for secular man who can no longer live comfortably
in the world without constantly looking backwards. Parsons
offers us a modern sociology for people who have accepted the
existence of a modern world as inevitable, and for people who
believe that modernity at least offers the possibility of egalitarian
universalism. This is not to argue that any adherence to
Parsonian sociology would lead inexorably to the conclusion
that we live in the best-of-all-possible worlds. On the contrary,
Parsons was perfectly aware of, and wrote frequently about,
inequality, racism, international conflicts and social conflicts.
He was also deeply concerned by the finality of death in a world

24 Robert J. Holton and Bryan S. Turner

without obvious religious comforts and consolations. However, Parsons thought that modern, complex societies were more developed and offered more scope for social rights than any other form of social organisation. While Parsons was acutely aware of the problem of egoistic utilitarianism and economic conflicts in the market place, he was concerned to understand those values, institutions and social movements which would promote and defend equality, universalism, and altruism. This was one feature of Parsons' optimism; he did not see the modern world in terms of a Fall from a pre-modern state of grace à la Marx and Weber. For Parsons, the modern secular world (in particular democratic society) is the legacy of Christianity as a consequence of a process of secularisation which Parsons obviously saw in beneficial terms (Parsons, 1963c).

Pessimistic sociology is obviously a reflection of a global political context in which nuclear war, followed by an ecological catastrophe, appears likely or even inevitable. The confident tone of Parsons' studies of American society and social change appears to be inappropriate in the contemporary crisis. However, the value of Parsons' socio-moral perspective on the modern world is precisely its absence of romanticism, traditionalism and nostalgia. Criticism of capitalist society is often hopelessly romantic in assuming that alternatives to capitalism would miraculously avoid two centuries of industralisation. In this respect, Marxists like Georg Lukàcs were the worst romantics. At least Marx, while condemning capitalism for dragging humanity through blood and fire, acknowledged the revolutionary nature of capitalism and commended its universalism over the stagnatory nature of China and India. In a similar fashion, Parsons recognised that evolutionary change had destroyed the cosy world of magic and religion, opening up a reality which is dangerous and threatening, but which also offers the chance of an egalitarian, universalistic culture. In this respect, Parsonian sociology is not a conservative defence of the status quo, masquerading as objective social science, but an argument in favour of social change – an argument which is often more radical than either Parsons or his critics adequately realised.

# 1
# Talcott Parsons and the theory of economy and society

*Robert J. Holton*

'It is vain to speak of the higher authority of a unified social science. No doubt if that existed Economics would gladly find shelter under its wing. But it does not exist; it shows no signs of coming into existence. There is no use in writing idly for it; we must do what we can with our present resources.'

(Alfred Marshall, 1885)

'Economic theory need not remain an "island" of theoretical specificity totally alone in an uncharted "sea" of theoretical indeterminacy. . . . Even though the general theory of action . . . is unevenly developed, we have been able to place economic theory within the general theory of social systems with considerable accuracy.'

(Talcott Parsons and Neil Smelser, 1956a)

Introduction

One of the characteristic features of modern western social thought is the representation of economic life as a discrete self-subsistent element in the social order. It is largely upon this basis that 'economics' has arisen as a distinct member of the family of social sciences, with its own internal body of economic theory as well as a separate academic identity. The question nonetheless arises as to the relationships that are taken to exist between the economy and society, and as a corollary between the inquiries of economics and the other social sciences. How in the first place, is the economy to be defined, such that its characteristic processes can be distinguished from other parts of society? What are the other parts of society, and how is the economy articulated with them? In the light of such questions how adequate is the view that the economy is (at least for certain purposes) self-subsistent, and able as such to exert a determinate, or even dominant influence on social life in general? How, finally, is the current prestige of economics as a theoretically coherent and yet self-subsistent social science to be understood?

Such questions have engaged a wide range of social scientists, most of whom have been critical of the perspectives on economy and society generated within the mainstream of conventional economic thought. Amongst the most influential of these are the work of Marx and Marxian political economy, Veblen and the 'institutionalists', and Polanyi and the school of economic anthropology. Less widely known but of equal interest is the theory of economy and society developed between the 1930s and 1950s by Talcott Parsons.

Parsons' work draws explicitly on the classical European sociological tradition of Weber and Durkheim, and on what might be called the sociologically informed economics of Marshall and Pareto. The Parsonian synthesis may be distinguished from the other three currents in two very interesting ways. First, an attempt is made to combine a generic theory of the economy with a concern for the importance of values and normative order in relationships linking the economy and society. While Parsons shares the former of these aims with Marxist political economy, and the latter with both institutionalism and economic anthropology, his *combination* of the two objectives is both highly distinctive and theoretically provocative. Second, Parsons seeks not to undermine or reject conventional economic theory as indefensibly abstract or as an apologetic version of 'bourgeois ideology', but rather to subsume it as an insightful but incomplete theoretical project within a general theory of society.

While this paper offers an exegesis of an under-appreciated side of Parsons' work, it has three further aims. The first is to

challenge the predominance of 'political economic' approaches
to economy and society within contemporary sociological
thought. Perspectives of this kind may be seen as inadequate,
as Parsons points out, both in terms of their handling of the
problem of order and in relation to their analyses of the structure of modern Western society. Secondly, it is claimed that
Parsons' contribution is not to have produced another evangelical manifesto in support of the diffuse importance of the
social context of economic activity, but to have identified a
systematic theoretical apparatus offering sophisticated analyses
of the relations between economy and society. The third aim is
to demonstrate that Parsons' economic sociology can be operationalised in empirical research and that the yield from what
might be called the Parsonian research programme seems very
promising. In all these respects there is good reason to argue
not for the 'de-Parsonising' of sociology, but for a process of
're-Parsonisation'.

*An initial technical note*

The concept of 'conventional' or 'mainstream' economic thought
deployed throughout this paper is associated with the major
tradition of Anglo-Saxon economic thought concerned primarily
with the functioning of market systems in terms of rational
action. This tradition links Adam Smith and Ricardo with the
neo-classical economists of the late nineteenth century and
twentieth-century traditions such as Keynesianism and monetarism. Use of this broad concept is not meant to imply that
economics is an homogeneous harmonious discipline. The
concept may rather be seen as a Weberian ideal-type expressly
designed to focus in a 'one-sided' manner on certain recurring
features in the logic of economic explanation. As such the term
'conventional economic thought' is a deliberate abstraction
rather than an empirical generalisation. Its function is essentially heuristic. The term represents a first approximation as to
the nature of economic thought, bringing some initial order to
a field, an order which may later be relaxed in cases of empirical
deviation from the initial concept. As such this concept initially
bears no more or less relationship to empirical reality than do

economists' postulates of perfect competition or rational economic man.


## The challenge of *The Structure of Social Action*

The problem of how to conceptualise and theorise the inter-
relationships between economy and society occupies a strategic
position in the development of Parsons' thought. This is evident
in his critique of utilitarian economics which formed much of
the basis of his 'voluntaristic theory of action', his discussion of
'power' as a circulating medium analogous to 'money', and
above all in the development of the four-function (AGIL) paradigm, for the analysis of social systems.

Parsons' engagement with problems of economy and society
may be separated into two phases. The first, in the late 1920s
and 1930s, setting out from his doctoral dissertation on theories
of capitalism, sought a basis upon which action theory could
be reconciled with difficulties prompted by the Hobbesian
problem of 'order' (see especially Parsons, 1934c, 1935a,
1937a).

In the light of this problem, conventional economic theory
was seen as still entrapped within the inadequate theories of
action of nineteenth-century positivism and utilitarianism.
While containing certain insights on the nature of means–end
rationality, economic thought must now turn to the reformul-
ated version of action theory developed by the classical sociologists of the late nineteenth century.

The second phase of Parsons' work in economic sociology
during the 1950s was predicated on his development of a
general theory of action which looked beyond the 'voluntarism'
of classical sociology. The elaboration of his general theory
within the theory of social systems saw the resumption of a
concern with the relations between economy and society. This
culminated in the publication of *Economy and Society*, jointly
with Neil Smelser in 1956.

The publication of *The Structure of Social Action* in 1936
represents the culmination of the first phase of Parsons' works
in social theory. The point of departure in this study concerns
certain internal problems within the leading nineteenth-century

variant of action theory – namely that associated with utilitarianism. While the terms 'utilitarianism' and 'utilitarian' have sometimes been used to refer to a system of social reform, Parsons' usage is directed towards those nineteenth-century action theories characterised by an 'atomistic', 'rationalistic' and positivistic approach to action.

The unit act in this atomistic schema is seen in terms of individual strategies to realise 'ends' irrespective of the 'ends' desired by other actors. 'Ends' moreover may be said to have both substantive and formal components. Substantively 'ends' are constituted out of values and are thus empirical phenomena. Analytically speaking, however, the formal concept of end in this *action* schema refers not so much to some valued 'anticipated future state of affairs', but more specifically to 'the difference between the anticipated future state of affairs and that which it could have been predicted would ensue from the initial situation *without the agency of the actor having intervened*' (Parsons' emphasis).

By 'rationality', Parsons refers in this context to the normative patterns that link the 'means' chosen to the desired 'ends'. In analytical terms 'means' do not refer to 'things' employed in realising ends in some general sense, but only to those aspects of means susceptible to 'control' by the actor. Rationality in this schema applies not to the status of ends which may be taken as a 'given', but to the appropriateness of the normative processes wherein particular means are chosen and deployed in a given situation to realise 'ends'. The 'rational' or 'irrational' nature of choice in this utilitarian context is seen moreover as capable of determination by scientific means – actors' strategies for verifying the appropriateness of chosen means being analogous to those employed by scientists. Parsons describes this assumption as 'positivist' in the sense that 'scientifically verified knowledge of the situation is regarded as "Man"'s sole possible significant, cognitive relation to external (non ego) reality, man as actor that is' (1937a, p. 61). It follows that departures from rationality within the utilitarian system can only be regarded as cognitively disprivileged, the results either of 'error' in choice, or 'ignorance' of available means.

A final, more explicit, feature of the system derivable from its other three characteristics is, according to Parsons, a view of the 'concrete' ends chosen by actors as 'random' elements. This arises as a result of combining the atomistic assumption that an individual takes no account of the ends of others, when setting his 'own', and the positivistic assumption that means-end calculation is not simply a conceptual device, but is also empirically descriptive of social action.

Having outlined these characteristics, Parsons locates a disabling theoretical instability in the system, designated as the 'utilitarian dilemma'. This may be seen as an immanent property of utilitarian action theory as it developed within nineteenth-century social thought in general, and nineteenth-century understandings of the relationship between economy and society in particular. The dilemma arises from the attempt to combine a sense of the autonomy of individual human agency and choice with the assumption of the randomness of individual ends. It may be stated as follows. In the first instance the atomistic assumption that individuals take no account of other ends may appear to safeguard the autonomy of agency. However, if individual ends are regarded as a random, then the difficulty arises as to how selection of ends arises. The indeterminacy which surrounds the notion of choice between random ends seems to reflect a patternless normative chaos in relations between actors. In attempting to overcome this unacceptable prospect, Parsons perceives that utilitarian action theory ran the danger of turning to an equally unacceptable alternative. This emerges when the problem of normative randomness or chaos is resolved by appeal to the causal significance of given conditions of action, external to the actor. Environmental pressure would be one example of such conditions. The problem with this option is that it is thoroughly inconsistent with action theory, since the autonomy of the actor is effectively undermined. The horns of the utilitarian dilemma are therefore, on the one side normative chaos, and on the other determinism. Parsons' general conclusion is that there remains no basis for resolving such difficulties while a positivistic theory of knowledge is maintained.

Nineteenth- and twentieth-century economic thought represents for Parsons the principal and most influential expression of utilitarian action theory and was thus especially vulnerable to the utilitarian dilemma. The essence of this argument, as it applies to economic theory, has recently been confirmed – apparently quite independently of Parsons' critique – in the work of Spiro Latsis (1972). Like Parsons, he demonstrates that economic theory contains not one but two logical structures of explanation. These are termed 'situational determinism' and 'economic behaviouralism'. Latsis demonstrates this dualism in economic theories of rational choice with particular reference to the theory of the firm. Reversing the order in which Parsons presents the horns of the utilitarian dilemma he starts, not with the problem of normative disorder, but with situational determinism. An important example of this is the neo-classical theory of the firm as visualised within theories of perfect competition or monopoly. On the assumption of independence of individual decision-makers, and rational choice in pursuit of self-interest, Latsis shows how economic theory, faced with either perfect competition or monopoly, sees only a single choice or exit involved in any decision. In this sense the outcome to action is determined exclusively by the conditions of the situation, since there is effectively no choice about what to do.

This 'situational determinism' is however seen as increasingly inadequate when applied to conditions of imperfect competition, such as oligopoly. Here it is empirically difficult to retain the assumption that 'ends' could ever be set independently of each other since so few actors are involved. At the same time there remains, according to Latsis, more freedom of manoeuvre for such actors allowing a multiple-exit situation. In the 'emergent research programme' of economic behaviouralism as applied to oligopoly, attention shifts from explanation of action 'as best decisions in constraining situations' to 'more or less good solutions in fluid and partially known or even completely misunderstood situations' (1972, 229). In the latter case, the only 'secure' variable becomes the propensities of the individual decision-maker. Latsis' conclusion is that this produces two incommensurable 'paradigms'. 'The neo-classical view stresses the situation and turns the decision making agent into a "cypher". The behavioural view on the other hand, focusses on the nature and characteristics of the decision making agent' (p. 234) but at the cost of relational instabilities.

Both Parsons and Latsis are clearly concerned with the

familiar problem of structure and agency as it affects the theorisation of economic life. Parsons' position diverges from that of
Latsis, however, in linking this issue to the further problem of
order. This arises in any attempt to maintain an individualistic
version of action theory where the connection between individual ends is regarded as indeterminate, chaotic or random.
How, in other words, is it possible for society to hold together
when faced with an atomistic plurality of actors each possessing
different psychological propensities and pursuing separate
ends? Is a normative theory of order at the level of such 'ends'
unnecessary, or are there alternative ways of producing a theory
of order consistent with the main principles of the utilitarian
action theory?

Such questions are of course highly pertinent both to general
theories of society and to any account of the relationship
between economy and society. If the economy is defined in a
conventional manner as that sphere where 'means' are
deployed to satisfy material ends, it makes a very great difference to any theory of society, as to whether the 'economy' is
taken:

    (a) to function without any need of normative order at the
        level of ends,
    (b) to generate its own normative order at this level,
    (c) to be dependent on external sources of normative order,
        or
    (d) to be dependent on some type of order, other than norma-
        tive order, e.g. coercion.

What room is there then within utilitarian action theory, and
utilitarian theories of economy and society, for an adequate
response to the problem of order? Parsons identifies the relax-
ation of assumptions about the randomness of ends as one
device by which this problem could be addressed with least
disturbance to the overall theory. This was achieved primarily
through the substitution of the notion of 'identity of interests'
for any strict assumption of randomness of ends. A solution to
the Hobbesian question of how to guarantee social order in the
face of an atomistic pursuit of individual advantage was found
not in some kind of social contract between ruler and ruled, but
in the assumption that rational action incorporated some respect
for the rights of others. Individual actors could still be regarded

as possessing disparate ultimate ends. But they also shared a common disposition to recognise that the pursuit of individual advantage is only possible if there existed a reciprocal obligation to recognise individual rights even where this conflicted with immediate interests. Following Locke, this disposition was located in the rationality of social actors, through which a minimum of normative order was brought to the conduct of social exchange. In this way, a means of accounting for order was offered consistent with the atomistic, rationalistic and positivistic features of the utilitarian action system.

Whether this amounts to a solution of the problem of order is however very debatable. Parsons points to the importance of a line of argument begun by Hobbes and developed by Ricardo and Marx, which provides an influential theoretical critique of the assumption of natural identity of interests. In this tradition, the parties to social exchange cannot be regarded as sharing reciprocal obligations to respect each other's pursuit of self-interest. The terms of exchange are rather dictated by conflicts of interest and resolved through the exercise of power – whether in the form of bargaining power or outright coercion.

This approach to the problem of 'order' has become immensely influential in contemporary sociology in large measure through the impact of Marxist political economy. Under capitalism, 'order' is conceived as the product of class 'power' exercised directly through the labour market, and in a more mediated fashion through the state. It follows that the political economic theory of economy and society is a theory of power conflict involving the institutional regulation of contradictory class interests. For Parsons, this position represents an important insight because it integrates institutionalised power conflict in such an arena as the capitalist workplace into the understanding of social action. This represents a development away from the individualistic bias of classic utilitarianism, shifting the analysis of means–ends relations to collectivities such as 'capital' and 'labour' within the enterprise. Marx also gave nineteenth-century action theory a historical dimension by stressing variations in the institutional context of action over time.

It is important to stress the many critical strengths of political economy in relation to 'orthodox economic theory'. There are of course different varieties of political economy involving important areas of theoretical disagreement, such as the debate between Marxists and neo-Ricardians over 'value' (Steedman, 1977; Steedman and Sweezy, 1981). The main thrust of the political economy approach has nonetheless been to deny the salience of economic theory in dealing with the links between market exchange and economic power, as it affects the organisation of production and the distribution of wealth between social classes. In developing the political economic insight that conventional economics is 'not a theory of a social system', Edward Nell (1972) has focussed on the importance of power conflicts over the distribution of income mediated through property relations, as the essence of the 'social' input into economic life. Order, at least in capitalist or class societies, is therefore a function of 'power', deriving from the pursuit of 'interests' by contending parties standing in differing relationships to each other in terms of access to property (or lack of it).

A number of twentieth-century Marxists have of course moved some way beyond this theory of order, combining political economy with a particular kind of concern for normative order and values. What has been referred to as the 'dominant ideology thesis' (Abercrombie, Hill and Turner, 1980) has become (however tacitly in some cases) a way of positing the need for an element of normative order or value commitment to the existing order within mechanisms of class control. A symptom of this is the wide use made of Gramsci's concept of hegemony. Such trends are important insofar as they introduce an element of action theory into Marxist analyses. The possibility of a counter-hegemony expressed in class resistance and class conflict also reflects the use of a framework designed to overcome the subject-less structuralism of some Marxist scholarship. If such resistance is episodic and counter-hegemony is seen as lacking at most points, this does not point so much to the spontaneous effects of economic relations (Marx's 'dull compulsion of economic circumstance') as to the efficacy of ruling ideas. Yet having recognised this degree of cultural autonomy, it is also evident that even 'culturalist Marxism' generally retains a strong instrumentalist 'quasi-utilitarian' view of norms and values. These are assimilated to one or other class-interest.

Considerable debate has taken place over the empirical existence of a 'dominant ideology' based on class-related norms and values within capitalism (Abercrombie et al., 1980, 1983, Chamberlain, 1983). Yet the protagonists of Marxist (and neo-Ricardian) political economy have not in general engaged in an explicit way with the problem of value commitments and normative rules as autonomous elements within economic life. This is reflected in the procedure of Nell who criticises conventional economics for its inadequacy as a theory of society, but then reduces such a theory to considerations of power conflict. The predominance of power relations over autonomous value commitments with respect to order is probably greatest in neo-Ricardian political economy, since Marxist theory has to find some room for the eventual transcendence of 'class' relations and hence the withering-away of power relations, to produce conditions for the emergence of a 'genuine' human freedom. While Parsons' comments on Marx, whether in *The Structure of Social Action* or in the two papers, 'Social Classes and Class Conflict . . .' (Parsons, 1954b) and 'Some Comments on the Sociology of Karl Marx' (Parsons, 1967c) are less elaborated than his exegeses of Weber and Durkheim, he does indicate what he believes to be the main reasons for this kind of obstacle within Marxism.

For Parsons the problematic treatment of value commitments in the work of Marx, stems from the common intellectual procedures he shares with utilitarian action theory. Of foremost importance here is the grounding of Marx' notion of interests in rational means–ends strategies by individuals involved in economic relationships. 'Men acted rationally for Marx because' within a given situation . . . the rational norm itself necessitates certain lines of action, precluding others' (Parsons, 1973a, p. 491). In this way the economic order, while constituted as the consequence of 'a multitude of rational acts', nonetheless comes to operate as a compulsive system. The economy comes to be seen as a 'great control mechanism' as self-regulating and hence self-subsistent. For Parsons, therefore, the conventional charge against Marx (and Marxism) of determinism is misplaced. Given the utilitarian roots of Marx's rationalistic political economy, no priority is given to the notion of overall systemic compulsiveness in preference to the rational pursuit of self-interest. On the contrary, it is the ordering of this pursuit by rational norms which eventuates in a 'compulsive' or 'imperative' quality of action.

For all its strengths including its historicity, and the breach with utilitarian individualism, Parsons feels that Marx's thought still remained trapped within other features of utilitarianism. Marx is still seen as committed to a rationalistic and positivistic approach to action, which leaves the utilitarian account of motivation and the focus on rationally perceived material interest unchallenged. Given that his hostility to the utilitarian picture of civil society based on competing self-interest was combined with an enduring materialism, Parsons in his later essay (1967c) suggests that Marx was left in the situation of having recourse to some alternative version of the 'natural identity of interests' to that postulated by Locke and his successors.

This argument points up (though Parsons does not say as much) the function of social ontology in the Marxist system as an underlying assumption about the emergent nature of the human species ultimately to guarantee 'order' once class society and power conflict were abolished. This kind of speculative philosophical anthropology is not, however, so easily reconciled with Marx's sociological account of the basis of 'order' under capitalism located within power conflict. What both such accounts of order lack is a concern for the sociological analysis of moral life within capitalism (or any other social system) with particular reference to the problem of order. Marx's residual utilitarianism it seems obstructed a translation of the metaphysical vision of order in the good society into a sociology of moral order in societies which fell short of that ultimate state. For Parsons this implied that 'order in the socialist society had, then, to be attributed to the "spontaneous goodness" of its members who, once freed from the corruption of capitalistic interests allegedly could not conceivably act in any antisocial manner' (1967c, p. 118). As a result Marx is left postulating a 'utopian' conception of harmony of interest of little sociological, though of immense philosophical and ethical, interest. One of the main problems with this approach is that it appears to leave no possibility of moral responsibility to individuals for their actions, except in the context of the ultimate good society.

It is doubtful whether Parsons' argument here gives due

weight to the post-Hegelian philosophical anthropology in Marx's overall project (Heller, 1976; Markus, 1978) nor to the implicit social ontology which Gould (1978) locates in Marx's treatment of labour, individuals, freedom and justice. Parsons' argument about the dualisms created by the utilitarian legacy within Marx's thought does nonetheless seem to have purchase on continuing instabilities and conflicts evident within twentieth-century Marxism. The phenomenon of the 'Two Marxisms' (Gouldner, 1980) rendered variously as 'structuralist v. culturalist', or 'scientific v. critical' is strongly reminiscent of Parsons utilitarian dilemma. This may be stated as follows. On a rationalist basis, social action may either be assimilated to the conditions of the situation – as in various forms of productive force determinism (Shaw, 1978; Cohen, 1978) – in which case the autonomy of the actor is lost – or alternatively, action is portrayed more voluntaristically as in teleological constructions of the thrust of (ontologically given) free producers to overcome alienation, but at the cost of an adequate sociological account of order.

In contemporary manifestations of the 'crisis of Marxism' such dualities are reflected in conflicts between the political economistic 'scientistic' theory of order, dominant ideology theorists, and more radical currents unable to accept a theory of society – even capitalist society – based on either or all of (i) material interest, (ii) power, (iii) class-contaminated values. One very interesting indicator of this is contained in the work of the Marxist historian E. P. Thompson which I have evaluated elsewhere (see Holton, 1981). His position is that the continuing existence of 'all those dense complex and elaborated systems . . . [such as] kinship, custom, the invisible and visible rules of social regulation, . . . religious faith, and millenarian impulses, etc.' (Thompson, 1978, p. 362) has been obscured by the materialist assumptions and logical procedures of 'Ricardian and Marxist political economy'. Such assumptions have been utilised so as to treat modern capitalism as an amoral social system in comparison with what went before. Thompson has found few of the resources with which to theorise moral phenomena under capitalism within the Marxist canon. Nor in a more general sense may an explicit non-utilitarian theory of action be found there.

These symptoms of contemporary theoretical impasse within the Marxist tradition make an interesting contrast with the fifty-year-old attempt by Parsons to locate and elaborate an alternative to the utilitarian theory of action. The announcement of such a theory in *The Structure of Social Action* drew very little from the work of Marx and even less from early twentieth-century Marxism. Parsons' voluntaristic theory of action, the foundation of his highly sophisticated theory of economy and society, draws instead on the combination of 'economic' and sociological thought represented in the work of Marshall, Pareto, Weber and Durkheim. Standing Lukàcs on his head, so to speak, it is to 'bourgeois' economics and sociology that Parsons turns to resolve the unstable dualism in all kinds of utilitarian thought, Marxism included.

In characterising the voluntaristic theory of action, Parsons takes as his principal starting point the logical status of ends within the utilitarian action schema. He begins in other words with 'residual' categories left unexamined in utilitarian-derived disciplines such as conventional economic theory and Marxist political economy. Instead of regarding ends as given with respect to the rational choice of means, the setting of ends is re-conceptualised as an integral part of the action schema. As a result, values and value commitment to a normative order become a crucial feature of any understanding of how means–ends strategies are constituted. This step is a radical one, because it challenges the atomistic, rationalistic and positivistic bases of utilitarian action theory.

The processes whereby 'ends' came to be regarded in this way in late nineteenth- and early twentieth-century thought are seen by Parsons as multiform and complex. One of the most important threads linking the work of the four theorists in question is the challenge to positivism. For Parsons, as we have seen, this is defined as that mode of cognition available to actors, dependent on processes of scientific verification. In utilitarian action theory, positivism in this sense is regarded as *the* only mode of cognition by which 'rational' action can take place. Such an assumption, however, left no place for the role of what can be variously referred to as 'irrational', 'non-logical' or 'ritualistic' aspects of social action. In each case these terms may be taken analytically to refer to means–ends relations where ends cannot be regarded as given and hence separate from the rational choice of means.

Instead there is reliance on alternative value-laden modes of cognition, whether of moral authenticity, as in Marshall's discussion of the uprightness of character underlying modern entrepreneurship, or 'symbolism' as in Pareto and Durkheim in their respective discussions of ritual and the collective conscience. It follows that positivism cannot be regarded as a 'generic' feature of any action schema.

This in turn brings a further pillar of the utilitarian action theory, namely rationality itself, into doubt. For if positivism is not the only mode of cognition of 'external reality', then the rational choice of the most appropriate means to reach given ends is itself only germane to one type of action rather than action in general. As Weber pointed out the notion of instrumental rationality is only one of several possible orientations to action (Brubaker, 1984).

*A. Marshall*

While such challenges began to emerge within the heart of utilitarian-derived economic theory itself, they did not necessarily bring the entire system itself into question. This is certainly the case for Marshall. His perception that 'activities' including the valuation of economic practices for their own sake, existed alongside the maximisation of utilities through the rational choice of means, is a typical example of a significant residual within mainstream economic thought, and Marxist political economy as well. This residual status is reflected, for example, in the tendency to treat departures from rationality as examples either of 'ignorance', 'error', or in the Marxist case 'false consciousness'. Such residual categories form much of the penumbra of what economists regard as the non-economic or social context to economic activity.

While Marxist writers have moved beyond an atomistic framework in linking 'false consciousness' to power relations, and, as already indicated, to dominant ideology theory, economic theorists have adopted alternative postures towards the analysis of 'ignorance' and 'error'. The most 'rational' is to consider information availability and information costs as an important element in economic exchanges. Alternatively there has been a tendency to brand actors displaying ignorance and error as 'irrational', 'wilful', 'whimsical' or 'irresponsible'. Goldthorpe (1978) has documented this tendency in economists' analyses of the role of the state and labour movements in money supply and cost-push theories of inflation.

In spite of Marshall's suggestive post-utilitarian comments, Goldthorpe's paper seems to suggest the continuing robustness of rational economic man and the research programme of utilitarian action theory. The robustness may on the other hand be more apparent than real, given evidence of an increasing divergence of opinion among economists as to the status of the *homo oeconomicus* assumption within a positivist framework. As Amartya Sen (1976, p. 325) has recently pointed out 'If today you were to poll economists of different schools, you would almost certainly find the co-existence of beliefs:

(1) that the rational behaviour theory is unfalsifiable
(2) that it is falsifiable and so far unfalsified, and
(3) that it is falsifiable and indeed patently false.'

While Marshall may have only pre-figured certain potential elements in a post-utilitarian theory of action, and as such left no permanent imprint on economists' treatment of social variables, Parsons' discussion of Pareto, Weber and Durkheim highlights a definite movement towards a voluntaristic theory of action among writers more closely aligned with the discipline of sociology. In spite of the disparate intellectual backgrounds from which they came, Parsons regards these three as presenting a profound challenge to the positivistic basis of utilitarianism and a far more elaborate discussion of the place of ends within social action than that offered by Marshall.

## V. Pareto

Pareto, for example, while eminent as a leading economist of his generation, was concerned to develop social science beyond the insights available from an elaboration of utility theory in the sphere of economics. Alongside his work on general economic equilibrium which yielded the concept of 'Pareto optimality', he also conducted a more far-reaching inquiry into the methodo-logical basis and substantive scope of a more general social science. In the former of these tasks, Pareto expressed consider-able scepticism as to the positivistic assumption that scientific theories must necessarily be truths about the empirical world. Any body of theory, as for example economic theory, is seen rather as a selective understanding of data, whose facticity is only observable in terms of a discrete conceptual schema. One important implication of this was that no single abstract concep-tual scheme could be expected to yield a comprehensive account of social phenomena.

While Pareto's initial social scientific work lay in economics, one important effect of this methodology was to encourage a *theoretical* interest in extra-economic phenomena. However powerful economic theory might be in explaining certain categ-ories of phenomena, its provenance could not be expected to be theoretically comprehensive. Alternative theoretical points of departure were therefore required, especially in the treatment of those 'ends of action' which were unintelligible in terms of the logical assumptions of economic theory. This position distinguished Pareto from Marshall who maintained a positivist, and indeed highly empiricist approach to scientific under-standing. For Parsons, this continuing commitment to posi-tivism on the part of Marshall inhibited a theoretical scrutiny of those phenomena, such as 'activities' which could not be explained through the resources of economic theory. On the basis of Marshall's positivism, the considerable empirical insights that could be derived from the rational choice assump-tions of economic theory left little or no scope for treating residual problems, such as the determination of ends and their relation with one another in terms of some alternative or additional theoretical standpoint.

It was Pareto's breach with positivism, and not any greater empirical awareness of the limited scope of economistic rational choice assumptions, which led him rather than Marshall to bring into theoretical discourse those 'residues' within social action which were neither amenable to the positivistic means-end schema nor explicable in terms of ignorance and error therefrom. Such residues represented ends or classes of action, such as ritual, which cannot be justified in terms of any scientific theory as means to other ends, but are deemed desirable as ends in themselves. Parsons goes on to argue that Pareto's residues could be theorised because they were not random but rather constituted a system of action. In these respects Pareto's conceptual schema creates space for the analysis of common values that may link together the ends of individuals, and as such represents a fundamental break with utilitarian action theory.

Parsons takes Pareto to be of special significance in elaborating a challenge to utilitarian action theory from within the mainstream of economic theory. He nonetheless draws fundamentally on the work of Weber and Durkheim in consolidating his picture of the convergence of theorists from different intellectual traditions on the voluntaristic theory of action.

*M. Weber*

Although Max Weber tended to regard himself as a social-economist rather than sociologist – at least until 1910 or so – his work does not stand in the same central position in Anglo-Saxon economic thought as that of Pareto. His economic writings on capitalism and economic rationality may nonetheless be viewed as a blend of the German school of historical economics, concerned with the analysis of historically particular economic mentalities and institutions and the pre-occupation of neo-classical economics for abstract conceptualisation and a means-end action framework. As is well known, this latter impact was felt not only in Weber's methodological commitment to the 'ideal-type method', but also within the concept of instrumental rationality (*zweck-rationalität*). For Parsons, Weber's contribution may be contrasted with Pareto in that it offers a general typology of social action, constituted in terms of different logical relationships between means-ends schema.

In this typology instrumental rationality exists alongside other orientations to action, most notably value-rationality. By this concept Weber sought to emphasise the coherence of action 'determined by a conscious belief in the value for its own sake of some ethical, aesthetic, religious or other form of behaviour, independently of its chances for success' (Weber, 1978, p. 25).

This type of action, which approximates to a good deal of what Pareto regarded as 'nonlogical' or a 'residue', could, following the ideal-type method, be regarded as having an internal logic referring to patterns of cultural meaning and their implementation in action. In both his sociology of religion and the Protestant ethic discourse on the spirit of modern capitalism, Weber emphasised the importance of value attitudes, not as intuitively grounded emanations, of 'spirit' as in so much of German idealist historiography, but in relation to a non-utilitarian theory of action. Actors could in other words have 'ideal' (that is value-related) as well as 'material' interests. This has two crucial implications for utilitarianism and Marxist political economy. The first is that the 'ideal' cannot be reduced to the 'material'. Value commitments may rather be rooted in cultural movements such as the ethic of ascetic Protestantism. Secondly value-commitments may influence the direction in which self-interest is channelled. This is encapsulated in Weber's celebrated aphorism that 'very frequently the world images that have been created by "ideas" have, like switchmen, determined the tracks along which action has been pushed by the dynamic of interest' (Weber, 1970, p. 280).

## E. Durkheim

Durkheim differs to a certain extent from the other three subjects of *The Structure of Social Action* in not having approached the resources of economic theory from some kind of internal viewpoint. The importance of utilitarian action theory and the problems therein are nonetheless a clear-cut feature of his work. From the outset Durkheim was profoundly concerned with the atomistic implications of economic individualism within market relations and the difficulties posed thereby for the problem of order in society. In Parsons' view there is a close, even a 'point by point' convergence of much of Weber's thinking on the problem of economy and society with that of Durkheim.

    The essence of Durkheim's position is contained in the influential notion of the 'non-contractual basis of contract'. Here he developed the view that the nature and binding force of the institution of contract could not be explained in terms of the sectional interests of contracting parties. It depended rather on the institutionalisation of certain kinds of solidarity through a normative order to which each party felt obliged to attach. Such a normative order, or set of 'ends', independent of individual interest, was thus present at the heart of economic life at least if it was to continue on a stable basis.

The corrosive effect of all this on the utilitarian action theory was of course considerable. For the operation of the economy depended not on a multitude of rational self-seeking atoms, but on a social system of relations between actors which relied on a normative bond. Utilitarianism, having failed to show how self-interest would not lead to an anarchy or war of all against all, should therefore be replaced by an alternative social theory. Unlike Weber whose intellectual background was heavily influenced by neo-Kantian epistemology, Durkheim found it harder to abandon the positivist assumptions of French rationalism. For a while his solution to the problem of order was therefore obtained at the cost of action theory, by assimilating norms to the external conditions of the situation facing the actor. The later Durkheim, however, came to believe that order was inconceivable without a more voluntaristic element involving belief (Lukes, 1973, p. 419). In other words it is the sense of moral desirability rather than obligation in the face of external sanctions, for example law, which produces order in contracts or elsewhere. Normative order therefore depended as in Weber on a measure of value-commitment.

Durkheim's particular substantive contribution was to explore such forms of solidarity, their genesis, morphology and reproduction through the symbolic bases of ritual. This paralleled much of Weber's work on the sociology of religion. While not without ambivalence (Lukes, 1973, pp. 474–5) Durkheim's view of the place of religion in the development of modern society is probably more optimistic than that of Weber. Thus instead of seeing the drying up of concern for ultimate values in the face of rationalisation, Durkheim sees religion as synonymous with the sacred core values of society itself. Such values are in constant need of re-affirmation and rehearsal if society is not to fall into a state of moral de-regulation. Such differences between Weber and Durkheim have some bearing on the discussion of the controversial role that Parsons gives to values and normative order in his analysis of modern society, and of the relationship between economy and society (see below pp. 56–78).

Parsons' *The Structure of Social Action* may be seen as laying much of the meta-theoretical foundation for the substantive theory of economy and society developed in the 1950s. He was of course to develop a far more elaborate discussion of the personality and psychic life within the further extensions to the general theory of action in the late 1940s and early 1950s (1950b, 1952a, 1953c). This work, stimulated in part by contact with the Freudian tradition of psychoanalysis, may be viewed as another important meta-theoretical development of Parsons' social theory into the expressive, that is emotional and subjective, as opposed to instrumental functions. Its underlying significance, as Parsons himself later pointed out (Parsons, 1961f, p. 318) was both to explore borderline problems between sociology and psychology, and to amplify the main thrust of *The Structure of Social Action* by exploring further 'the genesis of nonrational motivation', a problem neglected in conventional economic thought. In this latter sense, a strong sense of theoretical continuity with the earlier work is evident.

The main foundations laid within *The Structure of Social Action*, on which Parsons' later economic work was built, can be summarised as twofold. The first involves the claim to have located a basis for retaining the notion of the economy as an action system while rejecting utilitarian assumptions of the randomness of ends. Such ends, expressing value commitments are rather to be seen at work within and around economic life, linking the actions of individuals with one another. Ends function both as means of expression of individual values and as a means of producing social order. Here Parsons' economic sociology claims advantages not possessed in either utilitarian economics of Marxist thought. These amount to a solution to the problem of order without recourse either to environmental determinism, the social structural determinism of economic forces (for example the valorisation of capital) or to the device of assuming 'interests' at some level to be harmonious. Order is neither to be explained through rational adaptation to 'given' conditions, by the coercive power of dominant interests, or through a social ontology of the human species.

This position was itself built on an attempted solution to the

utilitarian dilemma, which combined a notion of social life as
both 'action' and 'structure'. The interpretation of *The Structure
of Social Action* presented here confirms the emphasis placed by
Münch (1981) and Holmwood (1983) on the combination of a
sense of 'compulsiveness' in the effects of the social system
on individuals, with the voluntaristic theory of action. This is
reflected in views of society as represented by a plurality of
unit-acts whose consequences represent emergent features of
social organisation at the societal rather than necessarily always
at the individual level. Parsons did not therefore discover the
'social system' in his post-war work. This interpretation would
only be valid if it could be shown either that the pre-war voluntaristic theory of action is inflected with a sense of unbounded
subjective will, or that his post-war references to society as a
system entail a sense of compulsive determination at the
expense of cultural meaning and value-commitment. Neither
can be substantiated.

There are nonetheless important limitations to Parsons' pre-
war writing on economy and society. The foremost of these
concern the conceptualisation of the economy in relation to the
other parts of the social system and the development of theories
explaining the articulation of the various sub-systems one with
another. Neither in *The Structure of Social Action* nor in his
important pre-war articles on economic theory, does Parsons
present much of interest in relation to a substantive theory of
economy and society.

Some idea of Parsons' current thinking on the substantive
scope of a theory of economy and society can nonetheless be
gleaned from his comments on the relationship between sociology and conventional economic theory. These are not defined
in relation to empirically distinct sets of subject-matter, but in
terms of their relationship to the general action schema. This is
characterised in terms of two dimensions. The first involves the
various components of the 'means-end' chain, the second
relates to the role of actors within the unit act.

Within this schema Parsons defines the theoretical object of
economics as the study of the choice of means in given
conditions to reach a given end, involving means-ends strategies applicable to the action systems of particular individuals.
This involves a conventional view of the economy as the setting

of scarce means to reach given ends. Sociology is to be found at the other end of the means-end chain, dealing with the relationship between the 'ends' of a plurality of individuals and with the choice of means in the light of such ends. The subject matter of sociology can thereby be summarised as 'the integration of individuals with reference to a common value system, manifested in the legitimacy of institutional norms, in the common ultimate ends of action, and in ritual and various modes of expression' (Parsons, 1973a, p. 768).

On the face of it, this amounts to an intellectual division of labour between economics (the domain of instrumental rationality) and sociology (the domain of value rationality). Theorists of economy and society should neither be seeking to supplant conventional theory, nor to subsume it under some encyclopaedic general sociology. Within a general approach to social theory (which was far more Parsons' ultimate interest than 'sociology') sociology should compliment economics – albeit on a theoretical rather than *ad hoc* 'residual basis'.

There is however a tension between this standpoint and the underlying substantive thrust of Parsons' argument that economic life cannot function in a self-subsistent way without the involvement of 'sociological' influences (for example value-commitments and institutionalised norms). In this respect Parsons' intellectual division of labour is combined with a strong sense of hierarchy. In this the problem of order takes precedence over the problem of want – satisfaction. What is therefore left unresolved in *The Structure of Social Action* is the nature of both the boundary relations and possible inter-penetrations between society and the economy. In resolving this issue, as we shall see, economic theory does eventually become subsumed under a more general theoretical framework, stressing the primacy of cultural determinism.


*Economy and Society*: the development of a mature theory

Between the publication of *The Structure of Social Action* and *Economy and Society* (jointly with Neil Smelser in 1956), Parsons consolidated and enlarged the scope of the meta-theoretical framework set out in his pre-war work. The most notable works

of this intervening period deal with personality and socialisation, and with the professions. They exerted an important
influence on Parsons' subsequent return to the problem of
economy and society through his formulation of the concept
of the pattern-variables (Parsons, 1953a) and the four-function
paradigm for analysing social systems (ibid.).

Parsons' pattern variables comprise a striking set of conceptual dichotomies, namely: universalism-particularism, achieve-
ment-ascription, diffuseness-specificity, neutrality-affectivity,
and self-orientation – collectivity-orientation. Underlying these
dichotomies is an attempt to chart the various dimensions of
modernity. For Parsons, following Durkheim, this involves at
one and the same time a higher degree of freedom of individual
action, set within a normative order founded on an increasingly
generalised set of values. Modernity is manifest through the
familiar process of differentiation or division of labour. Parsons
did not as yet address the problem of social change in any
explicit theoretical manner. The 'pattern variables' may
nonetheless be seen as a way of conceptualising the nature of
'modernity'. What is especially important here is the identification of individual variables with particular system 'needs' and
with the inter-relationships that exist between different sub-
systems of the action system.

Such problems of inter-relationship or 'interpretation' of
different sub-systems had first arisen for Parsons in his analysis
of the professional–client relationship. Here the client's need
for trust was felt to involve diffuse, affective and particularistic
bonds, while the professional links with his discipline emphasised specific, neutral and universalistic bonds. This particular
issue not only raised the question of what were the main social
sub-systems, but also of course how such systems might inter-
relate. These general questions led Parsons and his various
associates to specify the four-function paradigm (AGIL) of
system needs, and the mechanisms of interchange between
them. This schema sub-divided any social system into the
components of (A) adaptation of resources to environment, (G)
goal-attainment, (I) integration, and (L) latent pattern-
maintenance.

Parsons' pattern-variables, announced in 1951, had already
made an impact on sociologists interested in economic develop-

ment (Hoselitz, 1952, Kolb, 1954/5) prior to the translation of
the problem of economy and society into the four-function paradigm in 1956. This highly formalised framework now provided
Parsons and Smelser with a way of developing a far more
elaborate theoretical approach to the problem than anything
offered previously within the mainstream of economic sociology. This in turn led to a resolution of the problem of the
relationship between sociological thought and economics.

*Economy and Society* is dedicated to Alfred Marshall and Max
Weber as 'pioneers' in the integration of economic and sociological theory. The elaborate research programme, rich in
hypotheses, generated in this work, is founded on the four-
function paradigm as it applies to the logical structure of
conventional economic theory. Economic theory, in other
words, is no longer treated as a separate analytical science, with
a theoretical object distinct from that of sociology, but as a
'special case of the general theory of social systems and hence
of the general theory of action' (1956a, p. 306). Further 'On the
most general level which defines economic theory, there are no
specifically economic variables', the variables are those of the
general theory of action (ibid.).

This argument has two very important implications. The first
is that the functioning of the economy cannot be understood
except in terms of the interpenetration of 'economic' and 'non-
economic' processes. 'This applies to processes at the boundaries *and* within the economy' (ibid., Parsons' emphasis). In
this respect the economy cannot be regarded as self-subsistent,
even, as in conventional economic theory, for the purpose of
analysing a limited range of short-run market relations. In the
second place, however, Parsons retains an important place for
conventional economic theory by subsuming it within the more
general theory of action designed to analyse the interpenetration of economics and economic processes. This represents
a strikingly original invitation to sociologists to consider the
entire substantive canon of conventional economics in a positive
light. Equally, it invites economists to consider the possibility
of integrating economic theory in a systematic fashion within a
more unified social science. Equipped with the general theory
of action, Parsons felt he had successfully charted areas
regarded by economists as 'residuals'. By this means, a way

was opened to demonstrate the commensurability of central issues in economic theory, such as the operation of the labour market, or the theory of the trade cycle, with issues within the general theory of social systems.

## The economy as a sub-system of society

There are two main steps in Parsons' theorisation of the economy within the social system and action frameworks. The first is to view the economy as that sub-system of *society* dealing with 'adaptive exigencies' (A). On this level, the 'economy' is not centrally concerned with value-patterns (L), normative order (I), or even with the process of goal-attainment (G). Instead it concentrates on the function of production, adapting available resources to meet given goals in the face of environmental exigencies. Within this differentiated societal framework the economy is not self-subsistent, but rather engaged in constant 'boundary interchanges' with the three other sub-systems of society.

Parsons and Smelser elaborate the nature of such interchanges by drawing selectively on certain aspects of the logical structure of mainstream economic theory. The need for selectivity arises from the continuing presence of atomistic utilitarian assumptions within this body of thought. These are to be found mainly on the 'demand' side within such categories as 'utility', 'income', and 'consumption'. This set of concepts is usually defined so as to exclude the 'ends' underlying demand from the provenance of 'economic' (or any other kind of social) determination. At the same time space is left for the consideration of rational choice by individual consumers as part of the circle of economic activity linking 'demand' (or consumption) with 'supply' (or production).

For Parsons and Smelser, by contrast, the determination of ends is set firmly within the social system. It is not however subsumed to the atomistic means-ends strategies of utility-maximising rational economic man. The ends of consumer demand, and the transmission of such wants to the production sub-system are located in social relations located outside the economy in the other societal sub-systems. Consumption is not then in any sense a directly economic phenomenon. Consumption ends emerge rather within processes involving the socialisation of the personality and the institutionalisation of cultural values. 'Utility', 'income', or 'consumption wants' are therefore 'states and properties' of social systems not 'propensities' of individual atoms whose rational choices within the economy determine social processes.

With the proviso of this fundamental critique of the 'demand' side of conventional economics, Parsons and Smelser claim positive insights from other key aspects of economic thought. Two particular examples stand out. The first involves the analogy of input-output relations between elements in a system which is used to characterise the exchanges between subsystems of society. The second and more fundamental draws on the four factors of production, which are taken as representing congruent social system problems to those specified in the AGIL framework.

For classic political economy, land, labour and capital represented the three factors of production, which served as supply inputs into the system of production. The equivalent outputs (or factor incomes) were rent, wages, and interest. To this list, economists of the neo-classical epoch added a fourth factor input, namely 'organisation' (Marshall) or 'entrepreneurship' (Schumpeter), for which the appropriate output in terms of factor income, was 'profit'. Parsons links these four factors and their equivalent factor incomes to the four-function paradigm in the following manner.

'Capital' when defined as a stock of resources available for production, corresponds to the system need for means to realise or attain goals. It is linked as such to the polity or goal-attainment system (G). If capital is a major output from this system to the economy (A), this is 'balanced' by the input of 'interest' into the polity from the economy. Instead of the economic definition of interest as a reward for capital supply (a theory itself under challenge within economic theory), Parsons re-defines this category in societal terms. Attention is shifted from the monetary to the symbolic quality of interest rates. While 'on the one hand it represents the degree of the creditors' rights to intervene or power to control the relinquished capital funds . . . on the other hand, the interest rate represents one of the primary symbolic means of encouraging or discouraging enterprise' (1956a, p. 75). In overall terms these amount to expressions of political concern towards the state of the economy in general, and the productivity performance of the economy at current levels of credit, in particular.

Parsons' discussion of 'land' draws on the classical economist's notion of an entity whose supply is 'given' vis-à-vis current economic sanctions. This meaning is extended in a metaphorical way, in order to include certain 'human' resources alongside the physical entity 'land'. Such resources include scientific knowledge, technology, and the underlying commitment to work, all of which may be said to be 'given' vis-à-vis the adaptive sub-system. In contrast to the Marxist location of the 'productive forces' *within* the economic base – a location in which scientific knowledge never did fit happily – such 'land' factors are however external to the economy. They relate instead to the pattern-maintenance (L) function. It might be added that the inclusion of scientific knowledge in the pattern-maintenance system reflects Parsons' rejection of a positivistic rationalistic perspectives of 'science'. Commitment to scientific inquiry and the selection of particular fields of inquiry are rather reflections of value commitments, not least of which, as Weber pointed out, is the belief that the fruits of 'science' are worth knowing. In the case of science, like the other 'land' factors, the values contained therein 'will, within limits, be acted upon wherever appropriate, independent of cost' (1956a, p. 26).

The place of labour as a factor of production is more difficult to fit into this system. This is because two distinct processes are involved. The first of these involves fundamentally 'extra-economic matters like the underlying willingness to work'. This – as a cultural process – has been assigned (as we have seen) to the pattern-maintenance system. Labour can, however, be considered in a second light, namely in its 'economic' guise, responsive to short-term fluctuations within the labour market. As such labour supply may be seen as crucial to meeting the adaptive needs to the social system, with wages representing the factor income corresponding to labour input.

As far as organisation, the fourth factor input, is concerned, this is seen as 'balanced' by the income output of 'profit'. This notion of 'profit' is a technical one. It refers to 'income' that accrues neither to the input of 'capital' nor to the specialised labour inputs of management. Distinct from either of these is the money return to innovation.

Although Parsons and Smelser have some difficulty in fitting labour into the four-function paradigm, their over-riding aim is to establish a plausible logical congruence between the input-output relationships characteristic of the economists' four factors of production, and the analytical categories of the general theory of social systems. This aim serves two fundamental purposes. In the first place, it is on the basis of logical congruence between problems of sociological and economic theory that Parsons and Smelser rest their claim to have produced a *theoretically specific* account of the 'sources and destinations of these inputs and outputs' within the social system (see Parsons' later commentary in 1961 of pp. 351–2). It is as if sociology, in comparison with Marshall's day had finally come of age. Secondly, Parsons and Smelser go on to elaborate this logical congruence by treating the economy as a social system in its own right. Attention thereby shifts in the theory of economy and society from society as a whole, including the boundary-interchanges between its parts, to a consideration of the economy, its internal differentiation into four sub-systems, and finally, the articulation of each sub-system with the wider society.

The task of the theory of economy and society is not therefore restricted to showing the general theoretically determinate relations that exist between economic life in toto and the social context in which it takes place. Parsons and Smelser go well beyond Durkheim and Weber in this respect. For their claim is that a theoretically elaborate set of linkages exists between an economy, internally differentiated to meet four 'system' needs, and each of three other sub-systems of the wider society. The complexity of the Parsonian research programme for economic sociology is centred on its exhaustive but theoretically structured agenda, whereby relations are sought between the 'adaptive' goal-attainment, integration and pattern-maintenance sub-systems of the economy, and *specific* sub-systems of the goal-attainment, integration and pattern-maintenance sub-systems of the wider society.

## The economy as a social system

A detailed elaboration of the input-output boundary inter-changes between each of the economies' four sub-systems and the appropriate 'external' location in the wider society is beyond the scope of this paper. Three major 'interchanges' nonetheless stand out.

### (a) The goal-attainment sub-system of the economy

The first involves the goal-attainment sub-system of the economy (Ag). If the economy as a whole functions to adapt available resources to extra-economic goals through the production of goods and services, the goal-attainment sub-system of the economy functions to articulate such goals with the process of production. As a first approximation, inputs of goals from extra-economic sources are 'balanced' through this sub-system with outputs of goods. With what specific sub-system of the social environment, however, does the goal-attainment sub-system of the economy inter-relate?

In Parsons and Smelser's schema, the answer centres on the goal-attainment sub-system of the pattern-maintenance system (Lg). By linking 'economic' goals with the pattern-maintenance system, the intention is to emphasise that consumption wants or 'demand' is neither economically derived, nor simply the outcome of power relations. Consumption is neither to be theor-ised in terms of self-interested 'economic man' nor in terms of the coercive manipulation of the mass of consumers by concen-trations of corporate power orchestrated through advertising. It emerges rather from the sphere of value-commitments expressed within the pattern-maintenance system (L).

It should be emphasised that Parsons' discussion of the func-tion of commodity-exchange and the valuation of commodities is founded on an effective rejection of both key value categories in Marxist political economy, namely exchange-value and use-value. The notion that the value of commodities in exchange is generated from the 'supply' side through their role in the reproduction of capital simply ignores the importance of authentic consumer wants in determining the dissection of economic life. It was this neglect in classical political economy as a whole, formulated in an epoch prior to the advent of steadily rising real incomes for urban-industrial populations, which neo-classical economists later sought to overcome in the light of the subsequent rise of mass consumption. Parsons does not however take up the classical economists' notion of use-value as a basis for redressing this neglect. Like the neo-classical notion of 'utility' that succeeded it, this conception of commodity-valuation is strongly instrumentalist, effectively excluding any kind of cultural meaning or value-commitment. For Parsons, consumer wants and evaluations of goods are seen instead to have crucial symbolic and not merely instrumental functions in terms of status and prestige.

A further important feature of Parsons' discussion of consumption is that individual consumer demands on the company are not mediated through the societal integration system (I) which institutionalises values into a predictable and stable normative order. This indicates that Parsons and Smelser see consumption goals as a relatively unstable element in the social order and hence subject to change. There is still an implicit sense therefore of the 'irrational' ultimate values on which many such consumption decisions may rest. This is not however equivalent to the economists' conception of the randomness of the 'ends of consumption'. Since the functions of consumption are social and inter-personal, this must mean that individual relations of goods must be institutionalised to a certain extent to be effective. Neither 'status' nor 'prestige' can be expressed in consumption without some shared basis by which evaluation may take place. The socialisation of personality represents one important means by which shared values of this kind are inculcated.

If value-choices expressed in consumption cannot be reduced to individual atomistic preferences, it is equally misleading however to regard them as the outcome of some stifling value-consensus. In this as in so many other areas of Parsonian sociology, the interest in value-consensus is not from the viewpoint

of the functional inculcation of conformity and even less from
the need to control 'insatiability'. It lies rather in the emergence
of generalised enabling meachanisms permitting maximum variation in individual action. Value-commitment to consumer
sovereignty may be seen in this light, as a key component of
modernity.

While offering little empirical elaboration of this argument,
the theoretical space provided for an autonomous sociology of
consumption within the theory of economy and society
represents one of the most under-appreciated elements of
Parsonian economic sociology.

Within sociological discourse however, consumption remains
theorised in one of two alternative ways. The first, reproducing
the classical political economy of the nineteenth century, sees
consumption as governed by the distribution of wealth and
the general productivity of the economy. Normative elements
appear here, if at all, as residual, reflecting Marx's comment
that 'Besides the mere physical element of life, the value of
labour is in every country determined by the traditional standard of life' (Marx, 1970, p. 57). The second amounts to a
version of the 'dominant ideology thesis' in which Marxist
political economy is married with Freud's exploration of the
subconscious. Within Frankfurt School Marxism in particular,
attention is drawn to the communicative mechanisms such as
advertising, through which it is claimed that the imperatives of
capitalist mass marketing are internalised (Marcuse, 1964).
While the latter approach is not without insight, there have
been some recent, if somewhat sporadic calls to take consumption and the autonomy of consumers more seriously as objects
of sociological inquiry (Kellner, 1983; Moorhouse, 1983). This
reflects a growing resistance to the exclusive treatment of
'consumption' as an inauthentic expression of alienated
consumer consciousness under capitalism.

Alexander (1984, p. 233) has recently disputed whether
Parsons' and Smelser's discussion is an adequate way of
responding to the conventional neglect of values and norms
within the sociology of consumption. He sees their analysis
as 'one-sided', inasmuch as it 'vastly underplays the role of
instrumental rationality' in facing the situational exigencies that
are involved in consumption decisions. Although this criticism

may seem surprising in that Parsons and Smelser are committed at a theoretical level to assert the interpenetration of instrumental and normative elements, Alexander's point is that this commitment is not sustained in their substantive theory of consumption. At the same time he does not go on to suggest alternative lines of enquiry as to what a more adequate theory might look like. This is to neglect the very important recent contribution of Mary Douglas and Baron Isherwood entitled *The World of Goods* (1979). This goes much further than Parsons and Smelser in its elaboration of the symbolic functions of consumption. But it combines this with a review of recent attempts by economists to provide a more sophisticated account of the rational choice elements in consumption. The most notable of these is Milton Friedman's work on the importance of total lifetime calculations on consumer behaviour (1957).

Consumer goals represent the first major input into the goal-attainment sub-system of the economy from the pattern-maintenance system. This input is seen as 'balanced' by the output of consumer goods and services. There is however a second major boundary interchange between these two parts of the social system. This involves the input of human services from the pattern-maintenance system to the economy. For the economy to establish a goal-attainment sub-system of its own, the input of consumer goals must be combined with social actors who have been socialised to perform discrete occupational roles. This socialisation process involves value-commitments on the part of those seeking to fulfil these roles. Such commitments include 'acceptance of the responsibility to be a "good provider" for the needs and prestige of the household' (1956a, p. 117) wherein socialisation takes place. It also involves a commitment of 'trust' or 'loyalty' to employing firms, with whom those filling occupational roles are contracted.

An extremely important feature of this analysis is that 'consumption' is not considered as the exclusive basis by which extra-economic values influence economic activity. The emphasis in this double interchange is on the complementarity of consumption inputs and labour-service inputs from the pattern-maintenance system to the economy. Amongst other things this allows Parsons and Smelser to avoid the problem raised in much recent sociology as to the primacy of occu-

pational identity or consumer identity in modern industrial societies. The mutually exclusive manner in which such debates are
often conducted is inappropriate as a basis for theorising the
relationship between economy and society.

Beyond this general consideration Parsons and Smelser go on
to establish the extra-economic origin of the *system* of occupational roles (as distinct from the technical component of individual roles). This is not co-terminous with the economy. The
system of roles cannot be regarded as the spontaneous creation
of economic forces. Socialisation into this system is regarded as
extra-economic in origin, located in the household and
education system. Here Parsons explicitly rejects those economistic accounts which consider the 'human service' inputs simply
in terms of their function for economic life. Their critique of
conventional economics in this respect is also applicable to
certain recent Marxist discussions which have sought to assimilate domestic labour in the household, including the reproduction and socialisation of children, to the predominant
influence of the mode of production and such 'economic' mechanisms as the extraction of surplus-value.

It might be added in reinforcement of Parsons and Smelser
in this respect that the naive assimilation of human services
to economic imperatives leads straight back to the utilitarian
dilemma. Either personality formation and socialisation into
specialised roles are explained unilaterally in terms of economic
production imperatives in which case all sense of the autonomy
of agency and the cathectic side of personality becomes lost; or
the economy and role specialisation are conceived in a voluntaristic way in which case the possibility of normative order in
the regulation of individual 'choices' of role is jeopardised
through patternless chaos and conflict over access to roles.

The pattern-maintenance system is thus crucial, once again,
in explaining the origins of a fundamental input, in this case
human services, into the economy. The social values and value-
commitments contained within this system become crucial both
for the socialisation of children into particular roles, and the
tension-management of adults who fill such roles. Such
processes are located institutionally within the household and
represent a specific extra-economic input, alongside consumer
wants, into the economy. The adhesion of human services in

this manner is, however, 'balanced' by a further output from the economy, namely wages. This output is not to be regarded in an atomistic manner as a return to individual economic actors divorced from the wider society, but as an input into the household considered as an extra-economic unit. In this way Parsons emphasises that it is the household rather than the income-receiver that forms the major institutional unit of social stratification in terms of the distribution of income and wealth. This fairly simple point has nonetheless been systematically obscured in much economic discourse by the tendency to base discussions of standards of living on the atomistic unit of the 'income-receiver'.

In comparison with its neglect of consumption, sociological inquiry has had far more to say concerning the occupational division of labour, the relationship between 'social' and 'technical' aspects of the division of labour, and the connection between the input of human services to the economy in relation to the waged or salaried labour relationship. Work in these areas has not been exhausted either by unilateral economistic theories of the household or naive functionalist accounts of domestic life. Three particular currents stand out.

For some (Zaretsky, 1976) the household appears, as it does in Parsons, as the domain of sociability, personal life and individual values. This is not only seen as distinct from the economic order, however, but as profoundly antagonistic to it. The values of co-operation and expressive emotional bonds within the household are contrasted with the individual competitiveness and alienation of the workplace. This is, however, merely to rehearse the familiar duality of *Gemeinschaft* and *Gesellschaft*. What is not clear from these accounts is how the disjunction between the two spheres can be maintained, so that both 'economy' and 'household' can continue to function. How is it that household social relations of the *Gemeinschaft*-kind still manage to reproduce the socialisation of personalities capable of functioning in an effective and productive way in the economic life. It is difficult to explain the long-term dynamism of modern capitalism over the last 150 years, given the dysfunctional characteristics ascribed to household and personal life, unless the economy is after all regarded as causally privileged.

This of course leaves action theory once again in an insecure and residual position.

Of more theoretical interest is the recent work on gender, personality formation and role specialisation, both within and outside the occupational sphere. One of the major weaknesses of economistic theories of role specialisation is a failure to produce convincing explanations of the gender division of labour. The assignment of women to parenting and the predominance of men in certain economic occupations was taken more or less as 'given' – for some this given was located in 'nature' rather than constructed by 'society'. Recent studies of gender, informed in part by the work of Freud and to a lesser extent of Parsons, have shown by contrast the autonomy of processes of gender socialisation from either natural or economic determination (Chodorow, 1978; Mitchell, 1974). Socialisation has thereby been ratified both as a powerful mechanism for the reproduction of inequality, yet at the same time as a fundamental feature of social organisation, central to the formation of identity and adherence to norms. Inequalities associated with gender role specialisation can therefore be overcome not so much by economic change as by the reorganisation of socialisation, especially the socialisation of children. Theoretically then, much of Parsons' emphasis of the primacy of the goals of the pattern-maintenance system over the goals of the economy has been vindicated. This point is not compromised by the criticisms made by gender theorists of Parsons' institutional identification of the household with the nuclear family and of his ascription of affective socialisation roles to women.

A third set of commentaries focusses on what Parsons and Smelser refer to as the human service input-wages output boundary interchange. Leaving aside those criticisms which deny the salience of an action framework, much of the thrust of recent work in industrial sociology and class analysis has thrown doubt on the functional necessity of value-commitments to occupational role and to employing firms within the modern capitalist economy. As in so many other parts of Parsonian sociology, it is not the fact of social differentiation, so much as the assumption of normative order and value commitment that is in doubt. In this case, the question may be put as follows:

what, if any, is the non-contractual basis of 'contract' within the labour market?

A good deal of empirical evidence has been assembled to challenge the existence of value-commitment within the labour market. Much of this centres on the instrumental orientation of many categories of workers (Goldthorpe et al., 1968). In the case of manual workers, the traditional normative order of craft identity and pride, linked to notions of the 'dignity of the trade', is seen as undermined by processes such as de-skilling and the rationalisation of work tasks (Braverman, 1974).

Similar processes have been emphasised for many categories of white-collar workers (Mills, 1956; Mumford and Banks, 1967). The net effect for all those groups directly involved is seen as a decline in job satisfaction. An even more fundamental claim has been that such developments undermine the capacity of those affected to realise the achievement-oriented values of the wider culture. For Chinoy (1965, p. 133) 'the solution to the problems and meaning and purpose of their labour [for such groups] lies not merely in reorganisation of the job situation but in changes in the values of the larger society or in institutional changes which give them a greater degree of control over their fate'.

This kind of perspective helps to make sense of much of the resistance or anomic withdrawal found in industrial relations. It is not particularly useful, on the other hand, in dealing with phenomena such as 'loyalty' to the enterprise or value-commitments to an occupational role. The assessment of evidence germane to such aspects of Parsons' economic sociology of human services is, however, a very complex matter.

In the first place it is important to stress that Parsons is not committed to an exclusively 'productionist' explanation of such ties of loyalty, rather, the emphasis is on their development in the household and education system. In this sense at least, his position is consistent with the findings of the English *Affluent Worker* study, which also rejected the view 'that the ways in which workers view their firm and act in relation to it will always be primarily determined *within* the enterprise itself, as the result of in-plant activities and social relations' (Goldthorpe et al., 1968, p. 76). It was thus on the basis of extrinsic non-workplace influences that Goldthorpe and his associates organ-

ised their explanation of the clear majority of car assembly
line 'other manual and clerical workers who tended to see the
enterprise in generally "harmonistic" terms' (ibid., p. 74).

This study is an interesting one, in view of the outbreak
of an unprecedentedly militant strike shortly after the original
survey was conducted. This was taken by conflict theorists to
indicate the superficiality of the findings of relative industrial
peace (Blackburn, 1967, pp. 48–51). In the longer term,
however, what seems more important about such episodes of
militancy in Britain in the late 1960s and early 1970s is the
predominance of compliance, rather than a 'conflict' whose
roots are 'so deep' as to promise an 'inescapably unstable capitalist environment' (ibid., p. 50).

It is probable that the skewing of industrial sociology to
instances of conflict or breakdown has encouraged insufficient
attention to factors making for stability and integration,
however latent or tacit these may be. This having been said, it
remains problematic as to how evidence of relatively orderly
and conflict-free industrial relations is to be interpreted. Goldthorpe and his associates prefer to emphasise the instrumental
nature of workers' orientation to work and employment. Thus
'the generally positive attitudes towards their firms revealed by
the majority of our affluent workers would be seen as deriving
not so much from a moral but rather from a largely successful
calculative involvement with the organisations in question'
(ibid., p. 80). Whether it is possible to separate the instrumentalism of 'calculative rationality' and 'moral attachment' in this
way is rather doubtful. As Hirschman (1970) has argued, one
of the characteristics of 'loyalty' is the commitment to defer
'exit' from a situation, extending 'trust' to the organisation of
which one is a member to satisfy longer-term ends. It is probable
that the conceptual framework and underlying theoretical
presuppositions of the *Affluent Worker* team do not allow for the
interpretation of calculative instrumentalism and loyalty to the
firm in this way. As such, they neglect the possibility that
calculative rationality may have a moral component. This point
will be elaborated further in dealing with Parsons' discussion
of economic rationality as the principal component of the latent
pattern-maintenance sub-system of the economy (A1).

In addition, it is doubtful whether much of the extant

empirical evidence within industrial sociology has been designed in a sufficiently discriminating way to test propositions involving questions of loyalty to firm and commitment to occupational role. In both cases there may be a danger of looking for highly explicit examples of enthusiastic commitment. In this way the researcher who fails to find 'Quaker-like' statements of personal ethical witness may ignore the possibility that lack of strong feelings or 'indifference' to survey questions about moral issues may overlay tacit or latent commitments which are taken for granted. This expectation that values belong exclusively to the world of 'religious, ethical and generally humanistic discourse' has been persuasively criticised by Williams (1971) in his important essay on 'Change and stability in values and value systems'. The implication of such methodological problems is not of course that deep 'moral structures' can be assumed as ontological 'givens', but rather that research procedures should be sensitive to the different types of discourse wherein value-commitments might be found.

Notwithstanding these methodological issues, there are some *prima facie* grounds for regarding 'loyalty to the firm' in the Parsonian sense as a significant empirical feature of contemporary industrial societies. One possible indicator of this is the considerable evidence of stability in employment within a single enterprise. While the Japanese tendency to allocate individuals to particular firms as a result of the educational process may not be entirely typical of Western societies, there is some evidence in support of Dore's (1973) thesis of a growth of 'organisation-oriented employment' in many such societies. By this process

> the terms and conditions of employment are less and less
> influenced by consideration of the price a worker might
> get for his skill from another employer in the external market
> and more and more fitted into an internal structure of
> relative rankings peculiar to the enterprise and predicated
> on long-term employment (ibid., p. 12).

Such developments are reflected in the convention that long service *ought* to be rewarded as loyalty by giving preferential opportunities for long-serving workers when new employment opportunities arise, and the principle of 'last-in first-out' as means of organising redundancies.

It is also arguable that trade unionism, insofar as it operates in terms of company or plant bargaining, may involve the deployment of commitments to a particular enterprise on the part of employees seeking redress of grievances. For Parsons and Smelser (1956a, p. 148) there also exist semi-ritual functions of trade unions which

> integrate the individual worker and his household into a larger collectivity, membership in which enhances his self-respect and confidence . . . [This] in turn . . . can stimulate management, under the proper conditions, to give a larger output of contingent support and moral approval of the labour role to the household.

At this point it must be emphasised again that for Parsons the integration of labour into the enterprise is always as problematic as the development of social order itself. There is no functional necessity of social harmony. Unlike the extremely bland prognoses of 'industrial society' theorists such as Kerr et al. (1960), Parsons' position does not imply a benign 'end of ideology' in 'which the benevolent political bureaucracy and the benevolent economic oligarchy are matched with the tolerant mass' (ibid., p. 46). Within the modern labour market, with the development of effective trade unions to protect workers' interests, a repeated 'breakdown' in 'mechanisms of social control' is seen to be based on 'the exacerbation of the latent conflict of interest between management and labour' (Parsons and Smelser, 1956a, p. 149). In such cases it is important to note the 'non-economic' functions of trade unions in dramatising the anxieties and reinforcing the self-respect of workers through 'rituals, campaigns and therapy'. These help to balance the exigencies of the problematic situation whereby labour has 'to reconcile its inevitable involvements in both firm and household'. What is essentially at stake here for Parsons is a theory of the moral and symbolic aspect of trade unionism. This project is consistent with the recognition of conflicts of interest in industrial relations. With certain exceptions, such as the work of Holton (1978) on the crowd and social integration in modern society, very few analysts have sought to apply this neo-Durkheimian focus to the ritualistic features of the modern labour movement.

In addition to loyalty to the firm, there remains the more general question of orientation to occupational role. Here the case for instrumentalism looks somewhat stronger in those cases like the *Affluent Worker* study where survey data have found a greater commitment to 'pay' rather than to 'role' (Goldthorpe et al., 1968; see also Katona, 1964). Whether this is characteristic of the labour market in general is, however, doubtful. In the first place it is clear that in situations of occupational community, such as mining regions, waterfront areas, or one-industry towns identification with occupational role is high (Lipset et al., 1956; Hill, 1976). The *Affluent Worker* study may also not be typical insofar as its sample represented first-generation, geographically and socially mobile workers who had recently both changed jobs and settled in a new town without pre-existing community links.

Another way of disaggregating the labour force with respect to occupational role has been suggested by Goldthorpe (1982) in his discussion of the 'service class'. Here it is argued that the value-laden character of occupational role specialisation is far greater among managerial, professional and technical service sectors than elsewhere. The roles involved for such salaried workers are distinguished from labour-market relations elsewhere by a 'moral quality', namely trust.

> In the case of the wage-worker, the labour contract provides for more or less discrete amounts of labour to be exchanged for wages on a relatively short term basis; but the service relationship is such that the exchange in which employer and employee are involved has to be defined in a much less specific and longer-term fashion and with far greater moral content. It is not so much that reward is being offered in return for work done, but rather 'compensation' and 'consideration', in return for the acceptance of an obligation to discharge trust 'faithfully' (ibid., p. 168–9).

While such contrasts between the 'service class' and 'wage-worker' may identify an important area of heterogeneity in the character of commitment to occupational role, it is not certain whether a clear line of demarcation can be drawn between value-committed salaried 'service' personnel and 'instrumental' manual wage-workers. This is largely because wage-worker labour contracts, however short-term in the sense of formal periods of notice, may involve conventions of longer-term occupancy of roles and of some commitment to a diffuse 'service' ethic. This is probably most obvious in cases of public service manual workers in such fields as transportation, postal and telecommunications sectors.

Even if certain features of the 'instrumentalist' case for labour-market heterogeneity are accepted, however, this does not necessarily undermine all aspects of Parsons' conception of value-commitments and normative order surrounding occupational role specialisation. This is easier to appreciate if the system of occupational roles is seen as inclusive of, but wider than, employees within the labour market. Here the importance of socialisation processes involving value commitment is reflected both in the general unwillingness to accept 'unemployment' as a legitimate role (Bakke, 1933) and by the continuing salience of the gender division of labour whereby so many women want to be 'mothers', while so many men seek fulfilment in an active labour-market role. Parsons' conception of a strong sense of value commitment to occupational role specialisation remains plausible as an important social input into the economy. The functional significance of this contribution from the pattern-maintenance system to the achievement of the goals of the economy in the Parsonian schema should not be seen as necessarily excluded by instrumentalism in economic affairs, or by social conflict over particular features of the social division of labour between workplace and household. In this latter sphere the 'balancing' of the claims of the two different institutions is for Parsons always problematic and prone to 'strain'.

## (b) The adaptive sub-system of the economy

The second major boundary interchange between economy and society involves the adaptive sub-system of the economy (Aa). This sub-system may take the goals of the economy as 'given' at least in the short-term. Its concern is rather the acquisition of resources (other than human services) with which to conduct production so as to meet extra-economic consumer demands emerging from the pattern-maintenance system. In order to make commensurable the different types of resources involved, Parsons and Smelser utilise the notion of 'capital' as the generalised expression of such resources. As we have already seen, capital is not regarded as an exclusively economic category, but rather one pertaining both to the economy and the goal-attainment system or polity. This linkage is now taken a step further, with a more precise boundary interchange being posited between the adaptive sub-system of the economy and the adaptive sub-system of the polity (Ga). Here of course the political system is not co-terminous with government. Rather it involves all those institutions, governments included, which control the disposal of non-human resources such as 'capital' which are required for the attainment of social goals.

Within this schema, capital is quite clearly the first major input from the polity to the economy. By designating the adaptive sub-system of the polity (Ga) as that which inter-relates with the economy, Parsons reinforces the point that it is not social 'goals' which are exchanged between polity and economy but resources for the attainment of such goals. Capital transfers do not then amount to transfers of goal-imperatives. In this way Parsons does not offer a 'political economy' of economic life based on some kind of inter-action between the polity as the sphere of power with goals set by power-holders and the economy as the sphere of production. The place of the polity is far more delimited than this.

The substantive foundation of Parsons' critique of political economy concerns the separation of capital 'ownership' from economic 'management' in modern western societies. The full importance of this separation was not evident to nineteenth-century political economists like Marx. Their perceptions were based, however, on only a very transitional moment in the development of modern society, where capital ownership and managerial control were fused in the undifferentiated person of the nineteenth-century businessman. 'For a brief historical moment', write Parsons and Smelser, 'American capitalism appeared to be creating a new Schumpeterian "ruling class" of family dynasties founded by the "captains of industry". But this moment passed early in the present century and the trend since then is clear – the occupational manager, not the lineage-based owner, is the key figure in the American economic structure' (Parsons and Smelser, 1956a, p. 290). The implication of this argument is that modern industrial society, while unequally stratified, does not have a ruling class entrenched in the ownership of capital control of industry and pre-dominant in political power. The capitalisation of the economy does not therefore emerge from a unitary structure, but depends on input-output relations between a differentiated set of spheres.

Parkin (1979, pp. 51–4) has argued that Parsons' discussion of property, set in the context of the separation of ownership and control, serves to minimise the importance of private control over capital as a qualitatively different property right to those simply involving possession of objects. Alexander (1984, p. 198) has claimed that such inadequacies in the treatment of private capital prevent Parsons and Smelser from appreciating the economic constraints on Western government policy-making. Thus

> because capital formation is not in fact dependent on 'public'
> political decisions the national government does not
> receive the kind of adaptive inputs it needs to function
> effectively. National governments . . . rarely receive
> sufficient funds to achieve their public goals.

This line of criticism may be linked with more general difficulties with Parsons' discussion of 'power'. This has been seen as one of the most problematic features of his system insofar as it encourages a far too benign view of modern society, dominated by a pluralistic system of social exchange (Giddens, 1968). When applied to the discussion of capital, this pluralism maintains that neither the goal-attainment system nor the adaptive system may in the long-run deploy capital resources in an autonomous manner in defiance of the value-commitments and political loyalty of the pattern-maintenance and integration systems. In other words, the deployment of power involved in the capitalisation of the economy must remain more or less legitimate.

It is clearly the case that Parsons does assimilate power to social exchange theory. While this had not been fully elaborated in *Economy and Society*, his later works (Parsons, 1963f, 1966b) approach power as a generalised medium of exchange, analogous to money. On this analogy, power like money has no utility in and of itself; it is rather a facilitator of transactions. Having said this, Parsons' understanding of such transactions is not entirely benign, in the sense that negative sanctions may be involved in the enforcement of the obligations of exchange. Power 'exchanges' are not then simply a matter of freely willed, frictionless contractual arrangements. They are both enabling and constraining, and may involve coercion and conflict, as well as the satisfaction of need.

While Parsons does neglect the centrality of private capital to constraints on extra-economic goal-attainment, and as an institution whose legitimacy is profoundly disputed in modern societies, it is important to emphasise his awareness of the powerful and, in a sense, unequal property-rights that accrue to holders of 'capital'. These are evident when we consider the input-output relations between the polity and economy in more depth. In the first place, the input of capital funds from polity to economy is seen as balanced by a powerful right of intervention by the polity within the economy. Capital can thus always be withdrawn in accordance with prevailing rights retained by capital-holders, a sanction which gives considerable power to determine the nature and direction of economic activity. This kind of emphasis is compatible in a number of senses with Marxist emphases on the increasing dominance of 'finance capital' over the industrial process (Hilferding, 1910; Lenin, 1970) and with the notion that 'investment strikes' by capital represent a profound intervention by the holders of capital in the determination of economic life. There is nothing in Parsons' approach with respect to the provision of capital that rules out conflict or disequilibrium. In fact it implies the presence of such strains.

An interesting difference between Parsons' treatment of capital and that of Marxist political economy is his location of the capitalisation of the economy within an action framework. Capital transfers to the economy are not seen as setting inexorable system goals. In this way Parsons' position contrasts with the predominant tendency in Marxist political economy to treat capital as a self-expansive structural force deriving from the continuing generation of surplus-value within the production process. This expansiveness is grounded in Marx's argument that:

> The development of capitalist production makes it constantly necessary to keep increasing the amount of the capital laid out in a given industrial undertaking, and competition makes the immanent laws of capitalist production to be felt by each individual capitalist, as external coercive laws. It compels him to keep constantly extending his capital, in order to preserve it. (Marx, vol. 1, p. 555)

The expansive necessity of capital accumulation under competitive conditions is taken by most Marxist commentators to be manifest in a drive for profit-maximisation. In the process it is arguable that such problems as the institutional differentiation of capital owners, holders and users, and the role of value-commitments in investment contracts has been rendered epiphenomenal or invisible.

The predominance of 'situational determinism' over action theory in such formulations often produces a situation where capital becomes reified as a 'thing'. In spite of the attempt by many Marxists to treat capital as a relationship and not as a stock of resources, the discourse of political economy tends to speak of 'capitals' or 'fractions of capital' acting in this way or that. While Marx diagnosed a 'fetishism of commodities' in bourgeois political economy, it is tempting to locate an alternative difficulty, namely the fetishism of capitals in Marxist political economy. Following Marx, this might be taken to occur where the relationship between 'capitals' 'takes on the fantastic form of a relation between things'. This represents another of those occasions where 'the productions of the human brain appear as independent beings endowed with life and entering into relation both with one another and the human race'.

A tendency away from the compulsive lawlike depiction of determination by capital is evident in some versions of twentieth-century Marxist political economy. Just as the development of corporate oligopoly challenged nineteenth-century theories of the firm based on perfect competition, so the same type of phenomenon has challenged the competitive assumptions that lie behind theories of the expansiveness of capital. Baran and

Sweezy (1966), for example, emphasise the importance of the shift from individual to corporation as the locus of contemporary capitalism. Corporate 'monopolies' can, within limits, choose prices (ibid., p. 57) rather than accepting prevailing market-derived prices. At the same time price-making capacities are still set within a competitive system which demands profit maximisation. For Baran and Sweezy the cost-cutting emphases of the corporation result not in a tendency for the rate of profit to fall, as in Marx, but to a rise in the economic surplus. This is, however, premised not on the pressure of generalised social demands to satisfy wants by maximising productivity, as in Parsons' approach, but to system imperatives. In other words 'Maximum profits . . . become the subjective aims and values of the business world because they are the objective requirements of the system. The character of the system determines the psychology of its members not vice versa' (ibid., p. 42). It appears then that the shift to monopoly capital has not produced any fundamental change to the compulsive system imperatives of capitalism.

A more radical breach with Marx's competitive assumptions has been made by Friedman (1977). He argues that the diminution of competitive pressure has provided enterprises with 'a great margin of discretion over their policies'. While Mandel (1975) maintains that monopoly power allows the generation of super-profits, for Friedman this is often empirically not the case. Two reasons are offered for this. The first set engages, in a more positive way than Baran and Sweezy, with certain recent developments in the theory of the firm in mainstream economic theory. These speak either of maximisation of growth, staff or sales, or of the goal of satisfactory or optimum rather than maximum profits (Simon, 1952; Baumol, 1964). The second set of reasons involve the impact of labour-capital conflict and workplace resistance on levels of profitability. Here a neo-Ricardian emphasis on the distribution of income between classes is integrated into the micro-economic discussion of productive activity within particular firms.

Friedman's line of argument offers insights that appear unavailable in other currents of Marxist political economy, by freeing the capitalisation of the economy from an excessively determinist framework. At the same time it is still not clear that he gives sufficient weight to the differentiation between institutional suppliers of capital and users of capital in the production process. While clearly a good deal of capital is generated internally within the enterprise, this source is by no means predominant in securing the larger investment sums required for the more important corporate projects. Whether Marxist political economy loses any of its explanatory force by conflating capital users in the productive process with capital suppliers in financial institutions and elsewhere, depends on how much genuine differentiation exists between the aims and functions of the two sectors. This raises the issue of the sociological significance of the investment contract.

While a good deal of critical attention has been given to the problem of value commitment and the labour market, there is far less empirical material germane to the problem of the investment contract. The empirical aspect of Parsons' research programme at this point is entirely clear, involving an exploration of the 'common values' which link investors of capital and organisers of production. The hypothesis is that on the production side, both accept 'organization purpose, commitment to the goal of production and interest in productivity as a means of more effective production', while on the investment side there exists 'commitment to the responsibilities of "ownership", not merely with respect to a particular firm, but in terms of the "public responsibilities" of capital and its management' (1956a, pp. 128–9).

These relationships are traced by Parsons through a second important boundary interchange between the economy and the polity. This involves the input of various encouragements to particular kinds of productive enterprise (in such forms as tax relief, subsidies, and credit standing), balanced by the output of enhanced productivity. Control over productivity enables the polity to better meet 'system goals'. The mechanisms of control involved in these interchanges are 'political' for Parsons in that they do not arise spontaneously as a result of productive activities.

This is especially evident in Parsons and Smelser's interesting discussion of 'credit standing'. While the granting of such standing involves consideration of the degree of rationality with which applicants conduct their businesses, this is only one factor in the supply of credit. Two further elements are involved. The first concerns value-laden estimations of the 'reputation' and 'good faith' of the credit recipient. The second involves explanation of the pre-existing power position of the credit provider. This in turn includes value-concerns based on the proper management of capital funds deriving from investors of savings. To ensure an adequate flow of savings is not only a matter of attractive interest-rates but also of satisfying fiduciary obligations to lenders and depositors, such as the maintenance of adequate financial reserves.

Parsons' most fundamental claim in discussing the relationship between polity and economy remains the importance of a functional differentiation between both these two, and the remaining sub-systems of society dealing with integration and pattern-maintenance. It may well be that he underestimated the continuing importance of private capital ownership in reproducing social inequality in modern western societies. Yet this difficulty does not by itself dispose of his claim that the Marxist notion of the capitalist mode of production as a compulsive system based on the fusion of economy and polity has become increasingly undermined by other twentieth-century trends. These include citizenship rights (T. H. Marshall, 1950) by which loyalty to the political system is secured, and the influence of consumer goals and human service inputs expressed through the valuation of goods and activities. Marxist political economy, while encouraging an economistic theory of the state as the agent or facilitator of dominant class interests, has nonetheless proved incapable of treating 'value' as a cultural and symbolic category. The utilitarian echoes still present in Marxist discussions of value either displace the standing of culture and action frameworks altogether or else allude in a utopian manner to post-capitalist cultures of producer freedom.

## (c) The integration sub-system of the economy

The third fundamental boundary interchange in Parsons' theory of economy and society involves the integration sub-system of the economy (Ai). In developing the notion of the system function of integration with respect to the economy, Parsons and

Smelser draw on the realisation of both Marshall and Schumpeter that the combination of the various factors of production (land, labour and capital) does not occur spontaneously through the market mechanism. What is required, in addition, is a fourth integrating factor, designated (variously) as 'organisation' or 'entrepreneurship'. The organiser or entrepreneur is not seen merely as a routine business manager, but rather as a creative and imaginative innovator. In such endeavours, however, the entrepreneur draws on extra-economic resources to consolidate the role of economic integrator. These may include value-commitment to business as a vocation (Marshall) and the desire to found a family dynasty on the basis of business success (Schumpeter).

Schumpeter's work is especially interesting insofar as it offers a good deal of 'extra-economic analysis as to the sources and prospective fate of entrepreneurship in the modern Western world' (1961). In this he utilised Weber's notions of 'charisma', 'rationalisation', and 'the routinisation of charisma' (Weber, 1978, pp. 246–9). Entrepreneurship of the 'heroic' individualist kind played an especially important part in the early phases of capitalist development where innovation conflicted with the cultural preoccupations of stability, community, and a hierarchy of status. With the eventual triumph of rationalisation, however, the need for heroic cultural dissidents became undermined, leading to the routinisation of business activity. Schumpeter maintains that once the world has become depersonalised, automatised and accustomed to regular change, there remains no valid function for entrepreneurship. The anti-heroic, rationalistic thrust of capitalist development eventually overtakes the primary agents of capitalist emergence.

Notwithstanding this powerful scenario, Parsons and Smelser include 'integration' both as a crucial element in the coherence of the economy, and as a necessary form of boundary interchange with the surrounding society. The economy cannot integrate itself without extra-economic supports. These are seen as emanating from the wider society's integration system (I). This system, comprising norms of sufficient generality to bind together the 'societal community' in a stable form of solidarity, is for Parsons quite distinct from the latent-pattern maintenance system (L) wherein value-commitments are expressed and institutionalised. The major inputs of society's integration system to the integration sub-system of the economy are not then values pertinent to economic activity, but rather a stable normative framework wherein predictable economic activity may take place. This arises insofar as the norms in question are regarded as binding. This framework is identified by Parsons and Smelser with the institution of contract, as embodied in legal codes. Within the Parsonian schema, this is located in the integration sub-system of the societal integration system ($I_i$).

This particular sub-system of the integration system is selected because Parsons and Smelser regard the integration of divergent economic interests and social roles within a division of labour as a 'highly sensitive point in the social structure', indeed 'the paramount focus of society's integration problem' (1959a, p. 66). This appears to imply that the integrative problems posed by the economy are more significant for societal integration than those involved in the relationship between either the pattern-maintenance system or the polity and the integration system. In other words the problems of translating value-commitments into binding social norms, or of converting norms into politically effective policies, are taken to be of lesser significance in relation to society's integration problem. This position follows from Parsons' belief both in the possibility of general value-consensus and in the efficacy of democratic pluralist politics. While many of Parsons' critics reject these beliefs, it is somewhat ironic to find that he shares with them a conviction that the division of labour and attendant sectional economic relations, if left unregulated, contain an important potential for conflict and cleavage. At any event, given such presuppositions, it is certainly quite appropriate, on logical grounds to link the economy's integration sub-system with what might be regarded as the foremost integrative sub-system in the entire society, namely the integration sub-system of the integration system.

The function of contract in regulating the $I_i \rightarrow A_i$ boundary interchange is clearly crucial to Parsons' theory of economy and society. Looked at in its most general light, contract is regarded as the central economic institution without which economic exchange through markets would not be possible. However *'economic'* contract may be in its function of facilitating 'the process of bargaining for advantage', it remains fundamentally extra-economic insofar as fraud and coercion are avoided by means of 'socially prescribed and sanctioned rules' to which bargaining parties are subject (1956a, pp. 104–5). Such underlying extra-economic norms are essential, even if for most practical purposes they are regarded as 'given', such that contract appears as a purely economic phenomenon. Even entrepreneurs, so it appears, must be bound in some sense by norms.

Within the normative framework of contract, Parsons and Smelser go on to elaborate further 'activist', 'entrepreneurial' features of the boundary interchange between society's integration systems and the integration sub-system of the economy. Two important input-output relationships across this interchange are singled out for attention. The first involves the input of entrepreneurship, in Schumpeter's sense, into the economy. Here the source of entrepreneurship is quite clearly regarded as extra-economic rather than depending fundamentally on potential monetary rewards. The balancing 'output' for this input is profit, which again is regarded as a social category of extra-economic success as measured by profit. In this kind of economic sociology it is not the rate or scale of profit itself that matters so much as the wider societal valuation which may be extended to the profits of innovation.

If 'the prospect of profit does *not* account for the *genesis* of the motivation to innovate' (Parsons' emphases 1956a, p. 266) where then does this motivation derive from? This question is a complex one, involving amongst other phenomena the society's value system as it affects personality socialisation, and the institutional mechanisms which provide encouragement of new ideas. Part of this question depends therefore on the issue of how the role of entrepreneur emerges historically, together with the supply of individuals motivated to fulfil such roles. This issue has prompted a certain amount of attention among economic historians and social psychologists, influenced in part by Parsons' work (Hagen, 1962, 1967; Flinn, 1961; McClelland, 1961). Particular attention has been directed here to the influence of different religious and cultural practices on child socialisation involving achievement-oriented roles. McClelland (1961) has demonstrated the salience of child socialisation practices oriented to religious discipline for the pioneering capitalist entrepreneurs in eighteenth-century Britain.

Less widely explored is the linkage to entrepreneurial activity from consumer demand. Parsons and Smelser discuss this as the second major input-output relationship between $I_i$ and $A_i$. Here the input of demand for new product combinations from the integration system is balanced by the output of new products as a result of entrepreneurial intervention. Such outputs contribute to society's integration problems by allowing the incorporating of new product combinations into an increasing variety of lifestyles. Here once again is repeated the underlying Parsonian theme of the enhancement of individuation in modern society through the operation of generalisable or universalistic institutions such as the market economy and contract, a framework which at the same time promotes normative order. In the American case, Parsons goes on to identify 'the relative flexibility and lack of traditionalism of the American consumer' as an important factor in economic development (1956a, p. 267). This not only involves the application of entrepreneurial innovation to production but also to consumption, for example, changes in shopping associated with the development of the superstore.

Once again, Parsons' formalistic theoretical edifice yields at this point a number of empirical questions of considerable significance. These centre in the first place on the extent to which a normative consensus or positive social valuation is extended to innovatory entrepreneurs, helping to cement some kind of social integration. For Parsons, drawing on the American experience, the evidence indicates that 'people with somewhat visionary ideas are tolerated, even lionized. The "folklore" of capitalism is full of illustrations, of which the young Henry Ford is taken to be one' (Parsons and Smelser, 1956a, p. 265). Two further questions arise at this point. The first concerns the basis of the 'lionization' of Ford. If popular support of this kind is indeed widespread as Parsons takes it to be, is this indicative of support for entrepreneurship, or are other symbolic elements involved?

Recent work by Moorhouse (1983) on 'American automobiles and workers' dreams' testifies to a high degree of normative adherence to the personal capacities of Ford among many consumers of automobiles. Henry Ford appears in the 'hot rod culture of the 1940s' and to the millions who subsequently visited the Ford Museum at Dearborn, Michigan, 'not as industrial magnate, nor as the destroyer of skill, but as the producer of solid-cars and . . . as the prototype self-taught mechanic and backyard tinkerer' (ibid., p. 413). More generally, he is taken to represent an entrepreneur who brought car-ownership within the reach of large numbers, thereby facilitating the practical and 'fantasy' elements of much of the male population in activities such as 'general car expertise, the routine maintenance and upkeep of a family car' (ibid., pp. 413–14).

These findings support a certain positive normative adherence to one particular entrepreneur responsible for a major product innovation in contemporary Western society. They also indicate certain complexities in the 'lionization' of Ford as an entrepreneur of which Parsons may not have taken full note. For what is at stake in the symbolic success of Ford is not only heroic personal entrepreneurship linked to a prominent example of upward social mobility, but also a strong sense of technological and applied scientific advance involved in the emergence of the product. Moorhouse quotes the case of the 1939 World Fair in New York where the Ford exhibit – which attracted eight million people – invoked 'science' and 'progress' as the main themes of company development. This was symbolised in:

> A massive 28 foot high, one hundred and sixty ton press which punched out the steel shells used for hub caps while, alongside, a skilled worker using a variety of tools and hammers manufactured the same object. While he made one shell the machine turned out 2160 . . .

This exhibit was used by the company to indicate that 'if the contemporary Ford was made by craftsmen it would cost nearly $18,000 and be out of reach of the common man' (ibid., p. 415).

While Moorhouse understates normative support for Ford as an entrepreneur he does draw attention to an alternative source of support for Ford cars as examples of technological progress. Instead of heroic personal innovation this is linked, via Habermas (1971), to the existence of a normative order in modern capitalist societies based upon the benign effects of what appear as 'humanly unstoppable forms of technical and scientific change'. Here it is 'science' rather than the entrepreneur which appears as the 'integrative mechanism' capable of providing a technological solution to any problem. In this scenario, it is not individual human agency but 'structural' forces which are taken to predominate. Agency must simply adapt to 'high technology' and the computer. Whatever interpretation may be made of the particular case of Ford, the spectre of rationalisation raised again by Moorhouse introduces a second question prefigured in the discussion of Schumpeter but neglected by Parsons. This concerns the growing obsolescence of personal entrepreneurship in the face of 'science and technology'. Is the entrepreneur in the contemporary world really so central as an integrator of economic life?

In an empirical sense, it is by no means clear that personal entrepreneurship has been completely undermined. While Schumpeter thought primarily in terms of the heavy industry entrepreneurship of the nineteenth and early twentieth centuries, reflecting a 'productionist' bias, the post-war world has seen continuing examples of the emergence (and sometimes the failure) of Schumpeterian entrepreneurs primarily in the service sector of Western economies. Typical examples include Ray Kroc associated with the development of fast-food franchises (Macdonalds) and Freddie Laker (whose pioneering cheap transatlantic air-fares concern eventually failed). Such entrepreneurial innovations seem to undermine Schumpeter's case – at least up to a point. Once consumption and services are rationalised alongside production it may be that the obsolescence of entrepreneurship may assert itself. On the other hand, it may equally be that Schumpeter developed an excessively evolutionary interpretation of Weber's rationalisation thesis. Weber did not regard rationalisation as the exclusive force behind social change, since charisma could 'erupt' at any point (Weber, 1978, p. 245). In this way Parsons' emphasis on the integrative functions of individual entrepreneurship may continue to be apposite. An alternative possibility consistent with the Parsonian schema is that a further differentiation of entrepreneurial capacities is currently under way whereby teams of entrepreneurs, for example think-tanks or consultancies, replace heroic individuals.

A final, equally under-explored question raised by Parsons' discussion of entrepreneurship and integration concerns the relationship between normative support for entrepreneurship and support for the capitalist order in general. Here, some caution is required, since support for the innovatory projects of entrepreneurs need not necessarily imply support for a social system dominated by private capital. Entrepreneurial innovation may therefore have significance beyond the context of the economic system in which it operates. On the other hand, where capitalism is defined in terms of the individual freedom and liberty of action involved in private property, evidence of successful entrepreneurship becomes far more salient to the consolidation of such an ideology than the more routine activities of capitalist managers and bureaucrats. It may indeed be this identification of capitalism (or the 'freemarket system') with entrepreneurship which helps to explain the rather arbitrary popular association of rational bureaucratic organisation with public rather than private corporate institutions.

A 'sociology of entrepreneurship' is clearly integral to the research programme of Parsons' theory of economy and society. While the empirical contours of what such an enterprise might look like are not entirely clear to Parsons, they may be sketched without too much difficulty as a result of the confrontation between Parsons' discussion of integration and the contributions or 'silences' of recent research. From a theoretical viewpoint, Parsons' elaboration on the work of Weber, Marshall and Schumpeter allows a breach to be made in the dualistic approach to entrepreneurship deriving from positivistic or utilitarian theories of action. A coherent alternative is thereby offered both to the structuralist assimilation of entrepreneurship to the conditions of the situation, and to the voluntaristic depiction of entrepreneurial success as a heroic triumph of will. It is a very striking commentary on post-war sociology, that entrepreneurship has generally been regarded as a theoretically uninteresting category in comparison with structuralist accounts of the reproduction of capital, or the fateful march of bureaucratic managerialism.

## (d) The pattern-maintenance sub-system of the economy

The final constituent of the economy as a social system is the pattern-maintenance sub-system. This comprises the economy's value-system orientated to the function of maintaining common values and hence tension-management. The relationship posited between this sub-system of the economy and the wider social system is however considerably different to the three instances of boundary interchange and interpenetration considered so far. In such cases, the relationship of economy and society is conceived in terms of inter-active exchanges, involving input-output 'balances' between two discrete elements of the social system. Premised on the existence of a relatively elaborated division of labour, such contractually regulated exchanges deal with determinate 'quids' and 'quos' moving across the internal boundaries of the components of the social system. In the case of pattern-maintenance relationships between economy and society, by contrast, this model of input-output exchanges is inappropriate. This is because pattern-maintenance functions are 'cultural' rather than 'interactive' (1956a, p. 69). The notion of the 'cultural' in the context is holistic. Thus the individual pattern maintenance sub-systems of each social system cannot be regarded in an atomistic or fragmented manner vis-à-vis the values they embody. They are rather to be seen as expressions of 'the general value system of the total society' (ibid.). Whether such a general value system actually exists is of course one of the most controversial areas in Parsonian sociology.

One very striking feature of Parsons' discussion of pattern-maintenance and the economy is the assertion of value-commitments *within* economic life. Following Weber and Durkheim, he rejects the notion that the economy can be conceived as self-subsistent or autonomous with respect to values. The economy cannot be regarded in a purely instrumental manner, as some kind of device for satisfying externally valued 'wants'. This applies equally to differentiated 'modern' as compared to relatively undifferentiated economies. In this way, value-commitments enter both the market or capitalist economy, which Marx saw as an amoral 'cash nexus', and pre-capitalist economies wherein Marx saw moral bonds incorporating 'the most heavenly ecstasies of religious fervour, chivalrous enthusiasm, . . . [and] . . . sentimentalism' (Marx and Engels, 1962, p. 36). Within Parsonian economic sociology, value within the capitalist economy involves moral value not simply the political economic category of exchange-value.

The case advanced for the presence of value-commitments within the economic sphere stems in part from Weber's perception that the practice of instrumental rationality is not value-free. The instrumental commitment to find the most 'rational' means to realise given ends itself rests on a substantive value-commitment to instrumentalism. This latter commitment is fundamental, even if it remains 'invisible' to those practitioners of instrumentalism who have accepted 'the disenchantment of the world' at face value. Parsons and Smelser effectively combine Weber's argument with Durkheim's emphasis on the importance of normative order within contractual relationships. The result is a claim that economic relationships cannot proceed in both an orderly *and* meaningful fashion without value as well as normative regulation.

This line of argument is challenging, not only for conventional economic thought which takes ends as 'given', but also for those of its critics who seek to determine the limits of economic determination, in terms of the presence of moral constraints. This contrast of markets (that is the economy) with 'morals' (presumably located in cultural and religious practices) only reinforces the tendency to view the economy, at least in its modern capitalist or market form, as amoral or indifferent to value-concerns. Parsons and Smelser do not of course dispute that major sources of value-commitment lie outside the economy. Their view is rather that economic life – even in the modern epoch – partakes as strongly in value-concerns as any other sub-system of society.

What then does the economy's value-system comprise and how is this system related to the general value-system at the societal level?

For Parsons and Smelser the economy's value-system centres on economic rationality. This is defined as 'the valuation of the goals of production and appropriate controls over behaviour in the interest of such goals' (1956a, p. 176). This value-system is not diffuse, but directly related to the mode of organisation capable of effective attainment of production goals and related behavioural controls. Economic rationality in this sense is not seen as a postulate as in economic theory, but as a 'primary empirical feature' of the economy. The empirical referents of the economy's value system are manifest in the motivation of individuals through two kinds of process. The first involves the internalisation of the value system by individuals, the second involves sanctions on behaviour designed to stabilise and adapt behaviour to changing exigencies.

Before commenting on the empirical plausibility of this notion, it is important to clarify the relations between the economy's value-system and that pertinent to the general society. Here Parsons makes the point that the societal value-system cannot be defined simply in terms of economic rationality – or, one might add, any single substantive value-commitment. This is because the over-riding function of the societal value-system is to determine the relative importance of the various social functions performed by different sub-systems. The valuation of economic values in relation to other kinds of values is the crucial function performed at this level, which of course takes place in an extra-economic context within the societal pattern-maintenance system. It therefore becomes an empirical question as to whether or not economic values predominate. Here Parsons and Smelser argue that such values occupy a particularly high position in the value hierarchy in western society and possibly the highest position of all in the USA. In such cases economic rationality must be regarded as a property of a social system, not simply of the economy. This suggests that the achievement of a high status for economic rationality cannot be simply the outcome of a monocausal process of economic determination.

The empirical case for the existence of a strong value-commitment to economic rationality, in Parsons' terms, is founded on what is seen as the high and widespread valuation given to production, occupational roles and occupational success, a high valuation of productivity and of private and public activity geared to reorganising economy and society so as to maximise productivity and incomes (Feldman and Moore, 1969). The strength of these valuations may well vary between western industrial nations, and may be higher in nations like the USA and Japan than in Britain. At the same time party political evidence suggests that a strong commitment to economic rationality is shared by the dominant political parties of 'right', 'centre' and 'left', throughout the western world. 'Growth', 'productivity' and 'technocratic efficiency' also seem to be emergent features of both pro-capitalist and pro-socialist Third World societies, most spectacularly of all perhaps in post-Maoist China.

Two main lines of objection have been mounted against the existence of this kind of economic value-consensus in western-type societies. The first centres on conflicts *within* the economic sphere, most notably between capital and labour. Such phenomena as strikes, sabotage, factory occupations, movements for nationalisation and/or workers' control have been taken as indicators of a deep conflict of interest over economic and social priorities, rather than routine forms of bargaining pressure in a system whose parameters are agreed.

It is, however, arguable that many such conflicts are not necessarily incompatible with the economic values Parsons designates. For example, the high valuation of industrial production, the manufacturing sector and of occupational roles, lies at the heart of many militant labour conflicts, including those which seek to oppose plant closure, unemployment or de-skilling, within the labour process. Conflict with 'capital' over particular industrial relations issues is not by itself evidence of the lack of a general economic value-system, which may be shared by workers, managers and owners of capital. Flanders (1965) has gone on to argue that industrial relations systems, while often defined in terms of conflict-ridden processes of collective-bargaining, may nonetheless be seen as dependent on underlying value-commitments such as the freedom to pursue bargaining in a voluntary and peaceful manner. They function, usually in a latent manner, to prevent complete collapse into sectional power conflicts.

Having said this, Flanders also indicates that it is equally facile to regard any instance of conflict as compatible with (and hence functional to the reproduction of) some underlying order of value-commitment. In cases where value-commitments change or where some values are incompatible with each other, conflict may represent the breakdown of an underlying value-consensus. This enables him to approach the particular instance of Britain's troubled post-war industrial relations 'chaos' as representing a lack of consensus concerning the regulation of industrial relations systems.

Parsons and Smelser do not, however, take the British experience as the 'norm'. Nor do they dwell on the industrial relations sphere as some exclusive empirical arena wherein the nature of economic values may be ascertained. This stems from their location of American trends as far more indicative of a modern pattern of economic values than those of European societies, where pre-modern status cleavages may still be influential. This argument, outlined in Parsons (1967c) has two elements. The first treats the European experience of transition from feudalism to capitalism as an incomplete instance of modernisation. Social conflict in this context has been bolstered by the fusion of 'capitalists' and 'proletarians' with quasi-feudal status affiliations. Neither of the major contending Marxian classes is therefore fully emancipated from status considerations. 'The bourgeoisie', according to Parsons, 'may be regarded as frustrated aristocrats, and the proletarians frustrated peasants. Each is "alienated" from the true *Gemeinschaft* base of historic European upper- and lower-class status respectively' (Parsons, 1967c, p. 113).

The second part of the argument focusses on the development of American society, which never had an aristocracy or peasantry in the European sense. Here Parsons detects not class polarisation in the sense of a 'total, dichotomous interest-split', but a greater pluralisation and individuation. It is here that the pattern-variables distinguishing modernity from traditionalism along such axes as universalism v. particularism, achievement v. ascription and specificity v. diffuseness, have most purchase. Economic values are not then located primarily in terms of the interests of class collectivities as in so much European discourse. They are found instead within such phenomena as the high valuation of individual occupational achievement, and in the universalistic moral rules such as equality of opportunity whose generality is sufficiently inclusive to enable maximum variation in individual choice. It should further be emphasised that the existence of labour-capital conflict, or ascriptive obstacles to social mobility in post-war America, does not necessarily vitiate this line of argument. This is especially the case where the

rationale for conflict or challenge to the 'status quo' depends
precisely on the universalistic arguments, which Parsons argues
are central to the general societal value-system.

At this point, it is a common misconception to believe that
Parsons postulates some kind of monolithic general value-
system, involving the prominence of economic values, as an
emergent property of modern social systems. Parsons and
Smelser reject this possibility on the grounds that an important
distinction needs to be made between the value-commitments
of the social system and those of individual personalities. While
economic rationality may feature as a prominent if not predominant value at the system level, at the personality level this need
not be so. A large measure of interpenetration between social
system and personalities is of course required for societies to
maintain an orderly existence. Yet divergence between the two
is also to be expected as a result of the socialisation of the
individual within specialised differentiated agencies such as the
family and the educational system. Socialisation of children
does not therefore take place 'in and through the whole social
structure at once' (1956a, p. 177). Nor are the roles of individual
personalities restricted to their involvement in the economy,
since complex societies require individuals to have roles in a
variety of social sub-systems. Two important points follow. The
first is that different value-commitments pertaining to these
various sub-systems are internalised with varying degrees of
success and in various hierarchies. Second, no individual acts
only in terms of those values shared with others. This makes it
quite clear that Parsons rejects both a monolithic societal value-
system founded upon a conformist set of individual actors, and
a purely economistic interpretation of culture, in which personal
values are skewed to economic rationality.

These considerations indicate why a second line of attack on
Parsons, based on the existence of 'anti-economic values' in
the modern world, may be inadequate. In this approach, a
heterogeneous set of movements aiming variously at the
creation of 'alternative' lifestyles, ecological and environmental
conservation, or the primacy of 'welfare' considerations in state
policy, has been projected as a fundamental challenge to
supposed areas of value-consensus incorporating the mainstream of economic institutions. While 'utopian' and even

'millenarian' expectations may have characterised many such movements from time to time, what is equally evident is significant areas of incorporation of the reforms involved at a more general societal level. This has taken such forms as the commercialisation and routinisation of alternative lifestyles, the building of certain ecological controls into the normative regulation of economic life and innovation in the content of welfare policies.

Some part of this integration may be the result of the failures of different parties to reach consensus, leading to the imposition of, as it were, negative sanctions either by the economy on the wider society or vice versa. In the former case, for example, lack of income, diminished consumer choice and the occupational role confusion that may result from voluntary (as much as involuntary) abstention from the market economy may eventually encourage renewed involvement in markets as the means of furthering more muted conceptions of 'alternatives'. In the latter case, ecological and environmental controls may have been imposed by states upon private businesses not so much through value-consensus as by a bare minimum of voluntary compliance.

In spite of all this, however, it remains quite plausible to regard 'incorporation' in a more positive light, not perhaps as a triumph of altruistic value-consensus over sectional interest, but rather as a process whereby the mutual accommodation of different interests may be facilitated by general value-commitments. This is clearest in the case where beliefs that the economy *should* be responsive to changes in consumer wants, has aided the assimilation of new products from 'alternative lifestyles' (for example 'health foods') into the market sector. It is less clear in cases where regulative controls have been placed on private business by legislative action. Nonetheless, except in those cases where such controls involve unilateral imposition, it remains possible to interpret corporate commitments to act in good faith in the public interest, with or without legislative sanction, as part of a general value-commitment to act responsibly. Conflict over the substance of a 'responsible policy' in any particular case does not of course necessarily contradict the existence of some measure of general value-consensus between corporations, governments and social movements. Nor need corporate references to 'responsible action' be necessarily always taken at face-value in every particular case, as authentic manifestations of value-commitment. The notion of the 'soulful corporation' (Kaysen, 1957) may turn out to be apologetic in many empirical instances. There is, however, no theoretical reason why this should be so, unless we invoke conspiracy theory or move outside an action framework to embrace situational determinism.

One of the most important general consequences of Parsons' discussion of values within the economy and society is that it leaves open theoretical space for value-committed action on the part of economic actors. There is therefore no necessary contradiction between the 'cash nexus' of the modern market economy and value-commitment within the conduct of business. This may have been obscured by the tendency for critics of private corporate actions to mobilise moral arguments against what are taken to be inherently amoral operations.

## Concluding comments

One way of assessing Parsons' contribution to the theory of economy and society is to concentrate on the range of theoretical objects such as 'consumption', 'capital', 'entrepreneurship', and 'economic values' which are brought into sharper sociological focus than hitherto, within the vast formalistic edifice of the four-function paradigm. This general structure, while drawing on the central theoretical insights of the earlier generation of classical European sociology, clearly represents a step beyond the work of Weber, Durkheim and other turn-of-the-century theorists. The major claim that Parsons advances for this framework is not simply that it helps to bring certain neglected features of economic life into view, but that it does so in a comprehensive and theoretically integrated way. Underlying this theoretical integration is Parsons' attempt to understand 'modernity' as constituted by a set of universalistic, achievement-orientated, yet specifically differentiated social relationships, of which economic activity organised through market exchange is but one of several key elements. Assessment of Parsons' work merely in terms of certain substantive weak points in utilitarian-dominated theories of economy and society would certainly underestimate the scope of its ambition.

One immediate indicator of this scope is the theoretical robustness of Parsons' contribution vis-à-vis other theories of the relationship of economy and society. A particular theme of this paper has been to extend the explicit provenance of Parsons' critique beyond conventional economics to Marxist political economy. Underlying this argument is a strong sense that the high prestige currently enjoyed by political economy in sociological circles rests on limited and in some respects inadequate foundations. Parsons' critique can be elaborated with little difficulty to strike both at the heart of the conceptual system of Marxist political economy with respect to such notions as 'value' and 'capital', and in terms of the claim that 'capitalism' represents the quintessential form of western modernity.

The recovery of Parsons' neglected theory of economy and society, may then, in the context of earlier work by Weber and Durkheim, be read as a plea for the replacement of political economy by economic sociology. This project need not be interpreted as anti-Marxist, insofar as it complements at a sociological level certain of the themes raised by Marx in a more philosophical discourse concerning the social ontology of human existence. Foremost among these themes is the nature and conditions of emergence of a universalistic morality and normative order – a question which Marx's 'materialism' and residual 'utilitarianism' tended to suppress.

Within a broader comparative context Parsons' four-fold theory of economy and society represents a stronger and more coherent contribution to the economic sociology of social change and the development of modern society than either institutionalism or economic anthropology.

In the case of institutionalism, for example, Parsons' argument is simply that the accumulation of empirical evidence as to the unreality or abstraction involved in conventional economic theory has done little or nothing to reduce its centrality or theoretical standing within social science. Veblen, amongst the heterogeneous collection of American institutionalists, was accorded somewhat more attention as a social theorist who sought to incorporate 'psychology' and 'instinct' within a comprehensive theory of society (Parsons, 1934c). The more typical evacuation of grand theory by institutionalism, was however regarded by Parsons as counter-productive in that it did nothing to undermine the theoretical weaknesses of conventional economic theory. In this way economists could continue to treat the social context of economic activity as a 'residual'.

This verdict is less charitable to the potential of institutionalism to generate important middle-range theorising in substantive areas of social life. Many of the more important contributions of this kind in the post-war period have been connected with the labour market. They include work by Wootton (1962) on wage-determination, by Edwards, Reich and Gordon (1973) on labour market segmentation, and on labour migration by Piore (1979). Such work has done far more than simply dispute the empirical plausibility of conventional economistic models of human action. Yet it has been of little salience by itself in the construction of a general theory of economy and society. Nor has this latter project been strongly influenced by the revival of interest in Veblen stimulated by the publication of Seckler's recent work on institutionalism (1975). For Seckler, Veblen's work is of limited theoretical interest to economists as a result of its grounding of cultural action in a deterministic framework depending on an economic base (ibid., p. 75).

In spite of a mass of important middle-range studies, and the perception that Veblen's distinction between 'technical' and 'ceremonial' behaviour may be of some interest in articulating economic and non-economic action (Bush, 1981), it appears that the theoretical development of 'economic sociology' *per se* remains a low intellectual priority within institutionalist circles. Without a strong theoretical core of the kind projected by Parsons and Smelser it is difficult to see how it could be otherwise.

A more promising theoretical initiative, concerned with many of the same theoretical problems linking economy and society, was launched by Karl Polanyi and his associates in the post-war period (see especially Polanyi et al., 1957; Polanyi, 1977). As Pearson, Polanyi's associate, noted in his review of *Economy and Society*, Parsons and Smelser drew on the same theoretical heritage deriving from Weber and Durkheim as had influenced Polanyi himself and the economic anthropologists (Pearson, 1957). This influence above all else consisted in the rejection of assumptions that economic life could ever be self-subsistent with respect to society. Polanyi, like the classical European sociologists before him, spoke of the dual tendency of modern society to both expand its productive base and to 'protect' social order and secure social integration by regulating the economy. For Polanyi, as for Parsons, the work of Weber and Durkheim remained an illuminating if incomplete indication of the extra-economic normative basis of economic relations. Polanyi's economic anthropology differs nonetheless from the economic sociology of Parsons and Smelser (as the latter author pointed out in a later article, Smelser, 1958–9) in a number of key respects. Three particular contrasts are germane to the present discussion. First, Polanyi does not attempt a generic theory of economic life either around system functions or around any notion of problems in the allocation of scarce resources. This represents a fundamental revolt against the assumption that conventional economics provides a universal basis for the analysis of economic systems. Instead Polanyi's historical and anthropological studies of the ancient and non-European worlds (1957, 1977) are concerned to depict various 'substantive' patterns of economy. These involve different modes of integration, such as reciprocity, redistribution and market exchange. The generic criterion underlying this approach is a kind of political-economic geography. Polanyi thinks of the forms of integration as 'diagrams representing patterns made by the movements of goods and persons in the economy, whether these movements consist of changes in their location, in their appropriation, or in both' (Polanyi, 1977, p. 36). Thus perspective has recently become influential within the world-system theory of Wallerstein (1974, 1976) and others.

Polanyi does of course make some use of the same kind of differentiation model of social change that came to appear more prominently in Parsons' work in the 1960s (see especially Parsons, 1964d). Polanyi speaks of the embeddedness of early economies within social relations, and a subsequent historic process of what might be called 'disembedding' culminating in nineteenth-century laissez fairé. Little attempt is made, however, to explain what general relations exist between society and economy during this process. The notion of the 'protection' of society from economic processes is not elaborated in theor-

etical terms such as might challenge the theoretical provenance
of conventional economics on its own intellectual ground. We
are left instead with some implicit notion of regulatory norms.

A third major difference between Parsons and Polanyi is that
the latter thinker rejects conventional economic theory more or
less *in toto*. The ahistoric assumption of rational economic man
was ruled out simply by virtue of its inability to account for
historical variations in patterns of economic life. This weakness
was brilliantly exposed by Polanyi in his discussion of trade,
markets and money. The presence of any one of these should
not necessarily be regarded as an indicator of the presence of
homo oeconomicus, nor of the presence of the other two (1957).

Such propositions, which drew on Polanyi's vast historical
inquiries, led him to approach the logical structures of conventional economics in a thoroughly sceptical spirit. Unlike
Parsons, he regarded the postulates of scarcity and rational
choice as inherently flawed as generic features of social life. As
such they held out no promise as possible resources in the
construction of a general theory of economy and society which
could be applied to either historical or contemporary settings.

Underlying this position is a contrast between Polanyi's
cultural relativism and Parsons' evolutionism. The former
claims that each culture or civilisation may be understood
substantively in its own terms. The latter approaches the 'past'
only through the immanent or emergent features of the
'present'. In Parsons' case these centre on an integrated notion
of modernity, articulated within a differentiated social system.

Whatever general problems there may be concerning the
status of teleological assumptions built into evolutionism
(Nisbet, 1969), this kind of social-change theory depends on an
explicit set of generic criteria by means of which comparisons
between different 'stages' or 'case studies' are made possible.
Parsons offers a comprehensive and integrated set of such
generic criteria in terms of the four-function paradigm, where
the 'adaptive' sub-system or economy is taken to represent
a universal system need depending on means-ends strategies
approximating to Weber's category of instrumental rationality.
However 'embedded' this sub-system may be within other
political or cultural structures at various points in history,
Parsons' evolutionary presuppositions do allow the possibility

'that all human societies are economically rational to some important degree'. There is no 'prelogical mentality' to which the concept is irrelevant (1955a, p. 177). This possibility, whose empirical importance has recently been demonstrated in economic history (North and Thomas, 1973; Fenoaltea, 1975), is ruled out by Polanyi's cultural relativism, and by his use of the limited geo-political criterion of modes of economic integration as the principal generic basis for a comparative historical analysis of economy and society.

The ambitious scope of Parsons' theory of economy and society is not, however, exhausted either by its tighter theoretical definition of neglected areas of economic activity, or by its superior theoretical power compared with Marxist political economy, institutionalism, and economic anthropology. This is primarily because Parsons seeks to accommodate rather than reject what has hitherto been referred to as 'conventional economic theory'. This aim, as we have seen, is connected with his view that the strategies of instrumental rationality characteristic of economic action are of universal adaptive significance for processes of evolutionary social change and for the making of modern society. It is this perception which underlies the strikingly original claim of *Economy and Society* that the problem foci and theoretical structures of mainstream economic thought are susceptible to re-translation in a comprehensive and theoretically determinate manner within the four function paradigm designed to illuminate the differentiated nature of 'modernity'. Once Parsons had formulated the pattern variables and produced a multifunctional paradigm for the theory of society, the way was clear for the construction of a 'unified social science' embracing economic theory, of the kind which Marshall, writing in the 1880s, sought in vain.

Evaluation of the success of the Parsonian project for economic sociology is then partly dependent on the credibility of his analyses of boundary interchanges between economy and society, as it were from the economic side. While *Economy and Society* was reviewed quite widely in economic periodicals (Hutchison, 1967; Worswick, 1967; Ayres, 1957), the general reception given to it was a highly critical and sceptical one. This applies both to the project of a unified social science, which

T. W. Hutchison felt moved to describe as a manifestation of 'insubstantial intellectual Utopianism' (Hutchison, 1957) and to certain technical questions arising from Parsons' treatment of particular doctrines within economic thought.

One way of interpreting this scepticism is to posit a narrowing of the 'mainstream' concerns of economic thought since Marshall's day. What may have altered most since Marshall's time is the attitude to boundary inter-changes with the non-economic environment. These are known to exist, and are clearly prominent in certain applied fields such as development economics. Social inputs have nonetheless become more rather than less incommensurable over time with the increasingly quantitative mathematical foci of economic theory. Marshall's view that economic science should include the qualitative aspect of 'activities' as well as the quantifiable aspect of 'wants' expressed in money terms, reflects a somewhat broader approach than is evident among most contemporary economists.

Even Marshall, however, wished to postpone concern for the forging of systematic theoretical links between the economy and other parts of the social system to the longer-term, pending social scientific inquiries elsewhere. Like most recent economists, he looks to have been similarly unwilling to defer the immediate intellectual gratification that ensues from a delimited inquiry into market relationships, for the sake of longer-term more ambitious attempts to develop a unified social science.

In addition to the problem of incommensurability between 'quantitative' and 'qualitative' methodologies, another more fundamental reason for the sceptical reception of the Parsonian model may relate to differing normative conceptions of economic life. Goldthorpe (1978) has argued that economists mostly operate with a notion of economic systems as either inherently stable, tending to equilibrium, or, as in the case of Keynesianism, requiring institutional reforms of a kind which facilitate rather than obstruct the capacity of the economy to function normally. Such assumptions are clearly linked to a normative commitment to rational choice or decision-making in economic affairs by means of devices like cost-benefit analysis. The orientation of economic theory is therefore 'to help find rational solutions for economic' problems on the normative assumption that 'what the rational man would do, the plain man should do' (Hollis, 1979, p. 13). The task of theory is therefore to illuminate how certain internal adjustments to key variables may enhance 'rational' choice. This approach has a technocratic rather than social theoretical bias for 'where it does not explain, it shows men how to do better' (ibid.).

This orientation contrasts both with the aim of social theory to explain the fabric of social relations devoid of attachment to any particular technocratic vehicle, and with the theoretical claims of economic sociologists to have shown that economic life cannot be self-subsistent from the surrounding social environment. This has involved a greater interest among sociologists in the instabilities created by economic activity within the social structure, and a greater normative commitment to strategies aimed at 'integrative' solutions to instabilities arising from economic activity. Such solutions may envisage the abolition of the capitalist free market system, or, as in the case of Parsons, its subordination to democratic-pluralist values and political institutions. The fundamental intellectual obstacles to a rapprochement between 'economics' and 'sociology' come down to the persistence of a positivist epistemology both for the social sciences and for social actors, and a conception of rationality, restricted to instrumentalism.

Having said this, it is important to emphasise that 'conventional' economics has neither been entirely 'static' nor internally 'homogeneous' or 'stable' since Marshall's time. If the initial ideal-typical postulate of 'conventional' economics is relaxed, the shifting and heterogeneous character of the 'mainstream' appears considerable. This is nowhere better demonstrated than in Bronfenbrenner's depiction of 'the reigning economic thesis in the United States' during the 1960s (1966, p. 540). This is seen as combining

in an uneasy peace, elements of the previous Marshallian synthesis of the cost and utility theories of value and competitive price (with a variable adornment of imperfect competition) elements of the Keynesian theory of income and employment (embellished in various degrees by the 'neo-classical synthesis') . . . and elements of a neo-classical theory of economic growth and development.

To Bronfenbrenner the 'mainstream' appears like a 'smorgas-bord or chop suey' rather than an integrated discipline.

Notwithstanding such syncretic and ill-fitting components of the substantive theoretical repertoire, it is arguable that the basic postulates of positivism and instrumental rationality have remained intact in defining the boundaries of economic thought. Certain recent changes have indeed sought to tighten even further the self-subsistent character of economic thought behind boundaries that draw as little as possible on extra-economic influences. The foremost of these is the successful attempt to purge theories of consumer demand of psychologistic assumptions concerning the nature and function of utility (Hicks, 1956). Amongst these is the abandonment of hedonistic assumptions, and the drawing of a conceptual veil over problems pertaining to the origins of wants, by substituting the notions of 'revealed preference' or 'indifference curves' for that of 'utility'. In spite of Latsis' (1972) announcement of the emergence of a psychologistic paradigm of economic behaviouralism to rival the 'situational determinism of rational choice theory', Coats (1976) has indicated the remarkable consistency of the mainstream of economic theory in repulsing this type of challenge.

The continuing drive to purge economic theory of psychologism amounts to a far tighter boundary-mainstream device whereby to insulate economics from other theoretical systems. At the same time this gain is purchased at the price of a move in the direction of a de-limited and narrower economics more carefully sealed off from extra-economic considerations than before. Boundary interchanges between consumer demand and the social and psychological processes whereby 'personality' and 'wants' are formed, for example, become far harder to perceive and analyse.

Not all trends have moved in the direction of a narrowing of scope. One of the more interesting developments to have gained momentum in the last two decades is the analysis of 'property rights' (Gordon, 1954; Demsetz, 1967). Here economic theory has shown an increasing awareness of the normative and regulatory framework surrounding individual or corporate strategies to secure private economic advantage. This has proceeded on the assumption that individuals have to take account of each other's actions, interests and ends, even in pursuing their own self-interest. It has also stimulated some awareness of the historical character of the emergence of modern private property rights. Underlying this work may be found assumptions of economic rationality as a universally emergent feature of human society. In this respect there remains an economic rationale behind any particular pattern of property rights, whether over the medieval manor (Fenoaltea, 1975), or the collective-rights over American Indian hunting-grounds (Demsetz, 1967). The problem here is not that such interpretations may lack insight in particular cases. It is rather that an unexamined theoretical predisposition exists to regard economic rationality as a universally privileged explanatory device. In this way no interest is shown in problem issues such as cultural variations in the way economic interests are expressed, or in value rationality, whereby social practices may be valued as ends in themselves. As such the system problems of pattern-maintenance and integration are generally denied or regarded as residual. In this way the full force of the Parsonian critique of utilitarian constructions of positivism and rationalism remains unanswered.

A final area where economic models have influenced wider issues in social science is in the use of theories of market exchange in the field of 'politics'. Here the social exchange models of utilitarian action theory have been broadened to include interaction in the political market between voters and government (Downs, 1957; Buchanan and Tulloch, 1962). Parallels may be drawn between this work and Parsons' own deployment of social exchange theory, where market-like exchanges of an input-output variety may be posited between different components of the social system. A particularly striking parallel as we have seen is his treatment of power as a cumulating medium across system-boundaries analogous to money (Parsons, 1963f). What nonetheless differentiates this work from that of Parsons is the latter's concern for the problem of order. Individual contractual exchange theory of whatever kind remains incoherent without a non-contractual grounding in normative order and value-commitment. Within Parsons' four-function paradigm value-commitments from the pattern-maintenance system are not exchanged across boundaries. Their involvement in the social system cannot therefore be explained through some utilitarian calculation of advantage.

There are therefore both intellectual and institutional reasons why few economists seem moved to participate in the unification of economics and sociology desired by Parsons. The intellectual resistance undoubtedly springs from the pre-dominance of positivism and instrumental views of rationality, to which may be added the powerful normative and technocratic involvement of economists in processes of economic policy formation and management. Parsons clearly understood the intellectual incompatibility between utilitarian/positivist and voluntaristic theories of action. It is not clear, however, that he appreciated the institutional rigidities that have ensued within the academic division of labour, as a result of the credentialling of professional economists through proficiency in mathematical logic, and its application to 'rational' choices within the marketplace. At any event, there remains very little *theoretical* dialogue between economic sociology and the mainstream of economics. This remains the case in spite of Parsons' re-definition of the scope of action theory to include a place for most of the typical preoccupations of economic theory, and in spite of a number of recent studies by economists seeking to move beyond notions of economic man (Leiberstein, 1976; Bensusan-Butt, 1978).

Parsons' economic sociology appears *prima facie* more theoretically powerful than alternative theories of economy and society, while also demonstrating an impressive compatibility in principle with much of the apparatus of economic theory. Since his contribution in this field is either apparently unknown, or, where acknowledged, often treated in a cursory or misconceived fashion (Savage, 1981, pp. 166–95; Burger, 1977) there is good reason to skew these concluding comments to the establishment of this kind of general comparative plausibility. Yet there remains considerable scope for a more direct assessment and critique of Parsons' substantive theory of economy and society.

Much of the criticism levelled at Parsons has been directed at the high level of formal abstraction involved in his 'grand theory' (Mills, 1959). The mood of wholesale critical euphoria directed at Parsonian sociology in the light of influential criticisms of *The Social System* (1951) or structural functionalism did not encourage much interest in the research programme for a theory of economy and society opened up in *Economy and Society*. This not only comprised the formal apparatus of the four-function paradigm, but also a set of institutional mechanisms associated with the various sub-systems of the economy and society. In the latter case, a range of hypotheses amenable to empirical research were set out, involving such middle-range propositions as the centrality of a differentiated occupational structure to 'household' value-commitments, the function of consumption within the socialisation of the individual personality, the 'political' rather than exclusively 'economic' control of the capitalisation of production, and the existence of values within the economic sphere. All such propositions are amenable to empirical research, and tests of empirical validity or plausibility. The same applies to higher-order propositions, for example, concerning the dependence of economic life on social inputs, more especially value-commitment and normative order. It is not then impossible in principle to move from Parsons' formalistic theories of action and system to processes of operational definition and empirical testing.

An extensive review of the theoretical and empirical plausibility of the substantive research programme of *Economy and Society* is beyond the scope of the present paper. The sketches that have been offered of recent work dealing with issues that are germane to the Parsonian boundary interchanges have been hampered by two problems. The first is that, with the exception of a few close associates like Smelser (1959, 1963) and Dunlop (1958), very little empirical research has been framed within the theoretical parameters on economy and society set by Parsons. The second is that far fewer studies of modern society have been mounted in the tradition of economic sociology begun by Weber and Durkheim and continued by Parsons, in comparison with research orientated to political economy or some kind of institutionalism. In the area of values and the problem of order, studies such as those by Titmuss (1971) on the blood donor relationship and by Zelizer (1978, 1979, 1981) on the development of life and child insurance are comparatively rare.

These characteristics of the literature mean that at present we lack a translation of the empirical findings and theoretical implications of most work on economy and society into Parsonian terms. Given the lack of such a synthesis, there remains a considerable degree of uncertainty as to the current empirical standing of the various components of the boundary inter-change analysis.

Within such limits, the weakest area of Parsonian economic sociology is usually taken to be the discussion of value consensus and normative order. As noted above, one of the most influential challenges to this assumption concerns conflicts of interest between capital and labour and the asymmetrical power relations that are taken to exist between the two. One of the main difficulties in mounting a successful challenge to the Parsonian system in these terms, is the typical absence in such criticisms of consideration of the co-existence of conflict with value-commitments to some supra-economic principle of normative regulation. The existence of overt conflict and the demonstration of contested values in relation to the distributive justice of market relations structured by private capital is usually taken to be sufficient proof of the presence of fatal flaws in Parsons' theory. As such the two positions simply do not engage on this level.

What is ultimately at stake in such encounters is not so much a disagreement over value-consensus as such, so much as debate over the characterisation of contemporary western society. For Parsons, this is seen in terms of a 'modernity' which transcends the separate 'economic', 'political', 'religious', etc. domains, upon which Marxist conceptions of the capitalist mode of production are based. Capitalism, for Parsons, is but a transitional economic form, important in the emergence of European society, but destined to be overtaken by further 'modernisation' trends such as the differentiation of 'ownership' from both 'kinship' and 'management' (Parsons, 1967c). For Parsons such differentiation processes justify the treatment of the family and the polity as analytically distinct from the economy, though they do not in themselves prove the necessity of a strong sense of social integration. He can nonetheless point to an apparently greater degree of integration in 'modern' (that is differentiated) social structures like that of post-war USA, than that evident in European societies with a stronger legacy of divisive 'pre-modern' status traditions. The most perplexing problem for this analysis is not European-style conflict between capital and labour which is in any case subject to tacitly shared integrative forces, so much as the case of Japan which apparently combines a modern economy with an integrated yet traditional status system (Dore, 1983).

A more challenging general line of criticism is that advanced by Habermas in his discussion of the 'legitimation crisis' of modern capitalism (1976) and elsewhere. This approach embraces phenomena of moral evolution as well as political economic inequalities, within a theory of social change. The value-bases of normative order are not however deduced, as in orthodox Marxist political economy, from an exclusive emphasis on the structure of production relations. For alongside the technical rationality of the capitalist world, there exists another form of rationality, namely practical rationality based upon the 'life world' of inter-personal communication. While technical rationality involves a manipulative relationship with the social environment, practical rationality is founded on the adequacy of normative reciprocity between the intentional projects of social actors. Pathological crises in capitalism occur for Habermas, following the general arguments of Frankfurt-School Marxism when technical rationalisation comes to dominate or 'colonise' the 'life-world'.

Against this however resistance is possible insofar as universalistic expectations set during the course of capitalist development with the rise of political democracy are felt to be incompatible with the administrative management of the political agenda and of 'crises'. At this point Habermas advances a number of empirically related arguments whose effect is to bring into question many of the bases of value-commitment and normative order on which Parsons' notion of modernity rests. Amongst these, Habermas points to the decline in the grip of 'civic and familial-vocational privatism' on cultural life. This is reflected in a decline in the social conditions necessary to measure individual achievement against occupational success, and in the undermining of possessive individualism of a private kind within the sphere of consumption. Such elements of decline are seen in turn as the respective products of changing forms of workforce organisation which do not emphasise individually accountable achievement, and in the rise of collective consumption, in such areas as transportation, health care and leisure. All such changes, however, point in the direction of greater universalism.

This type of discourse engages far more directly with Parsons' project than does Marxist political economy, insofar as it embraces a multi-dimensional theory of action, a concern with the normative bases of social order, and a perception of the universalistic thrust of modern society, which must sooner or later displace capitalism. Habermas manages to combine these with a less benign view of the social structure than Parsons, a view which recognises the place of unequal exchanges of power and resources between capital and labour or citizen and state. In this way he is able to retain a conception of the continuing salience of inequality to the dynamics of capitalism with a concern for the autonomy of the normative basis of the socio-cultural system from both capital and state. By this means Habermas manages to produce a theory of economy and society, divided in much the same way as Parsons' four-function paradigm, while displacing social exchange theory from the prominent position which Parsons gives to it in understanding processes of boundary interchange. In addition to issues of empirical disagreement which may exist between Parsons and Habermas, as for example over the persisting importance of occupational role identity and commitment, this gives some indication that the meta-theoretical basis of Parsons' action schema is capable of yielding more than one substantive theory of the relations of economy and society.

At this stage in the development of economic sociology, there is still much to be gained from theoretical consolidation and further empirical exploration of Parsons' substantive theory of economy and society in comparison with kindred approaches such as that of Habermas. Until the rich research programme laid down in *Economy and Society* has been evaluated at this level, any verdict on Parsonian economic sociology based purely on meta-theoretical critique (Savage, 1981) seems highly premature. Without a more wholesale abandonment of positivist epistemology and a review of the limits of instrumental rationality, however, it is doubtful whether economists will wish to participate in this project in the manner that Parsons hoped for. Whether this exercise continues to be regarded by economists and political economists as 'utopian' depends on the extent to which the social sciences become even more overwhelmed than they are at present by the fateful progress of 'rationalisation'. Not the least of the merits of Parsonian economic sociology as compared with economics and political economy is that this spectre is both intelligible and capable of analysis in 'theoretical terms'.

# 2
# Sickness and social structure: Parsons' contribution to medical sociology

*Bryan S. Turner*

Introduction

The contribution of Talcott Parsons to the development of medical sociology has been neither fully discussed nor adequately assessed. This absence of a critical evaluation is peculiar, given the extent of Parsons' theoretical contribution to the analysis of sickness, medical professions and health-care institutions. Parsons was the major exponent of a distinctively sociological perspective on health and sickness. Although his particular approach to medical sociology has been the subject of criticism, Parsons' argument that sickness is a social not a biochemical condition provided the basic premise for the sub-discipline. To some extent, Parsons' contribution to medical sociology has been seen in terms of the concept of the 'sick role' (Parsons, 1951a); but this assessment of Parsons' work in medical sociology is too narrow and restricted. One might suggest that what Durkheim did for the sacred, Parsons did for health, namely to locate the dynamics of health and disease at the centre of the social fabric of modern societies. While Parsons made significant contributions to most areas of sociological investigation – law, family, religion and economics, there are a number of reasons for drawing special attention to the location of medical sociology within Parsons' sociology as a whole.

The problem of continuity and discontinuity in Parsons' sociology with respect to both theoretical and substantive issues has been much debated (Holmwood, 1983a and b). The importance of Parsons' medical sociology is that it pinpoints a major theoretical and substantive continuity in Parsonian sociology. More importantly, his analysis of sickness and health via the concept of the sick role indicates that sociology does not have to choose between either an action frame of reference or a social systems approach. There is only one sociology not two (Alexander, 1982). Parsons' concern for a sociology of sickness brings into sharp focus his general concern with the problematic of agency and structure, and thereby of voluntarism and determinism. In short, to what extent is human sickness a condition (an environmental constraint on action which guarantees our finitude) and to what extent do 'motivational factors' play a part in bringing the condition about? Parsons' answer was that it makes sociological sense to say that social actors choose to be sick, but this choice is itself an effect of the social and cultural features of modern society.

Parsons has often been criticised as the conservative apologist of professional power and elite institutions (Gouldner, 1971; Johnson, 1972). In particular, his view of health and the sick role have been regarded as 'medico-centric' (Gallagher, 1976) and it has been suggested that Parsons naively accepted a professional ideology which secures the compliance of patients to a medical regimen (Heraud, 1979). Much of this criticism is clearly valid and in recent years the Parsonian paradigm has been successfully challenged by what may be called a political-economy approach (Doyal, 1979; Navarro, 1976). Against such criticism, it is important to remember that Parsons' concept of the sick role provided a major challenge to the 'medical model' of illness, a model which is the ultimate legitimation of the medical profession (Veatch, 1973). Furthermore, Parsons assumed that the 'upgrading' of patients by an expansion of education would transform aspects of the asymmetry between doctor and patient, and that the bureaucratic reorganisation of medicine would transform the autonomous physician into a member of a team. In addition, he argued that medical practice and health could not be seen in isolation from wider changes in the social structure (especially the family and the occupational structure). Parsons' medical sociology had radical implications which neither his critics nor Parsons himself adequately appreciated. Parsons' medical sociology provides a theoretical site on which a more generous re-assessment of Parsonian sociology may be developed.

To achieve the status of a classical theorist in sociology, as in any other discipline, it is not sufficient to develop perspectives which are coherent, continuous and creative. Behind the theoretical rigour, there must lie a broader and more catholic vision of human beings, their location in the modern world and the importance of the sociological imagination in relating persons to circumstances. Classical theory is informed and instructed by values and personal commitments which are organised around a moral anxiety about the crisis of modern civilisation. One persistent theme of Parsons' meta-theoretical position is that no society could exist in terms of rationalist utilitarian individualism: expediency and self-interest cannot be the sole norms of action. Parsons' critique of social theory thus focussed on economism and emphasised the centrality of ultimate values for understanding human action and social systems. For Parsons, religion and medicine were the institutional embodiments of other-directed, disinterested actions which could not be explained by reference to rational, economic interests. Parsons' sociological interest in the functions of religion and the professionalisation of medicine flowed out of a prior commitment to certain moral questions. These religio-moral concerns remained a continuous feature of Parsons' sociology from the early essays on values and ideas (Parsons, 1935b; 1938b) through to his final reflections on the human condition (Parsons, 1978b). Like Weber and Durkheim, Parsons was centrally interested in the relationship between religion (nonrational, altruistic other-worldliness) and economics (rational, egoistic this-worldliness). Unlike Weber and Durkheim, Parsons retained an essentially optimistic view of the future of sacred values in an urban, industrial, capitalist society. It is not surprising, therefore, that medicine and religion are important links in Parsons' moral and sociological perspective on modern society and the human condition, since health and salvation are values which lie beyond the secular world of self-interest, calculation and rational planning.

The argument

To state my position controversially, 'medicine' is of no interest
to the sociology of medicine in the same way that 'religion' is
irrelevant to the sociology of religion. Medicine may be properly
the object of medical science and religion may be the topic of
theology, but the theoretical interests of sociology lie elsewhere.
When sociology takes medicine as its primary concern it is
converted into social medicine, applied sociology or at best
sociology in medicine. When sociology takes religion as its
object, it becomes religious sociology, not sociology of religion.
There is only one justification relevant to sociology for the study
of substantive topics such as law, the family, religion and medicine; this justification is simply that through the study of some
particular area we can come to a better understanding of social
structures and thereby develop the explanatory purchase of
theoretical sociology on social reality. Any deeper understanding of religion or medicine which may result from these
sociological inquiries is entirely accidental and secondary. In
this sense, sociology is scientifically entirely narcissistic, since
its aim is its own maturation and reproduction. The purpose of
medical sociology is to understand social structures and social
processes through the medium of health, illness, medical
professions and institutions. To drive home this point controversially, the criterion of theoretically valid medical sociology is
that it tells us relatively little about medicine and a great deal
about social relations. This was Parsons' project in medical sociology, for which medicine is the pretext rather than the context
for the exploration of sociological issues. These issues were
ultimately the problem of values in the explanation of human
behaviour, the secularisation of western culture, the development of universalistic standards and the character of American
capitalism.

For economy of presentation, it is possible to divide Parsons'
medical sociology into four broad areas. The first area concerns
the nature of professional values in relation to the economic
ethos of capitalist society, the development of scientific knowledge with special reference to the university system and the
impact of social change on the medical curriculum (Parsons,
1939; 1958b; 1960a; 1963d; 1964a; 1969a). The second area

includes the sociological approach to illness, the distinction between physical and mental health, the role of motivation in illness and the sick role (Parsons, 1951a; 1975c; 1978a). The third area is the effect of social structure (especially American society) on health, sickness and ageing, with special reference to the values of activism and the social strains within the nuclear family (Parsons and Fox, 1953; Parsons, 1958b; 1960f). Finally, there is Parsons' interest in death, sickness, religion and the human condition, where, particularly towards the end of his career, he brought together his distinctive concerns with medical sociology and the sociology of religion. These broad concerns may be subsumed under the heading of theodicy (Parsons, 1963c; 1973a; 1978b; Parsons, Fox and Lidz, 1972). There are other fields of inquiry which bear directly on Parsons' interests in medical sociology. For example, there is Parsons' profound engagement with the thought of Sigmund Freud and the relevance of psychoanalysis for the theory of personality. Parsons assumed that Freudian analysis had a clear relevance for clinical practice, but his adoption of Freudianism lies beyond the immediate focus of this argument and clearly deserves separate treatment. Although these four areas of Parsons' medical sociology will be considered specifically, the general point of my interpretation is that his interest in medicine and health is central to his theoretical perspective on modern societies, that his medical sociology largely survives criticism and finally that his view of illness has radical implications which have not been fully grasped or acknowledged.

## The background

It is well known that Parsons' academic aspirations were to be a biologist or a physician, being deflected into social sciences around 1923. This biographical fact may not be particularly significant; it is probably more important to note that Parsons retained a life-long interest in the relevance of biological theory for sociological theory. There was, for example, the early influence of Walter Cannon's *The Wisdom of the Body* on the formulation of the notion of the social system and the later influence of Ernst Mayr's distinction between 'teleological' and

'teleonomic' (Mayr, 1974) in the development of Parsons' paradigm of the human condition (Parsons, 1978c). Although there
was an obvious bio-medical input into Parsons' emerging focus
on medical sociology, his interest in the medical profession
and the sick role developed in a context where there was no
institutionalised sub-discipline called 'medical sociology'.
Parsons was thus highly influential in the formation of a new
specialism within sociology. Whereas Parsons' sociology of
religion was formulated on the back of an existing classical
tradition which embraced Durkheim, Weber, Troeltsch and
Malinowski, his contribution to medical sociology took place in
a context where there were few clear theoretical or substantive
guidelines. Medical sociology did not become clearly differentiated as a sub-discipline in sociology until the 1950s (Cockerham, 1982) and it has been suggested that medical sociology
remainded underdeveloped in terms of theoretical coherence
because of its subordination to professional medicine (Strauss,
1957; Roth, 1962).

   Although this interpretation of the late institutionalisation of
medical sociology in the sociology curriculum is superficially
valid, it is important to realise that Parsons' development of the
notion of the sick role and the doctor-patient relationship as a
social system did not entirely occur in a theoretical vacuum.
There were at least two important contributions from the 1930s
which were directly relevant to Parsons' approach. The first
was Louis Wirth's article on 'clinical sociology' (Wirth, 1931)
which argued that sociologists would come to play an important
role in the work of child-guidance clinics and anticipated the
development of 'sociological clinics'. For Wirth, the importance
of sociology for medicine was its perspective on the patient as
a 'whole person' whose illness could only be comprehended
adequately within a total social context. Illness could, therefore,
not be understood solely in medical terms. The second contribution came in two crucial articles by L. J. Henderson on the
doctor–patient relationship as a social system (1935) and on
the nature of medicine as applied sociology (1936). Henderson
argued that the clinical encounter between doctor and patient
is not unidimensional, but involves a social interaction which
is an important aspect of the basis for a medical diagnosis. Since
sociology is primarily concerned with such units of interaction

(that is, social systems), sociology ought to be a component of the medical curriculum.

Although Parsons acknowledged his intellectual debt to Henderson's treatment of the doctor–patient relationship as a social system (Parsons, 1964a), it can be argued that the sick-role concept is basically an elaboration of Henderson's insight. It is the case, however, that Parsons' development of a genuine sociology of illness and health took place in a context where there was little in the way of a corpus of sociological concepts and perspectives relevant to the analysis of medicine. In this respect, his contribution at the time was original and innovative. Parsons has correctly noted (Parsons, 1964a) that the debates in the 1930s were largely dominated by 'medical economics', where the primary concern was for the welfare problems of disprivileged sectors of American society in the context of New Deal politics. Sociology was somewhat peripheral to this debate and in this respect the recent revival of the political economy of health may be ironic. Parsons' early medical sociology can thus be regarded as the development of a theoretical alternative to the dominance of economics as the primary social science perspective on health issues.

Professions, self-interest and capitalism

The impetus behind both Parsons' development of the voluntaristic action schema and the analysis of the professions was the critique of utilitarian doctrines of self-interest, the predominance of economic models in the analysis of industrial societies and the centrality of positivism in the characterisation of rational action. For Parsons, the explanation of human action had to include reference to normative standards relevant to ends and to the exercise of choice with respect to both means and ends. Such normative standards could not be conceptualised within a reductionist framework. At the level of the theory of social order, the equilibrium of social systems had to be based on presuppositions about shared values, since coercive models of social order were held by Parsons to be incoherent.

Parsons' interest in the professions was directly related to these broader concerns, since what defined a profession within the occupational structure of modern capitalism was a code of behaviour which specifically denied that the professional was motivated by economic self-interest. It was from this study of the medical profession that Parsons developed the notion of 'pattern variables' (Parsons, 1951a). The professional orientation to the client was based on institutionalised disinterest in terms of universalist, neutral, collective and specific criteria which guarantee the delivery of a standard service regardless of the particular characteristics of the client. The ethic of the service professions was thus the exact opposite of the utilitarian notion of self-interest and furthermore the professional-client relationship was the opposite of a business relationship based exclusively on an economic contract. Indeed Parsons went on to argue that the effectiveness of the therapeutic function of the physician–patient relationship required a clinical situation in which market principles did not operate. The occupational order of capitalism could not, therefore, be defined simply in terms of the economic processes of competition, since normative standards are prominent in the service sector in determining the nature of professional performance towards clients. Medicine and medical professions thus played a crucial role in Parsons' theoretical development, especially in the critique of economistic conceptions of occupations.

Recent developments in the sociology of occupations have, however, established a perspective which is the reverse of the position suggested by Parsons. Contemporary approaches to the professions share an emphasis on professionalisation as a strategy to enhance occupational autonomy, exclusion of competitors and social status within the market place. The theoretical movement is away from definition of 'profession' in terms of normative criteria (universalism, technical competence and training) towards a view of professional labels as part of an occupational strategy to promote the interests of the occupation rather than to insure the quality of services delivered to clients. Within this perspective, 'professionalism' no longer refers to a system of ethics but 'becomes redefined as a peculiar type of occupational control rather than an expression of the inherent nature of particular occupations. A profession is not, then, an occupation, but a means of controlling an occupation' (Johnson, 1972, p. 45).

Sociologists have become more interested in the relationship between professions and the state (Johnson, 1982) as a crucial aspect of occupational control than in the standards governing relations with clients. Professional standards and training are no longer regarded as essential for maintaining the quality of service, but are treated as forms of credentialism and as aspects of social closure which seek to preclude competition (Parkin, 1979). Within medical sociology, this shift of perspective is especially prominent. The medical profession is seen to exercise 'medical dominance' (Willis, 1983) within the occupational market place, a dominance which functions to exclude alternative forms of service. Further, there is also a greater emphasis on the negative effects of technological medicine on health, the notion of 'iatrogenic disorders' (Inglis, 1981), and there is a growing literature on medical malpractice (Mechanic, 1977).

When contemporary sociology does turn to the doctor–patient relationship, there is a prominent concern to show that doctors do not operate in terms of universalistic, technical criteria. On the contrary, social class, gender and ethnicity are profoundly significant in terms of the quantity and quality of service. Variations in the length of medical consultations by social class are a simple measure of the absence of universalistic norms in practice (Cartwright and O'Brien, 1978). Finally, the feminist critique within the sociology of medicine has drawn attention to gender bias in recruitment to the profession, mobility within the professional hierarchy and in the treatment of patients (Clarke, 1983).

Medical sociology, like sociology generally, has taken a distinctly critical direction in the wake of neo-Marxist, feminist and other radical theories. This critical turn has rendered Parsonian versions of professions and professionalisation somewhat old fashioned and apologetic in character. It is not simply that Parsons' account of the professions is now held to be theoretically inadequate; modern sociology is implicitly anti-professional. The emphasis on professionalisation as social closure and monopolistic control is one of the few areas where neo-Marxists and neo-Weberians join hands in condemning functionalist and taxonomic approaches as formalistic and apologetic. Although the new wave of sociology of the professions provides distinct theoretical advantages over previous frameworks, it too is often more critical rhetoric than empirically grounded analysis (Saks, 1983). Furthermore, this critical rhetoric often amounts to an assertion that doctors have failed to adhere to the professional norms, especially of universalism. That is, to criticise doctors for a class bias in the treatment of patients requires an appeal to precisely those norms which Parsons stipulated as the defining characteristics of professionalism. Anti-professionalism presupposes universalistic values in order to mount a critique. Critical sociology accepts the standards of technical, universalistic competence as the criterion by which to criticise doctors for failing to act as professionals.

Of course, this critique is not all that the contemporary sociology of the professions has to offer. Part of its programme has been to understand the changing nature of the professions within the context of late capitalism, where state intervention is increasingly important in setting standards of service, training of professionals and in underpinning medical dominance. In this respect, Parsons' account of the professions is distinctly dated, since it was developed in the context of a laissez-faire economy, where an individualistic contract between doctor and patient was the norm. Parsons' model is not, therefore, wholly relevant to societies in which there has been a significant nationalisation of health care provision and in which the state plays an important part in regulating the cost of health care. In these situations, the traditional autonomy of the medical profession has been challenged, or at least called into question, by state intervention. Alongside these developments, there has also been some erosion of the status of doctors, especially general practitioners. The fragmentation of the profession, the erosion of traditional autonomy, and the expansion of the division of labour within health-care occupations, have led some sociologists to suggest that there is a process of de-skilling and proletarianisation underway within the medical profession (Johnson, 1972). Many of these changes have rendered Parsons' concept of the doctor–patient relationship obsolete.

The increasingly critical stance of sociology towards the medical profession has to be seen in the context of an enhanced public awareness of the limits and foibles of modern medicine. Although the medical establishment enjoys considerable prestige, there is also evidence of public concern over medical expenditure, medical technology, dependence on drugs and the irrelevance of traditional medical approaches for stress-related illness in industrial societies. Public interest in alternative medicine (Inglis, 1979) is at least one index of lay dissatisfaction with conventional allopathic medicine. The traditional power relationship within the doctor–patient encounter was based on skilled supply and unskilled consumption of medical services, but this relationship may have changed, at least marginally, in favour of patient involvement in the assessment of services. The growth of medical adversity insurance is one indicator of the change. Although Parsons' account of the doctor–patient relationship may be obsolete, he did at least recognise that this relationship would change with the growth of an educated, skilled population (Parsons, 1958b). The critical reaction to Parsons and the critical perspective on the medical profession may both be consequences of changes in the doctor–patient relationship which Parsons clearly anticipated.

The sick role

Although Parsons' analysis of the professions is well known, his principal contribution to medical sociology was the concept of the sick role which was first stated systematically in *The Social System* (1951a). The elements of the sick role are relatively simple, but the background and implications of the concept are highly complex. The central components of the sick role can be outlined succinctly. The difference between feeling sick and being sick points to the existence of a definite set of social expectations for the incumbent of a sick role, which Parsons claimed has four dimensions. The first is that it legitimates withdrawal from a number of social obligations, especially from work and family duties. There is the notion that a sick person ought to stay at home and rest. The second aspect of the role is that the person is exempted from responsibility for their condition; they cannot get well without external help and support. The third component is that the sick person has an obligation to get well; legitimation of sickness as a basis for withdrawal from social roles is conditional on the patient's acceptance of an obligation to get well by co-operating with the doctor's regimen. The final element within the role is thus an expectation that the sick person will seek out technically competent health-care, typically a trained physician. The sick role in fact describes a role-set or social system of the doctor–patient relationship, which is organised in terms of the pattern-variables, which Parsons had developed in connection with the analysis of professional roles.

Although the sick-role concept may look like common-sense ('When people are sick, we expect them to get better'), it is in fact a subtle and complex notion. Parsons developed the concept against an intellectual background in which the American medical establishment was beginning to take the notion of psychosomatic illness very seriously, and to realise that the social and emotional relationship between the doctor and the patient was an important aspect of the therapeutic process. Parsons himself had become aware, through the prompting of Elton Mayo, of the relevance of Freudian psychoanalysis for the study of sick roles, especially Freud's study of transference. These influences led Parsons to realise that there was an important issue of motivation in the process of becoming sick and that, given the nature of the action frame of reference with its voluntaristic premises, there is an important sense in which people decide to be sick. The essay 'Some theoretical considerations bearing on the field of medical sociology' in 1964 provides a useful summary of the implications of these psychoanalytic influences on Parsons' early conceptualisation of the sick role:

illness itself could probably be considered, at least over a very considerable range, to be more than an objective 'condition' which came about independently of the motivational balances of the social system, and which was merely 'acted upon' by a 'technology' in the therapeutic process. It was itself integrally involved in the motivational balance and hence *institutionally* defined. To be 'sick' was not only to be in a biological state which suggested remedial measures, but required exemptions from obligations, conditional legitimation, and motivation to accept therapeutic help. It could thus, in part at least, be classed as a type of deviant behavior which was socially categorized in a kind of role (Parsons, 1964a, p. 332).

It is worth emphasising these features of Parsons' definition of the sick role in order to grasp the innovatory character of his approach to the problem. The concept emerges in *The Social System* in the section on deviance and social control. Sickness, like crime, involves deviance from normal role expectations, and they are both forms of motivated action. The sick role legitimates this deviance, but it is also an important vehicle of social control since the aim of therapy is to return the sick person to conventional roles. Parsons' insight into illness behaviour as deviance was thus a remarkable anticipation of various deviancy-models of mental illness which subsequently became influential in sociology in the work of Edwin Lemert (1967) and Thomas Scheff (1966). There was thus an important link for Parsons between the role expectations of the doctor–patient relationship and problems of social control and legitimation at the level of the social order. Although Parsons is not noted for his contributions to the sociology of power, it is interesting that his discussion of sickness should have so clearly located the sick role in the context of an analysis of legitimation, social control and deviance.

Although the sick role has been recognised as an important contribution to medical sociology, it has also been subject to extensive criticism (Levine and Kozloff, 1978). At the core of these criticisms, there is the argument that Parsons' ideal typical model is based on a narrow, positivist model of organic disease. The model assumes that sickness is acute, the patient is passive, and the physician is competent and altruistic. The model has little relevance to chronic illness or physical disability. The relevance of the model becomes particularly problematic in areas where the use of the term 'sickness' is uncertain and unstable. These ambiguous cases would include mental illness, alcoholism, homosexuality or pregnancy. The thrust of these objections is that Parsons simply accepted conventional medical categories in the definition of what is to count as sickness. For example, although Parsons constantly drew attention to the activistic assumptions of western medicine, which postulates that in principle all disease can be cured, he did not question the

medical assumption that ageing falls outside the conventional
category of disease. Should ageing be regarded as a permanent
sick role that legitimates withdrawal from social roles (Caplan,
1981)? Parsons' model is limited because it refers to acute illness
(like appendicitis) where the doctor intervenes to solve a
problem which is morally neutral, unambiguous and life-threat-
ening, but short-term. The criticism of Parsons suggests that his
sick-role theory accepts naively the medical model of sickness.
Although Parsons offered a reply to his critics, in 'The sick role
and the role of the physician reconsidered' (Parsons, 1975c), the
reply was limited to rather narrow features of the debate.

The criticisms of the sick-role concept appear often to over-
look the radical implications of the model. For example,
although Parsons acknowledged that sickness was ultimately
rooted in biological malfunctions of the organism, the manifest
content of sickness was completely social. The crucial distinction
between illness and health was engagement in and withdrawal
from social activities and responsibilities in familial and occupational roles (Parsons, 1978a). These social criteria are particularly emphatic and central in the definition of mental illness.
Thus, Parsons (1958c) in 'Definitions of health and illness in the
light of American values and social structure' claimed that the
primary criteria for the definition of mental illness were in terms
of the social role-performance of the social actor. Mental illness
is primarily a form of deviance from conventional social expectations. Parsons was also fully aware that patients may be reluctant to get better and abandon the sick role since there were
many 'secondary gains' from sickness. People choose to be ill
as a defence against a social system in which they find it difficult
to operate or to cope successfully. Thus, Parsons saw mental
illness as a reaction of the individual to the 'strains' of the social
system. In a discussion of the 'vulnerabilities of the American
family', Parsons and Fox (1953) noted that sickness was an
attractive solution to the structural tensions within the nuclear
family. The sick role legitimises a withdrawal from such strains
and tensions within the family. For the child,

> illness can provide him with a method of escape from
> progressively more exacting obligations to behave in a
> mature fashion. . . . The aged individual, occupationless,

and with no traditionally assured place in the families established by his daughters and sons, through illness may once again become an integral member of a meaningful social group (Parsons and Fox, 1953, p. 35).

The idea that sickness is positively functional for the individual by permitting withdrawal has been developed by a variety of contemporary theorists, especially those with a psychoanalytic background. In particular, Claudine Herzlich (1973) has expanded Parsons' sociological perspective on sickness to analyse the individual and social representations of illness, which again brings out the positive functions of illness. For Parsons, of course, sickness could offer only a partial solution to these critics since the incumbent of a sick role is expected to struggle for recovery.

Parsons' sick-role concept is, therefore, not simply 'founded on the narrow organic disease model of positivist medical science' (Hart, 1983, p. 353). On the contrary, Parsons' conceptualisation of sickness provides a wide-ranging critique of the medical model. In the special issue of the *Journal of Social Issues* on 'sociocultural approaches to medical care' in 1952, Parsons and Fox rejected the dominant positivist perspective in which 'the invading microbe has reigned symbolically supreme as the prototypical cause of disease' (Parsons and Fox, 1952, p. 2). By contrast, Parsons emphasised the importance of socio-cultural factors (the 'strains' associated with modern work conditions and the isolation of the nuclear family) in the aetiology of disease. Under the influence of Freudian psychoanalysis, Parsons drew the attention of sociologists to the motivational factors in sickness and recognised the 'secondary gains' of the sick role. In brief, Parsons consistently denied that sickness was exclusively a biochemical condition and argued instead that it was an institutionalised role. The implications of such a view are that the medical profession does not enjoy a monopoly of relevant skill with respect to the patient's welfare. Parsons was perfectly aware of these implications since he argued that medical education would have to change in response to changes in social conditions and would have to incorporate developments in the social sciences, especially sociology and psychology. Having argued for the salience of socio-cultural factors in the aetiology, treatment and constitution of somatic and mental illness, Parsons could hardly remain content with a positivistic paradigm for modern medicine.


## Sickness and American values

It has been argued that Parsons' interest in medicine has to be seen as part of a larger sociological project, namely an inquiry into the nature of American capitalist society. For Parsons, the forms of illness and medical responses to sickness were profoundly shaped by the constellation of social values, which was an integral component of American activism and individualism. In his analyses of illness, Parsons constantly referred, with some degree of approval, to Robert Merton's study of individual adaptation to dominant American values (Merton, 1957). In Parsons' medical sociology, illness as withdrawal corresponds to Merton's category of retreatism as a form of deviance. Both approaches depend upon a particular characterisation of American society as the fulfilment of secular Protestantism, that is, a society with a peculiar emphasis on individualism, the achievement motive and social success on the basis of merit. In this sense, withdrawal and retreatism are forms of deviance which are specific to the American cultural context. Parsons' medical sociology pointed, therefore, towards a comparative sociology of values as determinants of constellations of deviance and sickness in industrial societies.

The argument that it is not possible to understand the nature of health and illness without a prior inquiry into the dominant values of a social system was a prominent feature of Parsons' sociology in the 1950s. Given the emphasis in American culture on instrumental activism, it is not surprising that in the lay definition sickness should be seen in terms of withdrawal from work, or that the aim of therapy should be to return the sick to effective participation in social functions. Parsons also observed that, following the centrality of activism as a value, the therapeutic process requires work from the patient, who is encouraged to try to get better. Therapy is a job to be done (Parsons, 1958a).

It is interesting, by way of digression, to note that Erving

Goffman in *Asylums* (1961) referred to the institutional history of the mental patient as a 'moral career', but whether such activist metaphors are peculiar to America is unlikely. Herzlich (1973) found in a French setting that illness was often presented as an occupation which involved ceaseless labour. Regardless of the comparative value of these observations, the importance of Parsons' emphasis on values is that, within any given society, there will be a selection in terms of deviance and illness from a continuum of possible forms of sickness. The presentation of symptoms will be highly specific to the particular value-constellations which are dominant within a society or in terms of cultural sub-groups within a society. Parsons' view of the crucial role of values in explaining variations or selectivity in the forms of illness behaviour, sick-role performance and symp-tomatology has been borne out by the research of Zborowski (1952), Campbell (1978) and Zola (1966). In this respect, the importance of instrumental activism in Parsons' account of the relationship between values and sickness provides a defence of the sick-role concept against two conventional criticisms. It has been argued that Parsons' model treats the patient as passive in contrast to the altruistic intervention of the doctor, but this situation is specifically denied by Parsons, who noted that the patient must engage in the doctor–patient dyad by regarding recovery as work to be done. Secondly, Parsons has been criti-cised for not paying sufficient regard to lay definitions of sick-ness, but this criticism is not entirely warranted, since Parsons argued that lay definitions of illness will vary between societies according to variations in their dominant-value system. Parsons was also concerned to study the variable impact of these values by age and sex.

In 'Toward a healthy maturity', Parsons (1960f) was particu-larly concerned with the consequences of instrumental activism on the ageing process and in retirement from the workforce. The emphasis on activism led to a corresponding 'accent on youth' in American society, which was combined with a denial of death. It is this combination of values on youthfulness and activity which renders illness, disability and retirement especially problematic in terms of the individual's self-definition as a worthy member of society. Some aspects of these strains in the American system had been outlined by Parsons in 'Age and sex in the social structure of the United States' (1942c), but it was not until the 1960s that Parsons began to see ageing within a broader theoretical context which embraced sickness, deviancy, retirement and personal identity as features of the problem of social control. Since health is defined as a capacity to achieve, sickness is deviant behaviour because it is withdrawal from activity. Where there are unequal opportunities for achievement, personal esteem and social prestige are constantly under threat. It was in this context that the ambiguity of the sick-role concept (and possibly the ambiguity of Parsons' own position) became most evident. Although there is an emphasis on working to get better, being ill on a permanent basis is a perfect legitimation of deviance as an occupation:

> sickness provides for the individual, perhaps, the most important single escape hatch from the pressure of obligations to achieve . . . illness is far from being an exclusive and unmitigated evil; it is also an important 'safety valve' for the society. . . . This seems to be preeminently true of the aging groups. It seems almost obvious that illness is a *particularly* important form of deviant behaviour for them (Parsons, 1960f, p. 172).

The parallel between Merton's typology of adaptations to discontinuities between culture and social structure is now obvious. In Parsons' medical sociology, the sick role is a legitimate, institutionalised resolution of failure with respect to standards set by instrumental activism. The aged, the poor, the uneducated and the disprivileged adapt to structural crises by a legitimised withdrawal into sickness. The gateways to deviance are monitored by the medical profession who are held to be technically competent to distinguish between malingering and madness.

Parsons' essays on age and ageing are not the most influential of his publications. They provided part of the theoretical basis of S. N. Eisenstadt's *From Generation to Generation* (1956) and his perspective on the contradictions between activism and ageing have been largely reproduced in more recent approaches (Johnson and Williamson, 1980). However, Parsons' analysis of sickness and deviance as adaptations to American culture in which physicians act as moral watchdogs rather than technically

neutral experts with a specific competence had radical implications which Parsons and his critics did not suspect or detect.
The recent 'radical' literature on 'medicalisation' (Friedson,
1970) and medicine as 'social control' (Zola, 1972) can be seen
in this light, not as a departure from, but as a consolidation of,
these Parsonian foundations. However, in order to understand
Parsons' perspective on American values and their bearing on
sickness as deviance, we have to make a further inspection of
Parsons' intellectual development by examining his final contributions to the sociology of religion. It is only by considering
the relationship between religion and medicine that we can
come to terms with Parsons' sociology of modern societies.


Death, religion and values

Religion, theodicy and the problem of death in relation to the
meaningfulness of life remained central to Parsons' sociology
of modern societies from his first encounter with Weber (in
particular the introduction to Weber's *The Sociology of Religion*)
to his final essays on Durkheim (Parsons, 1973a; 1981). It is
appropriate to include a discussion of Parsons' views on
religion, since they are pertinent to his approach to death in
American society. In the 1970s, Parsons began to engage with
the issue of the impact of medical technology on medical ethics
and with the implications of increasing life expectancy on the
meaning of death in the context of modern secular society. In
the course of these inquiries (Parsons and Lidz, 1963; Parsons,
Fox and Lidz, 1972; Parsons, 1978b), Parsons no longer saw
American values in terms of a denial of death, but brought
attention to a growing public debate about death. Parsons also
began to grapple with the problem of death in relation to the
adaptive capacity of the human species and the importance of
death for cultural diversity and social flexibility. A number of
general comments on Parsons' later writing on death are appropriate. First, they point to the comprehensiveness of Parsons'
approach to social phenomena in that he attempted to draw
together developments in biological sciences, medical technology, Freudian psychoanalysis and theology to develop a
sociology of the human condition in the twentieth century.

Secondly, Parsons' sociological writings have a powerful and obvious theological content (Robertson, 1982) which is reflected in Parsons' attempt to come to terms with the inevitability of death and the relativity of values in industrial society within a Kantian framework (Parsons, 1978c; Münch, 1981). Thirdly, Parsons' perspective was innovative in that it departed from what was then the standard argument, namely that death was denied within a secular environment (Ariès, 1981; Kubler-Ross, 1969). Parsons noted, for example, that the growing literature on death, of which his own work was simply a part (Shneidman, 1967), was hardly compatible with the denial-of-death proposition (Baum, 1982). Finally, health and religion were, for Parsons, not only two areas of human existence which could not be understood within a rationalist, utilitarian, economistic framework, but also provided markers for analysing the evolutionary development of western society.

To some extent, Parsons shares with Weber one basic assumption – that we live in a secular reality and that very secularisation makes sociology possible. However, Parsons' social theology is that of the liberal, Protestant, 'death-of-God', reformist, American theology. In this liberal view, three positions are typical: (1) God as a transcendent force becomes immanent in personal relationships; (2) the collapse of traditional Christian mythology and cosmology means that man can achieve a realisation of authenticity without the irritant of myth; and (3) Christian values and structures, rather than disappearing, are transferred into what appear to be secular political structures. It is interesting that Parsons (1973a) took Durkheim's aphorism that religion 'C'est de la vie sérieuse' to be consistent with Paul Tillich's argument (1952) that 'god' can be translated as 'our ultimate concern' while also praising Peter Berger (1969) and Robert Bellah (1973) for realising that all forms of secular *communitas* are essentially sacred. In this argument, it is not that 'God' is the symbol of 'Society' but that 'Society' is the incarnation of those common values which are our ultimate concern. Put differently, secular society is always to some extent an approximation to the blueprint of the Heavenly City.

We can also grasp the difference between Weber and Parsons by considering their divergent views on the impact of Christianity on western society. Although this is a somewhat controversial view, it can be argued that for Weber the origins of rational capitalism are located in the irrational quest for salvation and that the outcome of this quest is the irrationality of modern capitalism. In Weber, Protestantism was historically a mixed blessing: it was at once the root of rationalisation and of alienation. Furthermore, Weber argued that once on course capitalism no longer required any cultural push from religious asceticism. Parsons, while profoundly influenced by Weber, takes a very different stance. In 'Christianity and modern industrial society' (1963c), he argued that Christianity, especially Reformation Christianity, prefigured all the institutional characteristics of liberal, constitutional democracy. Christianity contained, latently, the following features: a notion of community independent of kinship ties; religious individualism; universalism; the separation of religion and politics; achievement orientation; and an appreciation of the value of secular knowledge. In short, Christianity provided the cultural prerequisites for the professional calling. In Parsons' view, secular society as manifested in the denominational pluralism of American democracy is not so much a falling away from religious standards as the modern embodiment of the Reformation tradition. Christianity, through a process of evolutionary differentiation, is now fully adapted to modern society. In particular, denominational pluralism is the most appropriate religious framework for the realisation of democratic pluralism and, because religion is now essentially a private affair of the individual within the domestic sphere, religion and the family provide ideal conditions for the socialisation of children. In Parsons' sociology of religion, Christianity did not decline or disappear with secularisation; rather religious values and practices were re-allocated, out of the public and into the private sphere of the individual and the family. Such a development was not inconsistent with Christian principles, but the realisation of their potential. In his essay on American religiosity, Weber was by contrast rather contemptuous of this domestication of religion, which he thought simply provided a rather superficial aura of legitimacy for business relations. Of America, he wrote 'Only the methodical way of life of the ascetic sects could legitimate and put a halo around the economic "individualist" impulses of the modern capitalist ethos' (Gerth and Mills, 1961, p. 322).

In *The Protestant Ethic and the Spirit of Capitalism*, Weber suggested that it was in America that the 'pursuit of wealth' had been converted finally into a 'sport' without ethical meaning. Capitalism was the unintended consequence of the drive for salvation and also its negation.

Two further comments on Parsons' view of religious values in modern society are pertinent. First, Parsons unlike many other sociologists makes a useful, however implicit, distinction between de-Christianisation and secularisation. For many commentators the problem of religion is solved by equating religion with the organised Christian churches; religion disappears conveniently with the disappearance of ecclesiastical institutions. The lesson Parsons takes from Durkheim's concept of elementary forms is that, insofar as the moral coherence of human societies is a necessary prerequisite for the constitution of a coherent individual, religion is not an epiphenomenal or ephemeral form of social life. On the contrary, religion is the grounding in which all social structures which transcend the epiphenomenal life-form of the individual pertain of sacredness. As Parsons correctly noted, Peter Berger's definition of religion as that phenomenon which completes the unfinished nature of human biology is an appropriate deduction from Durkheim's account of moral facts. The final outcome of that line of argument can be found in Robert Bellah's notion of 'symbolic realism', namely that it is not so much that religion resides in the social, but that the social is religious. Thus, Parsons defined religious ideas as

> the cognitive *definition of the situation* for action as a whole, including the cathectic and evaluative levels of interest in the situation. They . . . include the problems of 'meaning' in the larger philosophical sense, of the meaning of the objects of empirical cognition, of nature, human nature, society, the vicissitudes of human life, etc. (Parsons, 1951a, p. 367).

This definition is part of Parsons' more general argument, that the social actor is not simply a self-interested rational agent, selecting between ends in order to satisfy wants, but an agent who evaluates and defines the action situation in terms of meaningfulness. It is not enough for the world to be empirically given; it also has to be meaningful. We can also see from this definition why Parsons saw religion and medicine standing in close proximity. For Parsons, therefore, religion is a generalised system of beliefs which are concerned with the evaluation of being. Where these beliefs are commonly shared, social relations are experienced as morally coherent and meaningful. To my knowledge Parsons has never considered a social situation which could be regarded as meaningless or even systematically morally inchoate; the implication is that, while there is indeed deviance from moral norms, social systems are generically normative.

The second feature of Parsons' view of religious values and institutions is that, although they are highly diffused through the social system (indeed co-terminous with the social itself), they are specialised. As we have seen, the social function of religion within the social system, as a result of the evolutionary differentiation of Christianity, is to articulate and interpellate the individual. A socially competent actor in a voluntaristic framework must have knowledge of conditions and ends of action, but the actor must also have a capacity to discriminate and evaluate. As a specialised institution, religion is thus associated with the family in solving the latency and integration problems, that is of equipping social actors with motivation, values and expressive attachment to social relations.

If we combine these two features of Parsons' view of religion in society, we can approach them as a typical Parsonian combination of Durkheim and Weber. To solve the Durkheimian problem of order, there has to be a shared system of values. In modern society, the conscience collective has been distributed widely through the social system. There are no longer any prominent sacred places, objects or persons, but sacredness is to be found in somewhat muted form in 'civil religion', common values of civility or simply in culture. In Durkheim, the social core was a mountainous range of sacredness, its peaks set apart and forbidden; in Parsonian functionalism, the sacred is extended across a flat plain and access to these common watering-places of sociality is public and democratic. The social geography of the holy is essentially flattened by evolutionary adaptation. To solve the Weberian problem of meaning, each social actor has to be fitted out with a theodicy through family socialisation and involvement in primary groups. These theodicies need not have the formal coherence of Thomistic theology, but they must be adequate at the level of motivational commitments to action. Social actors for whom the social world has lost ethical coherence are unlikely to retain enduring, stable attachments to functionally important institutions. The two problems of order and meaning thus turn out to be the same problem, since the plausibility of systems of meaning hinge on the experiential facticity of social relationships. In the words of an earlier social theorist, it is social being that determines consciousness and our social being is an effect of our membership of social relations which exist outside our will. It is the security of social relations which produces coherent experiences of reality and in turn it is the coherence of these social experiences which support the plausibility of theodicy. Meaning is parasitic on order. It follows that a social being with a consistent (that is socially validated) personality must inhabit, indeed be the effect of, a social system which has simultaneously solved both problems of order and meaning.

The purpose of this review of Parsons' sociology of religion is to suggest that Parsons' view of medical ethics is part of a more general set of questions, relating to the impact of Protestant Christianity on American society. Specifically, instrumental activism is the cultural sediment of secularised Protestantism, but Parsons did not see American secularism as the antithesis of Christian other-worldliness. On the contrary, American values are the evolutionary outcome of Christian principles. It is possible to suggest, therefore, that the Hippocratic corpus (altruistic service to a patient on universalistic criteria in terms of a medical calling) is a specific instance of the Protestant calling in the world to human service. Medical professionalism is the unintended consequence of a secular, activist Protestant vocation in society. This perspective on Parsons' medical sociology takes us back, however, to the question of whether professionalism is best seen as an ethical code or a form of occupational strategy which attempts to maintain social closure.

## The state, values and professions

It is well known that Parsons found it difficult to develop an adequate theory of power and that his grasp of the role of the state is defective (Giddens, 1979). When, in response to his critics, Parsons attempted to develop a theory of power, he conceptualised power analogously to money, that is, power is seen as a system resource which facilitates the achievement of common goals (Parsons, 1963f). Power is not necessarily repressive or coercive; on the contrary, it is a public facility for bringing about desired conditions. Like money, it lubricates and cements the social system. Although there are merits to such an argument, there are some remaining problems with Parsons' view of the state. It is not clear, for example, why the state should not be conceptualised as a separate entity alongside the cultural, social, personality and organic systems. For Parsons, the state or polity is merely a sub-system within the social system. While most sociologists typically regard politics as merely a sub-field of sociology, there may be more compelling reasons for regarding the state as a separate system of action with its own autonomy and character. Given the prominence of the state in the modern period, it may be that Parsons does not give sufficient emphasis to the separation between the state and the economy, which many have held is the defining feature of modern capitalism. It should be noted, however, that the inclusion of the state as a separate system would not be incompatible with Parsons' general aim of producing a general theory of action.

We have seen that the problem of order was central to Parsons' sociology – it was the central and most persistent scheme of his life-work. The answer to the Hobbesian problem of order was the existence of a general system of shared values, but one problem for Parsons was to explain the source of these values. One answer for Parsons was essentially Durkheimian – values emerge out of the very process of socialisation and these values are thus both sacred and social. Now one interesting feature of modern theories of the state is that they typically regard the state as having a legitimating and cohesive function; it is the state which solves the problem or order in a capitalist society (Habermas, 1976; Althusser, 1971). These functionalist

theories of the state raise an interesting question: is the state or
civil society the fountain of those values which bind the society
together in a unity (regardless of whether that unity is contradictory or unstable)? Parsons did not regard the state as the principal carrier of such values as universalism, achievement and
disinterestedness. Parsons allocated these values to the
professions and it was professionalisation which in many
important respects brought about a general institutionalisation
of values in the social system. We might note in passing that
Parsons did not recognise the importance of the state in
supporting and guaranteeing professional autonomy, legitimacy and credentials. One reason for the gap is that Parsons'
political sociology was to some extent a reflection of American
conditions    and    values,    namely    constitutional,    liberal
democracy.

For Parsons, the state in a democracy may dominate the
public sphere, but it cannot be the source of general values and
it cannot provide values which are fundamental to the private
citizen, namely individualism. Parsons was not prepared to
consider the possibility which is central to much Althusserian
Marxism – the incorporation of the family into the state-system
as the basis of capitalist stability. For Parsons it is the privatism
of the family which is essential as a condition for the socialisation of individuals. Although Parsons gave a central role to the
professions in the maintenance of universalistic values, another
source of values is of course the continuity of the religious
tradition into modern society and the transfer (or upgrading) of
religious values to the polity (Parsons, 1963c). It would also be
compatible with Parsons' position to suggest that the democratic
process itself within the polity generates values (or at least
sustains them); these values would include justice, fair-play,
egalitarianism and individualism. Although it is possible to
identify these institutional locations of general values, the
absence of a Parsonian theory of the state in relation to the
values of citizenship appears to be an important gap in his view
of modern societies.

Evolutionary change: religion and medicine

As a conclusion, I shall present an argument about the nature of moral facts in modern societies, which will incorporate some aspects of Parsons' approach to religion and medicine in an evolutionary framework. This final section is in part, therefore, a justification for reading Parsons. The role of this section is to provide an application of aspects of Parsons' notions about the relationship between cultural differentiation and integration in the history of western cultures.

Let us consider a society in which the conscience collective is massive, all-pervasive and coherent. English society between the seventh and fourteenth centuries had such a moral system, in which there was little social division of labour and, in terms of the mental division of labour, there was a minimal separation between law, religion and medicine. Such a society possessed clear rituals of inclusion (baptism, confession and pilgrimage) which bound members of the society together and rituals of exclusion (excommunication and inquisition) which controlled social deviance. In such a society, there was no essential distinction between disease, deviance and sin. A primary illustration of this fusion of categories would be leprosy (Hepworth and Turner, 1982). Leprosy was recognised as a disease, but it had a moral aetiology and was a judgment of God. Lepers were excluded from society by a religious ritual – the 'office at the seclusion of lepers' – under the control of priests and it was by these ritual means that the sacred or moral core of society was kept free of contaminating dangers. The model I have in mind here is that presented by Mary Douglas (1966) in her *Purity and Danger*. The argument is not that every member of society was uniformly incorporated in the central moral system or that there was no dissent from the dominant institutions or that coercion was unimportant. It simply says that moral facts were prominent and subjectively experienced in all sectors of society. The argument also assumes most of the other features of Durkheim's model – the absence of individualism, the importance of retributive law and the elaboration of communal rituals. This form of mechanical solidarity began to break down in England with the development of an urban culture based on the merchant-burgher class. The change can be seen in the slow evolution of law, religion and medicine as three separate professional groupings which attempted to secure their status privileges through the process of social closure. The urban merchant class provided a clientele for professional services, and doctors in particular were able to draw upon certain scientific developments which, however primitive, formed the basis for new professional skills. Colleges for physicians provided an elementary basis for medical education and, with the backing of the state, doctors were able to prevent, or at least minimise, competition from the unqualified. The diseases of the body ceased to be moral and religious entities, and hence not an object of religious theorising. Disorders of the mind remained ambivalent and continued to be phenomena over which the clergy had a residual claim. These changes were reflected by a greater precision in the institutional treatment of crime, disease and sin. The expansion of knowledge created new spheres for the exercise of power and the surveillance of bodies; hospitals ceased to be dumping grounds for unclassified populations of the disorderly, and specialised treatment was now offered via asylums, prisons, hospitals. With the development of the germ theory, medicine emerged as an increasingly secular intervention into human misery, and disease ceased to have, at least overtly, any moral content.

In a society based on organic solidarity, the conscience collective becomes less central and prominent in social relations. At the same time the traditional bastions of civil society are undermined by the combined processes of industrialisation and urbanisation: the family, the church and the local community are marginalised and cease to be public institutions as they are converted into voluntary associations of the private individual. Citizenship rights are slowly extended throughout the society, embracing women and children on the basis of universalistic principles. What is crucial to this social system is the state as the guarantor of universal rights and this forces the state to intervene in the domestic sphere to uphold rights and obligations of citizenship. The possibility of rape within marriage as a criminal act is but one illustration of this situation. It is the state rather than the church which provides, or attempts to provide, the moral core of secular society; indeed the church becomes increasingly irrelevant in public life and the uncertainty of its social location is reflected in the fact that it is no longer clear what clergymen do in society. They appear to be vaguely located somewhere between social work and education. It is the state which now provides the cohesive factor in society and which provides the political supports for the two professions which dominate civil society: law and medicine. While disease, law and morality are differentiated, the medical profession expands to embrace wider areas of social behaviour within a medical framework: capitalist society goes through a process of medicalisation where traditional forms of deviance – alcoholism, homosexuality, political dissent and addiction – are reclassified as disease over which the medical profession has rights of monopolistic control.

Although medicine is now perceived as a neutral scientific practice with an unambiguous object of knowledge, diseases are not morally neutral. All diagnosis is in fact judgmental about what standards of health and behaviour are regarded as socially acceptable. In this respect Parsons' notion of 'the sick role' (1951a) was a major advance in the sociological appreciation of the complex relationship between disease, sickness, illness behaviour and deviance. Doctors, under the aegis of the state, have now replaced the clergy as the main guardians of public morality; they are essentially agents of social control who collectively decide what criteria constitute the 'good life'. Doctors are the new moral police (Foucault, 1973). The moral character of modern medicine is perfectly illustrated by the new plagues of the twentieth century: AIDS, herpes, veneral disease, cervical cancer, breast cancer and heart failure. The medical regimen presupposes a conception of the moral life. This world of medico-moral orders is, however, currently threatened by invasion from diseases which arise from 'immorality', especially promiscuity and homosexuality. The threat of AIDS has provided the grounds for an alliance between religion and medicine. The alliance is, of course, very old: salvation means health. The conditions for both in the modern world are either celibacy or heterosexual monogamy.

The sacred has collapsed in modern capitalist society; there are no prophets, gods or sacred places. The problem of order in modern society rests on the secular state in alliance with the professions. The orderliness of this society is precarious, given

the collapse of natural law, shared values and communal experiences. It is possible to conceive of such a society as having a
moral membrane which provides a thin, porous linkage
between individuals. This membrane has three features: (1)
national sentiment, which is based on common language and
citizenship – the state is after all typically the nation-state; (2)
episodic socio-dramas, which articulate the remnants of a
communal way of life – coronations, sport and national festivals
would be common examples; (3) a medico-moral universe in
which individuals, despite the scientificity of orthodox medical
theory, think out their existence in terms of personal responsibility and moral causation. The medical profession thus plays a
crucial role in legitimating society. Despite the rapid obsolescence of the household based on the nuclear family, medicine
provides the critical institutional link between the state and the
family, in alliance with its now largely moribund partner – the
church. Such a picture of modern society is compatible with
Parsonian evolutionism but does not entail any implicit assumptions about the superiority of liberal democracy. It is also
compatible with Weber, since it assumes that modern societies
are fragile and that morality is tenuous, given the relativistic
thrust of pluralism in culture. It assumes, with Weber, that
capitalistic society will also require as a last resort the coercive
apparatus of the state as that institution which enjoys a
monopoly of violence (Turner, 1982).

## Conclusion – agency and structure in the sociology of sickness

Medical sociology is often criticised for its lack of theoretical
development, its a-historical character, its narrow range of
substantive concerns and its subordination to the practical interests of the physician. In this perspective, medical sociology is
simply a tool of the doctor's art which aims to secure the
compliance of the patient. My argument has been that none of
these criticisms can be properly applied to Parsons' contribution
to the sub-discipline. Parsons attempted to provide a theoretical
basis for medical sociology in the basic concept of the sick role
which was addressed to the fundamental question – what is
sickness? Furthermore, as a result of his interest in the evol-

utionary development of western society, he provided a clear historical context for the study of medicine and the medical profession. It is equally clear that his substantive interests were far-ranging: death, sickness, religion, professions, American values, technological change, deviance, social control and secularisation. Finally, I have suggested that his analysis of the sick role was incompatible with the dominant medical model of illness and therefore his approach was never unambiguously supportive of professional status. Parsons' sociology was not medico-centric and furthermore it did not embrace an a-political view of the doctor–patient relationship. The scope and sophistication of Parsons' approach have not been fully acknowledged or adequately matched by either followers or critics.

We have to see Parsons' sociology of sickness as determined analytically by the paradigm of the voluntaristic action framework. The basic assumption of Parsonian sociology is that social actors exercise choice as between different courses of action in terms of norms, while the ends of action are circumscribed by values. Social actors are thus practical and knowledgeable; their consciousness of themselves and the conditions of action are an irreducible feature of what it is to be a social actor, and consciousness is a necessary feature of the distinction between behaviour and action. In this sense, sociology is not and never could be a behavioural science. As Giddens (1979) has repeatedly stressed, the 'knowledgeability' of the social actor is an essential presupposition of any adequate sociological theory. In terms of Parsons' medical sociology, it follows that sickness is not 'behaviour' but 'action' involving consciousness and choice on the part of a social actor. Since sickness is not simply a biochemical condition, it makes sense to say not only that we 'have' a sickness, but also that we 'do' sickness. Similarly we might speak sociologically about being occupied and preoccupied with *our* sickness, and also about the ways in which social actors take possession of sickness as *their* sickness. In the language of Winchian social philosophy, sickness entails rule-following action, where such rules are public and social (Winch, 1958). There are 'proper' and 'improper' ways of being sick, just as there are 'proper' and 'improper' ways of being mad. It is an interesting sociological paradox that to be berserk meant originally in old Norse culture to wear a bear's coat (bern-serkr).

The berserk was a sort of anti-role, but nevertheless a role governed by rules of what it was to be properly improper. To be sick, therefore, is not to be governed solely by natural laws (of a biochemical character) but fundamentally to adopt social rules of correct action. These notions – consciousness, knowledgeability and rule-following – lie at the centre of Parsons' simple but radical view of the sociology of sickness.

However, to argue that social actors 'choose' to be sick is to commit the double sin of idealism and methodological individualism. Parsons avoided these problems by noting that action always occurs within the context of limiting conditions and constraints over which the actor has little or no control. The two conditions of action which are crucial for Parsons' account of sickness are biological and structural. Parsons assumed that there are important conditions in terms of the biological endowment of an individual via the organic system which he regarded as the ultimate root of sickness. Parsons accepted the distinction between disease (a biochemical condition) and sickness (social performance) which has exercised philosophers of medicine in recent years (King, 1982). It can be argued against Parsons that 'disease' is not a neutral, descriptive category, but involves classificatory practices which are themselves fundamentally social. It is true that Parsons recognised that biological conditions are also transformed by social change. Changes in life expectancy would be one obvious example. Parsons was far more concerned with the social structural constraints on action than with biological conditions. His picture of the role of structural constraints operating on sickness activities was fundamentally Mertonian. Given the cultural emphasis on success, individualism and action, certain sectors of the population – the ageing, women at certain points in their familial careers, the unskilled and the disprivileged – are more exposed than others to the contradiction between means and ends (between opportunity and success). These sectors of the population are, so to speak, at risk and thus the sick role becomes a personal solution to the stressful demands of modern society. Sickness is simultaneously an effect of the conjuncture of achievement values, the isolation of the nuclear family and the demands of the occupational system, and the expression of such a conjuncture. Since Parsons was particularly interested in the relationship between medicine and religion, we might express Parsons' view of sickness in the words of Karl Marx:

> Sickness is at the same time the expression of real distress and the protest as a form of deviance against real distress. Sickness is the sigh of the oppressed creature. . . . It is the opium of the people.

Although this juxtaposition of Parsons and Marx may appear bizarre, it is worth remembering that Marx also emphasised the knowledgeability of the actor in the concept of *praxis* and regarded religion as a passive and deviant response to deprivation which stood in the place of politics. We might argue that in Parsons' sociology of sickness the sick role is a passive adaptation of sensuous, practical actors to deprivation brought about by social constraints over which they cannot exercise immediate or significant control. The doctor in such circumstances performs the functions of the confessor-priest. In this respect, we might argue that sickness is alienation, a withdrawal from the real world into a state of quasi-religious dependency.

In the last analysis, however, it is Parsons' relationship to Durkheim rather than to Marx which is significant. For Durkheim, the ultimate cause of crime was the existence of a legal and moral system which created a definite social boundary between normative and deviant behaviour. In this respect crime could have a functional contribution to the preservation of a moral order in that the punishment of offenders may reinforce the sense of a common consciousness. In this perspective, crime can be regarded as normal 'because it is bound to the fundamental conditions of all social life' (Durkheim, 1978, p. 184). The normality of crime is a consequence of the ubiquity of social norms of a common life. Different types of crime are the outcome of different forms of social structure. There is a parallel between Parsons' treatment of sickness and Durkheim's perspective on the normality of crime. Although it has been emphasised that the key element to Parsons' sociology of the sick role was the centrality of choice, this choice is in response to structural limits and constraints on the social actor. Furthermore, we can argue that sickness is distributed in society according to a set of highly specific causes or determinants (class, gender, age and ethnicity). In this sense, the social actor has to select a specific sick role, depending on the forms of sickness which a society makes available. In the twentieth century, bewitchment is not available as a sickness in industrial societies. The implication of Parsons' interpretation of the contradictory pressures of achievement, youthfulness and domesticity in America is that sickness, like crime, is a ubiquitous social fact which is normal because it is bound into the basic fabric of all social life. Sickness will not disappear, and it is not a finite phenomenon. By their very nature, societies constantly reproduce sickness and, so to speak, invent new categories of sickness to correspond to new strains in the structure of social relations. It was Parsons' recognition that sickness is normalised deviance which has been one of his major contributions to the development of modern sociology.

# 3
# Parsons, Schutz and the problem of *Verstehen*

*Roy Fitzhenry*

A central problem of sociology was given its most famous expression in these words of Max Weber: 'Action is social in so far as, by virtue of the subjective meaning attached to it by the acting individual (or individuals), it takes account of the behaviour of others and is thereby oriented in its course' (Weber, 1947, p. 88). This is a definition which firmly places the category of action as pre-eminent for sociological thought, and at the same time, by the ambivalent terms 'attach' and 'orient', gives social action the compound sense of behaviour and meaning.

That Weber here defined the cornerstone concept of his entire approach to sociology, to which all his other formalised concepts can be systematically traced, is part of the discipline's conventional wisdom. That this tracing involves a number of difficulties, some of them obdurate, provides part of the subject matter of Weber criticism. Parsons and Schutz have been the outstanding sources of much of this criticism. The category of action, as defined by Weber, gave each a basic orientation and a departure point for his distinctive theorising.

These departures form the topic of this essay. Parsons and Schutz will be examined in terms of Weber as a reference point in their thought. Yet this involves a degree of bias: the importance of Durkheim and Pareto to Parsons (and also Henderson and Whitehead), and the debt of Schutz to Bergson, Husserl and the German sociological tradition apart from Weber (including Simmel) will necessarily remain somewhat subordinated. But at the outset it needs to be noted that this bias affects the two theorists differently. Schutz was oriented throughout his life to Weber's problem, in a way which did not involve the rest of classical sociology, nor of cognate social sciences, in detailed criticism and review. The only other major sociological theorist to whose work Schutz devoted much critical attention after his student days was Parsons himself.

By contrast Parsons defined his interest early as 'general sociological theory', was committed from the beginning to a comparative methodology in theory-construction, and so displayed a constant view of issues as arenas, in which, like players, the classic sociologists might be humbled but never expelled. The 'state of play', however, was subject to long-term shifts; the mentioned bias seems quite justified in the case of Parsons' early work when the 'action frame of reference' was elaborated. Later, its inclusion within successively more abstract schemas of analysis, culminating in a system of 'the human condition' just before Parsons' death in 1979, makes it increasingly difficult to sustain. However, the object of this essay is to consider Schutzian and Parsonian concepts of action and it is with their earlier work that I shall mainly be concerned.

It is with a common attitude that I shall begin. The quotation from Weber is indeed a definition and the basis for another, of social relation as:

> . . . the behaviour of a plurality of actors, insofar as, in its
> meaningful content, the action takes account of that of
> others and is oriented in these terms. The social relationship
> thus consists entirely and exclusively in the existence of a
> probability that there will be a meaningful course of social
> action – irrespective, for the time being, of the basis of this
> probability (Weber, 1978, p. 267).

Here relationship is defined as a finite course of mutually oriented behaviour in such a way that its probability of occurrence depends directly on its meaningfulness (Gay, 1978). It should be clear from this that his concept of chance or probability cannot be detached from the problem of the meaning established in a course of action. That is, probability theory in the formal sense, applied to observed outcomes of social actions, is not warranted by Weber's use of the term.

This pair of definitions displays Weber's characteristic mode of formalisation – as he develops these each new concept is deeply embedded in its predecessors – so that the definitional structure has, as Schutz remarks, 'a mutually confirmatory character'. Both he and Parsons sought in their different ways to subject the content of this structure to criticism in the positive sense, in order to draw out the category of action as a refined and universal basis for concept formation. The assumption of each is that Weber's definition of social action is a culmination of, or distillation from, his substantive studies, such that it and the derived formalisations form the appropriate object of criticism.

While this is very clear in Schutz's work, which nowhere takes up Weber's sociological interpretations, and therefore presents only a torso of his thought to the naive reader, Parsons does indeed engage Weber's analyses of religion and European social change. Yet in *The Structure of Social Action* (1937a) his entire discussion of these is angled through a window formed by the formal Weberian categories. From this point of view Parsons finds the analyses deficient because of the incomplete state of the formalisations, and certain errors which he argued stemmed from Weber's inconsistent view of science. In other words, despite the more careful exegetical appearance of his treatment, there is the same subordination of the vast bulk of the substantive work to the definitional formal rump.

I am suggesting here that a common attitude of Schutz and Parsons, prior to the development of any thematic contents which parallel or 'converge' in their work on Weber, is a 'theoreticist' one. A distinction is implicitly drawn between 'interpretation' and 'theory'; the latter is held to summate and express the former, so that a reading of it is predicated upon what import it holds for the theoretical 'core' of the writer. From the point of view of the production (and reproduction) of 'theory' this is an economic principle of reading Weber. It may, however, violate his overall stance toward the problem of sociological analysis.

This essay began with a quotation which was described both as a definition and the expression of a problem. I have just implied that a reading which shears off the latter, the better to provide a technical problem of theory, and a coherent view of a founder of sociology, may have to pay high costs. That the 'essential' Weber could not be revealed by such an exercise was argued already by Karl Löwith in 1932, the year of the publication in German of Schutz's *Phenomenology of the Social World*. Against the reductionist approach which took Weber's definition of action as its departure Lowith insisted (p. 104):

> Even the immense casuistry of his conceptual definitions in *Economy and Society* has a *dual* purpose; not only to capture and fix reality in definitions, but at the same time and *above all* to establish the opposite sense of an open system of 'possibilities' (my emphases).

One such cost is Weber's conception of historical sociology. For Weber the goal of his substantive work was the construction of ideal types of 'historical individuals', analysed in terms of their capacity to construct meanings and types of social relationship. But these were elaborated from '. . . the focal points for *possible* "evaluative" attitudes which the segment of reality in question discloses and in consequence of which it claims a more or less universal "meaning" – which is to be sharply distinguished from *causal* significance.'

Lassman, after quoting this passage, notes that it was 'a fundamental axiom of Weber's methodological approach [that] there cannot be an ultimate system of social concepts' and that for Weber 'the social and historical sciences are sciences of "eternal youth" whose ideal types can only be transient' (Lassman, 1980, p. 105). A certain minimalism, if not anarchism, thus dominates Weber's view of the object of his historical sociology and the result of this position is the tentative state of his formal conceptual structure as explicitly addressed in his writing and about which, in their separate ways, Schutz and Parsons complain.

If this much and no more was common to their departure points from Weber it may provide some insight into the fact that from their opposed positions some decades later their followers developed methodologies which were virtually silent on the problem of sociology's classic critique of history.

Another aspect of Weber's sense of problem in relation to the category of action can be gauged from the following:

> Actual conduct is carried on in the large part of its
> manifestation in semi-consciousness or unconsciousness of
> its 'intended meaning'. . . . Only rarely, and only by a few
> in collective action, will a meaning (whether rational or
> irrational) of an act emerge into consciousness . . . that
> should not preclude the fact that sociology forms its
> concepts through the classification of objectively possible
> intended meaning, as if conduct were carried on
> consciously in a meaningfully oriented manner (quoted in
> Schmalenbach, 1982, p. 105).

One does not have to accept the criticism of Schmalenbach
and others that Weber's category of action is thereby weakened
fatally, to read such passages as an expression of serious reserve
by Weber regarding the overall system of concepts he
constructed abstractly. If sociology's central problematic is the
construction of meaning by actors, this meaning will often be
ineluctable within its immediate context of expression. Yet this
was no statement of disengagement. Weber's immersion in
problems of substantive historical sociology proceeded
unabated and all of these were concerned with the meaning
contained in conducts, affective, traditional, rationalising, etc.
Rather it is an expression of Weber's suspicion of the definition
of context-free concepts, an uneasiness with a universalistic
category of actions. As I have noted, it was the category of
action at precisely this level of abstraction which Schutz and
Parsons sought to refine.

If one considers, in the light of these remarks, the wide range
of Weber's substantive interests, each of which was an instance
of a sociological problem, then a perspective on his methodological position opens, which is not explored in either Schutz or
Parsons. Weber was evidently content with a view of the discipline as an interpretation of interpretations, that is an empirically based critique of historical and social theory. Marxism,
'historismus' and idealism, as philosophies and *as concrete
analyses*, were equally targets for this critique of his cultural
present, chosen not from an abstract principle (this would be
the position of a 'specialist without spirit') but according to his
own value-relevances (*wert beziehung*). Clearly, Weber general-

ised from this personal position to that of the act of sociological observation.

But if this relationship to values entered actively into the determination of an empirical problem then it followed that no single methodological emphasis could be pre-defined with a high degree of clarity. For Weber, but not for Parsons nor arguably for Schutz, the value-positions possible within a culture, to both observers and the observed were manifold. No single method could capture this multiple possibility. It could be argued that Weber thus adhered to a version of the uncertainty principle: use of a given concept systematically obscured facets of a phenomenon whose relevance for the observer increased paradoxically as the one-sided penetration of the phenomenon increased.

Schutz, however, did approach this perspective in several places, for example in his strictures on the limits of methodological prescription:

> Methodology is not the preceptor or the tutor of the scientist. It is always his pupil, and there is no great master in his scientific field who could not teach the methodologists how to proceed . . . In this role the methodologist has to ask intelligent questions about the technique of his teacher (Schutz, 1964, p. 64).

Yet the question raised by this statement is whether Schutz' selective approach to Weber could deal adequately with those techniques.

The position Weber adopts is not eclecticism but methodological diversity. The observer cannot specify in advance which facets of a phenomenon, chosen according to value interest, will be accessible. This determines what emphasis may be used methodologically. Thus in some places Weber lays stress on the clarification of motives of actors engaged in a developing relationship – a 'mutual subjective orientation' (Weber, 1978, p. 27). Indeed, this is a residual necessity in *all* cases because without some degree of mutual orientation being identified, sociological explanation is impossible. But he also declares that 'Action, especially social action which involves a social relationship, may be guided by the belief in the existence of a legitimate order' (Weber, 1978, p. 34). Here Weber is pointing to a different guidance of action where the stress is upon the insti-tutionalisation (or materialisation) of idealised forms of action, for example ethical institutions or canons of 'taste'. If the analytical distinction between these two guidance-principles cannot be sustained for long, a point which occupies both Schutz' and Parsons' critiques, that it is made at all is due to Weber's interest in capturing the *inter-relation* of methods, rather than the essential properties of social structures.

After Weber, the grounds of the debate over the importance of the subjective in social scientific work changed considerably. The social context of this shift was the emergence of a socio-logical profession in the United States with a focus upon social criticism and urban 'social problems' and hence with a concern to elaborate its methods of observation. The two most influential critics of Weber, whose entry into the debate was almost contemporary, approached his work with a concern that was quite congruent with this need. Participant-observation reportage, psychological/survey instruments and historicist interpretation tended to dominate the investigation of these problems. A definition of the social as a relatively autonomous field, and the subordination of these techniques to a distinctive principle of method: these were the quite practical needs of an emergent academic discipline with a reforming perspective on society. The methodology of subjective understanding – *Verstehen* – formed in the debate over methods in German historiography was one of the proposed central methods of an *observational* social science.

Levine has argued that between 1909 and the 1930s American sociology moved towards a 'theoretical vacuum'. The formal sociology of Georg Simmel, partly translated from the German, provided a minor theoretical focus, which he argues was temporarily erased by 'the Parsonian synthesis' (Levine, 1971, p. lvii). This view partly rests upon the somewhat dismissive treatment of Simmel in *The Structure of Social Action* (Parsons, 1949d, pp. 772–3). Since an exposition of Weber, and an insist-ence on the importance of studying subjective meaning was part of this re-orientation, the question arises: what role does *Verstehen* play in Parson's concept of social action?

Parsons' actor

At once, however, it needs to be noted that in Parsons' thought
a significant change occurred in the status of the *Verstehen* and
that this change is presaged by an ambivalent attitude. In 1937
it was 'the fundamentally important concept', which marked
the 'objective differences' (Parsons, 1959d, p. 583) between
natural and social sciences. In line with a Kantian position
which forty years later he re-affirmed, the social sciences had
to deal with phenomena qualitatively different; these were not
merely data but thought-data. Thus for Parsons the data of
sociology were simultaneously objective and subjective in that
this discipline had to analyse the conceptual and symbolic structures of actions which processed 'raw experience' into meaning
(Tiryakian, 1980, p. 59). In this, Parsons' view of meaning as an
operation of an actor's mind fits broadly with the neo-Kantian
position of Weber. For Parsons, Weber's concept of *Verstehen*
'meant essentially the accessibility of the subjective aspect of
other people's action as a real process in time. The object of
this verstehen is to uncover motivations' (Parsons, 1949d,
p. 635). The centrality of Verstehen as method for Weber's
substantive research aims was acknowledged by Parsons as this
later comment shows: Weber 'felt strongly, and rightly that only
through relating the problems of the dynamics of the whole to
the motives of individuals could he achieve a genuinely
scientific level of explanation' (Parsons, 1947b).

But already in this work Parsons claimed that Weber failed
to distinguish 'between motivation considered as a real process
in time' (that is as an ongoing construction of meaning by
actors in a concrete social relation) and 'atemporal complexes of
meaning as such' by which he means 'real things or events . . .
significant only as symbols with no intrinsic significance of
their concrete properties' (Parsons, 1949d, p. 636). Atemporal
complexes of meaning as a term prefigures what Parsons later
called 'the cultural system', analytically distinct from but inter-
related with 'the social system', by virtue of its atemporal status
'outside' history but realised in and through social action.

By 1949 the cultural system was being given a theoretical
importance which overshadowed actors' motivational
processes, or rather the motivational was seen by Parsons as

partly determined by the configuration of the elements of a given cultural system. The concept of culture provided Parsons with the means to 'de-historise' Weber's thought (Zaret, 1980) and at the same time to downplay the importance of actors' wilful construction of meaning. In 'Values, Motives and Systems of Action' (1951), written with Edward Shils, a cultural system contained 'patterns of regulative norms' functioning for actors to guide choices of action. These norms were action-directed specifications of the 'value systems, belief systems and systems of expressive symbolism' which constituted a given cultural system (Parsons and Shils, 1951b, p. 55). In the same essay Parsons and Shils concluded: '. . . the importance of culture is almost synonymous with the importance of what in motivational terms are sometimes called "symbolic processes"' (Parsons and Shils, 1951b, p. 242).

Taken by itself this would seem to involve a cultural determination of social action which some critics of Parsons have called the normative paradigm (Wilson, 1971), seeking to stress the victory in his thought of Durkheim over Weber. But this was not Parsons' position. Earlier he had stressed the 'Weberian theorem' that 'value-systems are diverse; there is a plurality of different possible systems' (Parsons, 1949d, p. 593). 'Incompatibilities' between actions and actors are thus inevitable, for which the transmission of cultural elements (in their diversity) is itself directly responsible. Now this in itself is not an avoidance of cultural determinism with its reduction of action to a dependent variable. But Parsons' 1949 view was that the incompatibilities of actors and actions constituted a continuous source of destabilisation of the social system, prior to any self-conscious forms of collective action within a society. If the stability of a social system had meaning as a sociological problem – and this had now moved to the forefront of his interest in general theory – then the basic 'mechanisms' which reduced this had to be described. They, however, could not be derived from the theory of motivation of actors (*Verstehen* of intended meanings constructed within relationships). To do so would be to confuse the sources of stability with those of change, and again to over-emphasise the causal significance of culture. Instead, they had to be discovered in the self-regulative properties inherent in any scientific description of a 'system', a system of 'action' no less than any other: 'Insofar as the system remains a system, some mechanisms must come into play for reducing these incompatibilities to the point where coexistence in the system becomes possible. . . . Some conception of *functional imperatives* . . . are [sic] necessary.' (Parsons and Shils, 1951b, p. 241).

At this point it should be clear that the category of action in Parsons thought was capable of considerable displacement, if not outright change. Throughout his work he continued to claim the continuity of his thought with respect to a *voluntaristic* action frame of reference, developed from the 'unit act' whose description and analysis occupies part of *The Structure of Social Action*. But two years after the formulation of functional imperatives, in *The Social System*, the displacement of voluntary action from a notion of creative possibility – its central meaning for Weber – to that of a situation of choice between limited alternatives is far-reaching: 'Value orientations . . . always constitute definitions of the situation in terms of directions of solution of action–dilemmas' (Parsons, 1951a, p. 351). And:

> contrary to the view held by the author in *The Structure of Social Action* it now appears that [the study of action from the point of view of the actor] is not essential to the frame of reference of action in its most elementary form. It is, however, necessarily involved at the level of elaboration of systems of action at which culture, that is shared symbolic patterns, becomes involved (pp. 543–4).

An example of what Parsons means by 'necessary involvement' here can be found in his long analysis of modern medical practice in the same study. There he analyses the inter-locking or complementarity of role performance and expectation by the doctor and the patient. The entire discussion is predicated upon their joint possession of a symbolism of health and illness acquired by each in the process of socialisation. Their inter-subjective relation is a particular version of the various kinds of association which societal members can develop from the 'shared symbolic patterns', i.e. culture, as these are mediated by the complex of institutions.

These are statements of the changes which a voluntaristic concept of the act had to undergo when Parsons integrated Weber's problem of meaning with anthropological conceptions of culture and the idea of the symbolic. After 1951 Freud and Durkheim occupied increasing attention in his writing. The importance of the latter had already been acknowledged in 1937. In *The Social System*, 'the geometry of erotic attachments' within the modern family, his first significant borrowing from Freud, is part of his analysis of the internalisation of social value-orientations, a discussion critical to Parsons' argument that socialisation, or personality-formation, joins the 'energy' of the individual organism to cultural prescriptions so as to produce *patterned* action. Action, henceforth, is always treated by Parsons as involving effort and cost. Subsequently, Freud also supplied Parsons with ideas for the analysis of expressive symbolism which took on increased significance in his late writings. The turn towards these two theorists is earlier signalled in *Values, Motives and Systems of Action*: '[The] institutionalization and internalization of value patterns, a connection independently and from different points of view discovered by Freud and by Durkheim, is the focus of many of the central theoretical problems of action theory' (Parsons and Shils, 1951b, p. 240).

These influences strengthened Parsons' tendency to interpret Weber's problem of subjective meaning in the direction of the second 'guide' of the social actor mentioned earlier, that is the symbolic systems of value and thought, or 'legitimate order' in Weber's terms, which provided solutions to the 'dilemma' of action.

The pattern of norms specified from these systems liberates the individual from the unpredictability of the other. He is then free to act 'voluntarily'. This is the core meaning of voluntarism in Parsons' work. His writing is genuinely free of any ironic inflection when he associates the institutions of individualism in modern western society with the fullest realisation of voluntary action. It was precisely this, however, which Weber described as an 'iron cage'.

Proctor has claimed recently that Parsons' 'metaphysical voluntaristic position' on action *never* emphasised the 'purposive, reasoning and self-conscious qualities of the action of concrete individuals' – which Weber's insistence on the study of situated motives entails (Proctor, 1980, pp. 311–12). Proctor thus argues against the line of criticism by such writers as

Martindale and Atkinson who see Parsons shifting from an
action-centred (Weberian) to a systems theory. On the contrary,
Parsons' concept of action was limited from the outset with
respect to the voluntarism of the social actor. Thus it was
congruent with the later development of the structural-functional systemic theory and no shift occurred. In making this
claim, Proctor restricted himself to work published up to the
end of the 1940s, thus excluding *The Social System*, to which so
much of Parsons' work after 1945 was directed, and the essay
with Shils.

According to the view of these studies proposed here, Proctor's argument is partly supported. However, I have been
concerned with the fate of the method of *Verstehen* in the work
of Parsons. In terms of this interest, my argument has been that
while Parsons began with a partial revision of the place of
*Verstehen* in sociological explanation, about 1950 a strong preference for the causal role of external symbolic systems of action
emerged, with the consequent redefinition of motivational-
processual *Verstehen* as a necessary but secondary investigation.
In this displacement Parsons' original commitment to a
comparative method in theory criticism and construction seems
to have been as important as any early definitive attitude to
action.

Parsons employed the sociologies of Pareto and Durkheim,
in which action was a passive category, for a revision of Weber's
radical view of the differences between natural and social
sciences. This view held that because

  all knowledge of social reality is always knowledge from
  particular points of view, then sociology progresses
  through a perpetual reconstruction of its central concepts
  and this process itself reflects or is tied to the cultural and
  social problems of the age within which the investigator
  lives (Lassman, 1980, p. 102).

Such a view required that 'motivational' *Verstehen*, whether for
historical or contemporary observational problems, function as
the central method of sociology. Parsons' rejection of this 'too
rigid' viewpoint in order to accommodate Weber with the other
theorists, entailed the eventual displacement of the method.

The practical consequence of this was that Parsons never

subsequently refined the concept of motivational *Verstehen*. No clearer indication of its displaced status can be given. The concept of action remained in stasis. It is this immobility which mainly constitutes the 'continuity' of the category of action in his thought.

By the same token, Parsons' position towards anyone who would raise the problem of the construction of meaningful action as a process of inter-subjectivity was necessarily hostile. Of these, Schutz (for reasons to be mentioned later) was treated as a consistent adversary. In his last work (1978a) Parsons disparaged 'certain phenomenologists, in the tradition of Alfred Schutz [who tended] to interpret scientific theory as "fictional", in their case of course attributing "reality" to "subjective experience rather than to external objects".' (Parsons, 1978a, p. 400) As early as the 1940s, in an exchange with Schutz on the latter's lengthy commentary on *The Structure of Social Action*, this 'fictional' stance had been the centre of Parsons' objection. It is interesting here that in attacking Schutz he was virtually re-stating his own (1937) criticism of Weber, namely that the latter arrived at a 'view of the "fictional" nature of social science concepts' (Parsons, 1937, p. 593) via a mistaken conviction that there could be no single system of social-scientific theory. In Parsons' final judgment (1978), Schutz was a modern representative of Rousseau, 'the apostle of direct motivational "experience"' (Parsons, 1978a, p. 413) as the basis for social theory. If cognitive empiricism in the tradition of Hume represented the polar opposite of this, then Parsons took his stand in opposition to both positions. The whole passage is worth study for its epigraphic quality.

> Many practitioners of cognitive enterprise tend to allege that our knowledge of the external world is directly 'given' by the 'nature' of that world and that humanly formulated 'theory' unless inferred by the strictest rules of *induction alone* is distortion. However, there is an equally, indeed recently even more prominent, tendency to maintain that humans have directly authentic experience of organically grounded motivation and that to 'free' such authentic motivation from alleged distortions it is necessary merely to brush away the symbolic structuring of human action

systems. In this sense, if Hume be the great apostle of
cognitive empiricism [in the *Treatise of Human Nature*] then
Rousseau [in *Emile, or Treatise on Education*] must be
identified as the apostle of direct motivational 'experience';
Schutz [the reference is to the *Collected Papers*] stands in this
prophetic line. Both extremes are equally unacceptable to
an unreconstructed Kantian like myself.


Schutz and the problem of attention

Parsons, then, placed Schutz within the tradition of romantic
social thought but in doing so implicitly aligned him with those
elements of Weber's sociology which he felt had to be rejected.
Schutz's irrelevance in Parsons' view was that of a rearguard
which fights for an army already defeated. The question of
Schutz's relation to Weber therefore deserves careful study.
Periodically expressing his profound respect for the substantive
content and projects of Weber's work, but avoiding all direct
treatment of its topics, Schutz's work is in this respect a curious
example of sympathetic criticism. It has already been suggested
that he shared with Parsons an attitude of abstraction, which
attends to Weber's work in a particular way, 'bracketing', so to
speak, the substantive studies in order to concentrate upon a
group of formalised concepts. As to these, Schutz was aware
that Weber changed his views on methodology (Schutz, 1976,
p. 244); nevertheless what was constant in his work was 'the
problem of the ideal type as the central problem of all the social
sciences' (Schutz, 1976, p. 226) or in other words, the method
of the objective interpretation of subjective meaning contexts –
*Verstehen*. The entire project of the *Phenomenology of the Social
World* is the philosophical grounding and the sociological extension of *Verstehen*. This may be contrasted with the position of
Parsons, for whom the ideal type as a conceptual vehicle for
the analysis of subjective meaning was rejected in *The Structure
of Social Action* and who later subsumed the meaning-
constructing actor under the theory of system. Parsons sought
to transcend Weber, Schutz to complete him. What follows is
a brief account of how this was attempted.
    No attempt will be made here to outline the whole structure

of Schutz' critique of Weber, nor the positive programme of interpretivist sociology which can be derived from it. I will begin in fact with a relatively minor problem – in terms of the space Schutz devoted to it the problem of history. In considering 'the problem of history' as one structured by the peculiar inaccessibility of an observer's 'predecessors', Schutz occupies a ground of vital importance to Weber himself, that of long-term social change treated as 'complexes of interaction' (Hall, 1981, p. 134). The latter had argued that the interpretation of meaning could occur in three modes: as the grasping of 'actually intended meaning for concrete individual action' (the historical context), or in the case of 'mass phenomena', the variations and average of the actually intended meaning (the statistical context), or, finally, the meaning of a 'scientifically formulated ideal type of a common phenomenon' (such as bureaucracy). Weber's ideal type stated the course human action would take *as if* the actors were logically governed and dominated by single unequivocal ends. This sociological context was a deliberately one-sided construct, unrealisable in life because of these conditions of its construction.

Its purpose (the usefulness of the 'puppet' thus created, Schutz would say) was thought-experimental: to explore the range of meaningful actions possible within an artificial social context. The empirical discovery of selection by historically typical individuals from this range, or of their failure to recognise alternative courses of action within it, generated the problem: how to account for this pattern of selection or neglect. However, this formulation is oversimplified because in substantive analysis Weber always used multiple ideal-types. These were juxtaposed antithetically (the Protestant ethic and the spirit of capitalism) or sequentially (charismatic prophets and their churchly successors). It is precisely because of its artificial quality that no ideal type can be used singly; used in a multiple strategy, ideal-types were, for Weber, useful *approximating* devices for historical interpretation. This is to say, that the validity of an ideal-type cannot be determined purely by an internal inquiry. The *relation* between two or more ideal-types must also be examined. To do this, however, means that the distinction between formal and substantive theorising in Weber's work must be set aside. It must be treated as a whole.

There is no way in which, for example, Weber's concept of rationalisation can be evaluated fully without being situated in his analyses of the city, of capitalism and of religion. I have perhaps laboured the point that Schutz avoided this form of conceptual analysis. My intention has been to underscore the partial character of Schutz's critique in order to situate its positive contribution.

In his treatment of Weber, Schutz is blind to the actual conditions of use of the ideal type. Yet he does appreciate a different aspect of Weber's idea of inter-related methods when he notes that the latter 'allows that all three methods of understanding meaning (Sinn-Verstehens) [i.e. 'historical', 'statistical' and ideal-type] are valid for interpretive sociology' (Schutz, 1976, p. 227). Schutz shows that 'even when social science is dealing with the action of a single individual, it must do so in terms of types' and this also holds true for the statistical treatment of 'mere phenomena' (Schutz, 1976, p. 227). Hence ideal-typical constructions are present in all three of the methods; what separates them is only levels of abstraction between historical, demographic and sociological research aims. Schutz's purpose here is to show that Weber's concept of ideal-type is overly restricted. Whenever an explanation following logical rules of inference (as opposed to, say, intuition) turns to the subjective context of meaning it must *always* operate with ideal-types, even implicitly, and so sociology is not distinguished from other cultural sciences on this ground. They are *all* characterised as 'objective meaning contexts of subjective meaning contexts' (Schutz, 1976, p. 223).

Specifically, sociology is not thereby distinguished from history. In Schutz' view Weber sought the wrong criterion. The real one lay in the two possible modes of explaining the actions of predecessors.

The 'objective meaning' of past actions may be the departure point of the historical sociologist, that is action will be approached in terms of correlation and cause; the result will be a 'history of facts' (Schutz, 1976, p. 214). Such a history is based upon a set of ideal-types about courses of action and kinds of person; however, these are treated as constants. In other words they are not topics but resources of the investigation in question. For example, war, trade and imperial boundaries have this

constant character as ideal-types in Teggart's historical explanation of invasion patterns of the Western Roman Empire
(Lyman, 1978). It is the fact that historical actors can only be
studied with a maximum of indirectness that makes such an
objectivist stance toward investigation not only possible but
apparently required. Yet even in the case of history an alternative framework of explanation is possible. 'A history of human
behaviour' (Schutz, 1976) requires that investigation begin with
subjective meanings. In the case of an ideal-type such as trade,
this would mean that its highly objective character – precisely
that quality which allows it to function usefully as a constant –
be suspended by the investigator. To suspend, however, does
not mean to deny. It is because the investigator does not deny
the objective character of trade that its meaning to the historical
actors becomes a problem of high salience. Thus the alternative
which Schutz identifies – an interpretive historical sociology –
is not simply 'subjectivist' but one which takes the subject –
object *relation* as its topic. The specific task of this history is to
relate step-by-step the highly 'anonymous' and objective ideal-
types by successive approximations to the 'cultural locations of
actors' or their 'cultural being'. Weber's *The Protestant Ethic and
the Spirit of Capitalism* was a demonstration of this alternative,
but, bearing in mind the many criticisms made of it, is also a
cautionary example.

In terms of action the world of predecessors lacks an 'open
horizon': the absence of any possible relationship between the
observer and the actor precludes the possibility of clarifying the
motivational constructions of historical actors in the way open
to an observer of a contemporary event; here, at least in principle, the actors and the actions may be approached. In contrast,
the 'signitive' material upon which the actions of the past may
be interpreted consists in records, monuments, traces and past
interpretations (such as letters, memoirs, reports, histories). For
Schutz the problem is to make the observer's interpretive
schemes coincide with the expressive scheme of the predecessor
in question. Even when the expression is of a stipulated sign
system, such as language, music or formalised political doctrine,
one which can be treated confidently as 'objective', the problem
remains, for it is a problem of the use made of, and the meaning

given to, the system by an actor or a group. The problem seems formidable.

Schutz notes that all kinds of product and cultural object can be treated as signs of meaning – construction: and suggests '. . . we can start out from the external sign itself . . . trace it back to the original actions and subjective experiences of its inventor or user' and in doing so make the transition from objective to subjective context (Schutz, 1976, pp. 217–18). Thus one way of reducing the difficulty inherent in *Verstehen* approaches to the historical past is to trace usage and meaning from the relatively objective evidence of symbolic structures. We may note here that while Weber's formal sociology is indeed poorly developed in terms of this problem, his substantive work engages it. For example, his essay on the city adopts such an approach in his tracing of the subjective meaning complex of urban institutions intermediate between the bourgeois and aristocratic circles (Weber, 1958). His concept of institutionalisation is built on the possibility of creative response by actors to their social existence, and its establishment as regularly meaningful and realisable in their everyday projects of action. To use Schutz's terms borrowed from Husserl here, the urban festivals and ceremonies co-produced by bourgeois and aristocrat were invested by the idealisations of 'I can do it again' and 'and so forth'; that is, they were made natural instances of the lived urban world. But this is perhaps to find in Weber's interpretation rather more congruence with Schutz' position than is warranted. Certainly, the latter's discussion seems to call for a far greater attention to what would now be called the reflexive or self-interpretive activity in a past situation. It is the interpretive schemata of action in use which provides the vehicle to a 'history of human behaviour'.

Schutz takes another step beyond Weber's historical *Verstehende* sociology when he poses history – or temporal modes of understanding – as a cultural object in the sociologist's own present, that is as an activity of contemporaries. History as a form of social action itself can be seen in its active or vivid sense as a continuous trans-historic relationship 'of variegated content and ever changing partners' (Schutz, 1976, p. 214): the contemporaries and their successors become predecessors and history is a mode of cultural understanding formed on the base of a 'pre-predicative' awareness of mortality and heritage. Without it, in fact, there would be 'no reason to assert the unity of the social world', for without a continuous process of the creation of objective accounts of the actions of predecessors, the subjective meaning of being a contemporary would have no unity. A *sense* of 'pastness' is a non-temporal, essential feature of the structure of social experience. To the extent that it can be investigated directly, as a problem of *Verstehen* investigation conducted on *contemporary* actions and actors, a further possibility emerges of a 'history of human behaviour'. Our knowledge of the past, by being part of a continuous process, contains 'supertemporal' categories (Schutz, 1976, p. 212). Elucidation of these provides a framework for the investigation of predecessors' construction of the meaning of *their* present: the focus is changed from a set of 'facts' which are held to constitute a problem of history to the framework of interpretation in which the consciousness of time structures experience. From such a change in focus, Schutz implies, the particular modalities of recording and interpreting experience current in a past society provide a basis for approaching the conventional concerns of historical and historical-sociological research. Again, such a view is separated widely in emphasis, though not fundamentally different from Weber's. Schutz implies that the primary step of historical sociology, *to the extent that the researcher departs from a strictly objective approach*, is an interpretive sociology of knowledge.

Schutz' direct treatment of this problem, however, occupies just a few pages of his 1932 work and it was only slightly developed subsequently. His theory of our knowledge of other selves contains the remark that 'the problem of subjective and objective meaning is the open door to every theology and metaphysics' (Schutz, 1976, p. 138). Immediately following is the chapter entitled 'The Structure of the Social World', where he turns to examine the types of knowledge, the forms of subjective understanding, which are possible in a social world which is essentially heterogeneous. This 'multiform' structure is spatio-temporal and its differentiation radically limits the knowledge of the other, or inter-subjectivity. The problem of the *Verstehende* sociology of the past just discussed is a problem of understanding for *any* societal member who confronts the question of the motives of a predecessor. Both the evidence and the possibility of investigation are similarly limited in the cases of the naive and the specialist interests.

Schutz's general point underlying this is that motivational *Verstehen* by the ideal type is a *normal* method of reflecting on the behaviour of another and of cultural objects in general. In this sense it is 'the experiential form of common-sense knowledge of human affairs' (Schutz, 1962, vol. 1, p. 57). But reflection in general is not a continuous state of consciousness. Reflection is only awakened as a method under definite conditions of interest and attention. In everyday life, governed by pragmatic and practical interests, the Schutzian actor approximates to the social scientist whenever instead of 'merely experiencing' the other he attempts to account for the other by means of a scheme of interpretation (Schutz, 1976, p. 140). The approximation, says Schutz, is primitive to be sure, but the activity occurring is nevertheless (a) directed to accounting for behaviour of the other as meaningful, (b) in motivational terms, (c) contained in a scheme of interpretation, (d) which employs ideal types of social action. A major shortcoming of Weber, in Schutz' opinion, was the failure to recognise interpretive activity as such as a form of social action. This led to Weber's neglect of *Verstehen* as a primitive or elementary form from which the sociological method had to be developed. Another inadequacy was the undifferentiated state of the Weberian concept. Weber failed to consider that mundane *Verstehen* was a shift of attention from social experience to social reflection. In other words, what lay 'below' mundane *Verstehen* was not mere behaviour, or the a-social, but deeper strata of social awareness of the actor (Schutz, 1976, p. 13).

The description of these strata, employing a combination of Husserl's early phenomenology and Bergson's vitalist philosophy, occupies much of the *Phenomenology of the Social World* and of Schutz' subsequent work but cannot be followed in any depth here. In *The Structure of the Social World*, striving to summarise the results of his previous chapters, Schutz contrasted experience with reflection in the following terms:

> While I am directly experiencing you and talking with you, the whole complicated sub-structure of my interpretation

of you escapes my *attention à la vie*, has other goals at the
moment. However I can at any given time change all this
and bring these acts within the focus of my gaze. I may ask
. . . the questions that I am forced to ask every day in my
relations with other people. The moment I raise such
questions I have abandoned my simple and direct
awareness of the other person, my immediate grasp of him
in all his subjective particularity. . . . I no longer experience
my fellow man in the sense of sharing my life with him;
instead I 'think about him'. But now I am acting like a
social scientist (Schutz, 1932, pp. 140–1).

'Pre-predicative' knowledge (awareness) is therefore a foundation for subjective understanding. A sociological *Verstehen*
must on the one hand show the conditions under which 'understanding' arises as a mundane practice in order to comprehend
the difference between the mundane and the scientific use. To
the extent that Weber achieved neither of these aims, Schutz
considered that he had not provided the essential epistemology
of interpretive sociology nor generated adequate basic concepts
for its use in research.

The social world then, receives its multiform character from
the stratification of consciousness in which understanding,
whether the scientist's or the actor's, is one among several
attentional states. There are, however, at least five other principles of its structuration which occupied Schutz and it might
be convenient to list these as:

1  strata of consciousness;
2  domains (or 'realms') of experience;
3  attitudinal stances: the natural attitude and the scientific
   attitude;
4  provinces of meaning and realities;
5  relevances.

Of these, the last is barely mentioned in Schutz' conclusion and
is treated in depth only in his later writings. The second
emerged briefly in the foregoing discussions of the strata and
historical sociology. As in the case of the strata, the second,
third and fourth will be raised below only in so far as they
contribute to the problem of *Verstehen* methodology and to a
final discussion of the 'Schutz-Parsons debate'.

Schutz' purpose is twofold: firstly to show the multiformal structure which conditions the possibilities of thought and knowledge for a human subject: this structure, insofar as consciousness of the subject is concerned, involves a description of 'the invariant, unique, a priori structure of the mind, in particular of a society composed of living minds' (Schutz, 1976, p. 44). Retention and reproduction of experiences, a typology of intentions, the relation of projects to actions and the unity of the latter, conscious and unconscious actions, the temporal structure of motives – these are among the 'invariants' described according to a method derived from Husserl and Bergson. Of this method Schutz remarked:

> Our studies of the constituting process in internal time consciousness will be carried out within the 'phenomenological reduction'. Therefore they presuppose the bracketting (disconnection) of the natural world and therewith the carrying into effect of a complete change of attitude (the *epoché*) towards the thesis of the 'world-given-to-me-as-being-there' (Schutz, 1976, p. 43).

The result, 'a psychology of pure intersubjectivity', formulates human capacity to act in social life and at the same time describes the states of knowledge which are 'primordially' given to the subject in such acts as memory, self-reflection and orientations to others.

Secondly, as the social is approached, the perspective is shifted from the solitary ego to the 'general thesis of the alter ego' (Schutz, 1976, pp. 97–8), the generalised acceptance of the social other as 'basically similar' in the form of his consciousness. This thesis constitutes the natural standpoint of man-in-society, the unity of the social world, whether viewed from mundane social life or from that of sociology. But in order to describe the structure of this unity Schutz abandons the strict form of reduction which guided him earlier. It is necessary, he says, to accept the natural standpoint as given if the object is to explore the structures of self- and other-understanding in it. The realms of experience are one such structuring principle.

Schutz remarks that in the everyday world others are understood 'in different conceptual perspectives'; 'I live through their subjective experiences in various degrees of intimacy' (Schutz,

1976, p. 142). In the realm of directly experienced social reality the immediate co-belonging to one 'Here and Now' anchors the self 'by spatio temporal community' and knowledge of the other is dominated by 'directness of experience'; the other has 'simple givenness' (Schutz, 1976, p. 176) and this point applies as much to strangers who are bodily co-present as to lovers. A concrete, or 'actualised' we-relationship exists to the extent that a person bodily experiences the other.

The other exists for the self as the other who existed prior to this duration of bodily co-presence, and simultaneously as *this* body, experienced in vivid contrast with the 'conceptual perspective' characteristic of the situation in which he is 'known about' but not directly experienced. The ideal types of knowing-about, drawn from the common-sense stock of knowledge, have their integrity as knowledge based in the anonymity of the subject to which they refer. The presence of this subject in an encounter always entails a shift in the basis of, and potentially in the nature of, the experiential ideal type of the knower. The knowledge-types of the other formed in the we- relationships are, in short, of a different and opposed order to those formed in impersonal and 'anonymous' conditions.

From this description of one existential limit on the social world as a meaning-structure Schutz moves to the 'social world of contemporaries which "coexists with me and is simultaneous with my duration"' (Schutz, 1976, p. 142). Like the 'fellow men' of the directly experienced world one can be both observer and actor in this world; but in contrast with them 'I do not directly and immediately grasp their subjective experiences but instead infer, on the basis of indirect evidence, the typical subjective experiences they must be having' (Schutz, 1976, p. 142). And 'My whole knowledge of you [the contemporary] is mediate and descriptive' (Schutz, 1976, pp. 181–2). As against the thou-orientation of fellow-men in the concrete we-relationship, the attitude of contemporaries is a they-orientation, for their conscious experiences are apprehended by their interactants as *anonymous* processes.

Indirectness characterises the social relations established in the contemporary domain, and this stems directly from the anonymity of the other self encountered there. Schutz means by anonymity the fact that others' experiences are seen as the

'individuation of a type' and this individual is only supposable
or possible – there is no direct experiential basis for the knowledge that one is for certain dealing with an instance of a type
that exists. The personal ideal-types that mediate my encounter
with a contemporary stress objective meaning contexts over the
subjective precisely to the extent that this contemporary (person
or cultural object) is not encountered in a bodily co-presence.

These two domains are referred to by Schutz as the *Soziale
mitwelt* (confusingly translated as the social world of contemporaries). Contemporaries and consociates (or fellow men) can be
grouped together not on the basis of their mere co-duration but
their mutual convertibility. I can enter a formerly anonymously
known group of contemporaries and I can 'lose a friend', that
is, replace my knowledge of him by increasingly anonymous
personal ideal-types of his actions and motives. However these
domains do not exhaust the social worlds of which a social actor
is knowledgeable, although the forms of knowledge typical of
these worlds vary yet again. The *Vorwelt* (predecessors' world)
is a world which everyone enters. As to those who are already
predecessors, knowledge of them approaches the maximum of
anonymity and objectivity, since no one can be an observer in
that world. The world of successors (*Folgewelt*), however, is
even more closed and can only be typified by extrapolation
in the vaguest sense. Neither the objective nor interpretive
understandings possible in the case of the *Vorwelt* are accessible
here. By implication, to the extent that the world of successors
is relevant to the contemporary, distinctive forms of knowledge
will be involved. Weber's concepts of prophecy and religious
authority provide exemplary discussions of the social construction of knowledge of the *Folgewelt*, and his entire sociology of
religion is implicated in it but, typically, Schutz does not engage
them.

Mention has already been made of the natural standpoint or
attitude. Each of the domains are particular versions of the
'general thesis of the alter ego' which Schutz sees as the foundation of the natural attitude. Its main anchoring, however, is
in the lived world, where projects are formed and past actions
may be reflected upon under a general orientation which is
'pragmatic'. Schutz notes at several points that the mundane
actor may conduct himself like a scientist but such acts are

contained within the orientation. They do not break the frame
of the natural attitude. Thus they do not amount to scientific
action which, for Schutz, is action governed by a different and
opposed attitude. Although Schutz recognises that mundane
actors form rational projects of action to the extent that they
formulate 'known intermediate goals' (Schutz, 1976, p. 61) and
deploy a wide variety of rational standards to evaluate
completed acts, he argues that 'clearness and distinctness in the
strict meaning of formal logic do not belong to the typical style
of everyday life' (Schutz, 1952, vol. II, pp. 64–8). These qualities
do distinguish the scientific observer of the social world who is
'not practically but only cognitively interested in it'. Here Schutz
is using a conception of social science which Weber advanced,
as committed in its mode of inference and reasoning to canons
of formal logic. This Schutz treats as the essence of science,
while he recognises that science is also a 'social phenomenon'
and the scientist therefore subject to value-preferences and to
power. For Schutz, however, only this attitude which the scientist has to adopt toward his problem distinguishes him from
the mundane actor's observation and questioning of the world.
This ideal-typical construct of science as an attitudinal stance
clearly has a number of major consequences for the analysis of
social meanings.

We can approach these by noting again that the everyday
social world is the main anchor of the natural attitude. This
world is the pre-eminent source of conceptions of reality and
factual orders. All other worlds will be either special derivatory
forms of it, as in the case of the domains, or they will be
antithetical organisations of knowledge with radically different
bases. Art, science and religion are examples. But each of these
is both penetrated by the everyday world (consider the use of
ordinary language and of everyday motivational accounts in a
science laboratory) and subordinated to it. In short, the world
of contemporaries can be likened to an empire of facts which has
a number of provinces of meaning within which fundamentally
different conceptions of reality (facticity) are preserved, but with
difficulty.

Thus, for Schutz there is a primitive correspondence between
mundane reasoning and the scientific. However an absolute
qualitative difference exists when science is practised with

cognitive interest in and detachment from the mundane world. Logical reasoning forms the criterion. But this is perpetually threatened by the massive 'facticity' of the everyday world. The fact that the scientific form of reason is not typically found in the everyday world means that the actions of mundane actors are evaluated by an observer with a standard which is alien to those standards of rationality which are typical. Furthermore, these standards themselves are not reducible to one basic form. The social world is characterised by diverse rationalities. A special problem exists, therefore, in the application of a scientific attitude to social action. Schutz confirms Weber's insistence that sociological explanation must conform to the mode of scientific reasoning in general. But before logical procedures are usable the sociologist must have identified the principles of meaning-construction, which are native in the mundane procedures of the socio-cultural world he is investigating. To use Kaplan's phrase, the 'logic-in-use' must be grasped before there is a possibility of reconstructing this logic in terms of a scientific understanding. As Schutz put it: '. . . the constructs of the social sciences are, so to speak, constructs of the second degree, that is constructs of the constructs made by the actors' (Schutz, 1962, vol. 1, p. 59).

Weber's interpretive method, then, is affirmed by Schutz as the indispensable basis of sociological inquiry, but its relation to the character of its topic, the life-world, has been radicalised. Where Weber's formal thought took the incorporation of the 'subjective' within an 'objective' framework as relatively unproblematic, the experiential form of common-sense, that is, practical mundane reason, is itself shown to be a finely struc-tured *Verstehen*. The first task of *Verstehende* sociology is to pose the question of how this structure works to produce the possibility of social relationships. Sociological *Verstehen* is not a step which, once taken via some ethnography of the 'meanings' actors use, frees the investigator to engage in formal behaviour-istic, i.e. 'objective' theorising; it is a *continuous* methodological principle which controls the distance between first degree (actors') and second degree (sociologists') constructs. Without it the very possibility of objective theorising about social experi-ence is subverted.

Accordingly, to the rhetorical questions: '. . . why form

personal ideal-types at all? Why not simply collect empirical facts? Or, if the technique of typological interpretation may be applied successfully, why not restrict oneself to forming types of impersonal events, or types of the behaviour of groups?' (Schutz, 1962, vol. 2). Schutz developed an answer which embodied his defence of ideal-type analysis within the special problem of the social science as he saw it.

He allowed that a 'very great part' of social science can and does operate without precise reference to the construction of meaning by actors. Nevertheless such work is 'nothing but a kind of intellectual shorthand' and in specific reference to Parsons' 1937 volume, the actions are reconstructed abstractly with 'maximum anonymity', which amounts to the same thing. Because the *problems* which such abstract theories of action have to solve eventually make necessary a shift in the level of explanation, 'to that of individual human activity' such theories must always be constructed in such a way that the concepts may be decoded from the abstract to the concrete level. In the longer work on Parsons' 1937 volume, of which this discussion is a fragment, Schutz made clear his belief that the concept of social action which Parsons advanced did not enable this to be done, for the very reason that the process of typification, itself a part of 'social action' had been atrophied. If Parsons' last word on Schutz re-echoed what had disturbed him in Weber, here we find Schutz with his radicalised version of *Verstehende* sociology, denying the validity of the grand synthesis in which Parsons domesticated Weber.


Conclusion

Since 1980 the broad assessment of Parsons' contribution to social theory has intensified. One strand of this was begun two years earlier with the publication of the whole of Schutz' 1940 critical study of *The Structure of Social Action* and the correspondence of Schutz and Parsons (Grathoff, 1978). Natanson has claimed that the themes of this correspondence 'are still vital to an understanding of the logical foundations of social science' since what is continually at issue is the relation of philosophy with social science (Grathoff, 1978, p. ix). Natanson noted that

neo-Kantians could have a fruitful encounter with phenomenology, citing Natorp and Cassirer as examples; that the neo-
Kantian Parsons could not Natanson puts down to misunder-
standings over terms, for example 'philosophical naiveté', used
by Schutz, and to Parsons' excessive pragmatism which would
allow 'philosophy to enter the discussion only when it is
needed' (Grathoff, 1978, pp. xiv–xv). Since Schutz held an
opposed position on this basic question, essentially sharing with
Merleau-Ponty the view that 'at the moment of interpretation
[the sociologist] is himself already a philosopher', no dialogue
between the two theorists could develop (Merleau-Ponty quoted
in Grathoff, 1978, p. xvi).

Natanson's brief comment is ambiguous. He lists the areas of
overlapping concerns which are essentially those which have
been treated in the earlier sections of this essay, as containing
'some positive features' and he refers to 'the philosophical
differences between the two thinkers' (Grathoff, 1978, p. xiv).
Yet he makes it clear that for him Parsons has a stunted view
of the role of philosophy in social science. On his view of
Parsons it is difficult to see how the latter could describe himself
as the 'unreconstructed Kantian'. But the continued engagement with philosophical problems at a quite explicit level in
much of Parsons' work surely defends him against this judgment. Especially is this true of Parsons' later work and his
attempt to ground that Freudian theory of symbolism within
'general sociological theory'. Natanson's judgment might be
more accurately addressed to the 'Parsons-effect' in modern
sociology, with its occasional reliance upon the 'scientific philosophy', proposed by Reichenbach (1968) and others. Considered
as a comparativist in theory building, Parsons reveals himself
as a daring innovator in the zone between philosophy and
sociology.

Recognition of this emerges clearly and more charitably in
Grathoff's discussion of the issues between Parsons and Schutz
in the same volume. Among these issues Grathoff identifies the
'Kantian Problem' in the following terms:

. . . Kant had to ask how it is at all possible that men's
perceiving, cognitive constructing and experiencing can
reach the world as an empirical world of vivid creatures.

Kant proposes that this can be achieved by the application of what he called 'schemata' of understanding. [These are the mind's] means to reach the world of objects as objects known. . . . However the origin and constitution of these schemata remain an open problem, which Kant refers to as a secret of the human soul.

Parsons' whole work is an attack, from a highly abstract base, upon this 'open problem'. For him the symbolic orders in culture are the empirically discoverable schemata, governing what an actor can know about his social world and hence, how he may act. But, precisely because these schemata cannot be reduced to history or to psychology, the method of discovery must employ a system frame of reference – outside time and the mind – which can itself order and incorporate both. Thus time and mental structure are its objects of inquiry.

That Schutz positively appreciated Parsons' *project* is made clear by the former's letters to Parsons: 'I realized immediately the importance and the value of your system and also the fact that it starts exactly where my own book ends' (Grathoff, 1978, p. 97). Schutz expressed his agreement with much of Parsons' thought in *The Structure of Social Action*, for example the view 'that cultural systems may be considered as *products* of processes of action' (Grathoff, 1978, p. 99). However, from his point of view the theory was flawed by the level of abstraction from which its concepts were generated. This had no serious consequences for its internal validity but reduced its capacity to analyse human interaction, a result highly paradoxical in a voluntaristic theory of action. Schutz's unwelcomed advice to Parsons was therefore to 'radicalise' this theory by means of the perspectives he developed in *The Phenomenology of the Social World*. One can only speculate that it was to this end that he included in his critical study as an excursus, a summary statement of his theory of motives (Grathoff, 1978, pp. 33–7). In any case Schutz asserted that Parsons' claim that 'the subjective point of view is the only acceptable one for any theory of social action' (Grathoff, 1978, p. 43) *entails* an adequate account of motive. Once this was done, however, it appears that for Schutz the Parsonian synthesis could indeed formulate a general sociological theory as a paradigm for the discipline. The level of

potential compatibility is attested throughout Schutz's treatment of Parsons, for motives, or rather systems of motives,
are historically objectivated schemata, coded in language and
cultural objects, and in terms of them: '[human beings] have
pre-selected and pre-interpreted this world which they experience as the reality of their daily lives. It is these thought-objects
of theirs which determine their behaviour by motivating it'
(Schutz, 1962, vol. 1, p. 59). Thus in one sense at least both
Parsons and Schutz have the 'Kantian Problem' as their joint
concern, and it issues in a common agreement on the empirical
object of sociology: the analysis of sign and symbol and the
social forms through which these are articulated.

In Grathoff's view, the fundamental difference between
Parsons and Schutz, which set to nought the common interest
just discussed, was over the problem of rationality. He noted
that for Parsons the distinction between common sense and
scientific reasoning is one of gradation on a continuum. The
position of a human being's thought on this continuum is determined by its 'environment', or social location. No special
problem confronts an observer located at the logically sophisticated, or scientific end; since rationality is axial, the observed
actor can in principle be assigned quite readily to a degree of
rationality. However, to understand this actor sociologically is
to comprehend the force of non-logical, moral constraints (the
structure of the environment) on his action (Grathoff, 1978,
pp. xxi–xxii, and 129–30). As the last section sought to show,
Schutz's conception of this problem is more complex. Formal
reasoning is one of the modes of rational action to be found in
everyday life but it exists there as a member of a family of
rational modes, selection of which is governed by motivational
relevance. To grasp the 'concrete actor and his performances'
(Grathoff, 1978, p. 129) the concept of formal rationality as a
continuum, itself a cultural perspective, must be suspended or
bracketed in order to discover how action is judged. In Schutz's
view it is not that Parsons is wrong but that his concept of
rationality must systematically obscure the way in which action
is assigned orderly or disorderly properties in social life. On
this question turns the whole 'problem of order' which Parsons
addressed.

This is the 'Schutz–Parsons divide' which constitutes the

'debate' which Grathoff considers should be erected over a forty-year-old exchange of letters, since it articulated the fundamental action-dilemma, so to speak, of the sociological observer. Evidently, Grathoff does not consider the purpose of such a debate to be reconciliatory but to pose starkly the necessity of a phenomenological underpinning of interpretive sociology; and the clear implication of this is that more or less rapidly the whole superstructure would have to change. Post-Parsonian sociology would be a non-Parsonian enterprise.

Yet there may be grounds for doubting whether the differences between Schutz and Parsons, even those concerning the actor's interpretation of action, would lead, via a debate, to a confrontation of paradigms. It was maintained, early in this essay, that Parsons saw himself as a worker in a distinct tradition of social theory. Thus his perspective is that of a comparativist and mediator between the ideas of a tradition which have their roots in Kant. With this stance he could identify evidence of 'convergence' in the work of such sociologists as Weber and Durkheim, who in other respects are irreconcilably opposed. While it was possible by a process of interpretation to manage some of these differences, the work of Parsons stands as a monument to these differences as much as to the convergence. From this point of view Parsons' systems theory lends stylistic unity to a highly selective reading. His reading of the classic sociologists is true to an evolutionary and progressive interpretation of social thought in western culture, an essentially liberal and Enlightenment perspective not dissimilar from the history of ideas represented by such writers as Lovejoy in *The Great Chain of Being*. This would suggest that, despite the high level of system formalisation which Parsons and his followers have built upon his original synthesis, it cannot be rendered into a clear epistemological position – an antagonist against which a 'phenomenological' alternative could define itself.

Nor is it possible to discern in phenomenological sociology, as it has developed from Schutz, a fundamental agreement about method and problems which can provide a candidate theoretical synthesis to sociology. Between Luckmann's essay on European religion (1967), his work with Berger on knowledge (1966), the 'phenomenological' sociology of deviance (Phillipson, 1974), the various tendencies within ethnomethodology and more recently the insertion of Schutzian and related perspectives into anthropology (Kapferer, 1983), radical differences of approach to the actor and his performances exist. What many of these studies demonstrate is the remarkable facility with which products of phenomenological reduction can be incorporated within an essentially unmodified Durkheimian view of culture, and operate there to resolve some of the antinomies between action and system. Perhaps it is this which has encouraged commentators such as Jules-Rosette (1980) and O'Dea (1976) to argue for a rapprochement between structural-functionalism and phenomenology. What is recommended has in fact partly occurred. In any case, this view might find reinforcement in those appreciative remarks of Schutz to Parsons mentioned earlier. These studies have also demonstrated the usefulness of Schutz's perspective for concept-criticism, as the analysis of legitimation in Berger and Luckmann's *The Social Construction of Reality* shows; more recently Thomason's (1982) discussion of Schutz, his critical analysis of Berger and Pullberg, and his reformulation of the concept of reification has extended this to other fields in sociology.

If Parsonian sociology is by no means so internally consistent as its systematic appearance suggests it may even be capable of a regression to that point where Weber's insistence on the creative possibility of action was overlaid. This is the burden of O'Dea's sympathetic criticism of it. Social phenomenology, recent polemics notwithstanding, seems less of a paradigm challenge than a critical mode, inhabiting the space between the classical sociologists and the act of research. Valuable and productive though each of these tendencies may be they do not appear to be the stuff from which re-vitalising debates are made. Sociology's encounter with the various Marxisms over several decades provides a vivid contrast. From that debate no protagonist emerged unchanged and its effects on theory, problems and research styles was profound.

My point here is not that phenomenological critique is incapable of significantly changing the substance of sociological work. It is that precisely *as* critique it has that potential, while as a revolutionary 'paradigm' in search of the key debate over 'the relation of philosophy to sociology' it is likely to be self-neutralising. The epistemological foundation of interpretive sociology is unquestionably a problem for each of its practitioners but as a problem it cannot be separated out from all the other levels which constitute that practice as a particular form of action in the social world. It is in this sense that one can agree with Schutz that the methodologist (as provider of epistemology) has little to teach the practitioner, while granting that his questioning may be the critical means of progress. The epistemology which a disengaged philosopher can provide to a sociologist is based upon a separation of theory from practice which necessarily reifies the former; yet it needs to be added that the sociologist who neglects Merleau-Ponty's warning that while he observes he philosophises is condemned to idealistic empiricism – the faith in the 'factual'. In this essay my argument in relation to Schutz was that his inquiry in *The Phenomenology* was an appreciative criticism of immense subtlety. Its limitations lie in the arbitrary splitting of the Weberian corpus into theory and substance. The methodologist, in the broad sense of this term, must take his object entire; nothing warrants the parcelling-out of the cultural object he explores, if it was his aim to preserve the integrity of that object as itself an intentional subjectivity.

Weber sought a sociology of the present which would ground itself in a critical re-interpretation of history, continuously enacted from particular self-conscious value-standpoints, and hence constantly changing. Both Schutz and Parsons reject this anarchist vision of method and problem. Neither of them could abide a scientific mind which treated so marginally the scientific conventions concerning explicitness, reproducibility and the accretion of knowledge. The idea of sociology as a critical practice living within and between other cultural practices, but itself homeless and without a stable fund of established 'findings', was unacceptable.

That such an uncompromising view of the nature of sociology was indeed held by Max Weber – and is the 'dark side' of his whole thought – is a matter of contention. It has informed this essay, but has not been established here. Therefore it may be appropriate to turn finally to the appreciation of Weber by Maurice Merleau-Ponty, whose role in the development of social phenomenology equals that of Schutz, but who, in contrast with him, lived his intellectual life between Marx, the

Marxist movement and phenomenology. In 'The crisis of the understanding' Merleau-Ponty (1978) ascribes to this 'unsystematic phenomenologist' the role of having shown 'under what conditions a historical dialectic is possible'. Merleau-Ponty documents that version of liberalism – 'completely new because he admits that truth always leaves a margin of doubt, that it does not exhaust the reality of the past and still less that of the present, and that history is the natural seat of violence' (Merleau-Ponty, 1978, p. 193) – which Weber developed. This view of Weber, although only briefly sketched, notes that his methodological reflections come after his substantive work and asserts that it is in the latter that his unique approach to social meaning may be discovered.

If Schutz and Parsons failed in their interpretation of Weber to the extent that they de-historised him, perhaps this is symptomatic of the much wider movement of social thought in the first half of the twentieth century in which the concept of meaning was polarised either as the individual's attitudes or as structurally generated ideology. That each dissented from this polarisation and attempted to construct alternative routes to the study of social action, using Marx and Weber as a chart in this endeavour, is a sufficient reason for building a debate from these three dead voices.

# 4
# Parsons and his critics: on the ubiquity of functionalism

*Bryan S. Turner*

Introduction

Talcott Parsons had one of the longest and most productive academic careers of any modern sociologist. The diversity and extent of his publications clearly verify this claim. Although Parsons began his career very much writing against the mainstream of American behaviouristic social science, his structural-functionalist perspective became the dominant theoretical paradigm of American sociology in the 1950s and 1960s. Two important consequences follow from this rather bland opening comment. The first is that Parsonian sociology has been subject to more critical scrutiny than any other contemporary theoretical framework. The second is that, given the sheer quantity of Parsons' theoretical output, it is not surprising that certain aspects of his work appear to stand in a contradictory relationship to other features. There is for some critics an 'early' and a 'late' Parsons, just as there is an 'early' and a 'late' Marx. Indeed the comparison is apposite since both Marxism and Parsonian sociology addressed the dilemma of agency and structure. It is not clear whether Marx's humanistic emphasis on sensuous human praxis in the 'Theses on Feuerbach' can be reconciled with certain deterministic views of the mode of production which appear in *Capital* (Althusser, 1969); it is not clear that Parsons' voluntaristic action framework can be wholly integrated into social systems analysis (Scott, 1963). In the case of both Marx and Parsons there is much debate as to the presence or absence of a thematic unity in their work (Alexander, 1983; Holmwood, 1983). Despite the disputes which surround Parsons' sociology, it can be said that at least one thematic unity running through this corpus of publications is the argument that sociology requires a theory and this theory has to be general. Parsons saw the task of sociology as explanatory rather than merely descriptive or interpretative; the point of sociology is to explain how social order is possible. This explanation takes the form of structural functionalism, namely the explication of the functional contribution of certain structures to the overall coherence and continuity of the social system. In this chapter I wish to consider some of the major criticisms raised against Parsons' sociology and especially against structural functionalism. At the same time I want to offer a modest defence of functionalism, partly by showing that most critics of functionalism are themselves functionalist. One further extension of this argument is that historical materialism is simply a variant form of functionalist analysis, especially in terms of a comparison of Althusserian and Parsonian structuralism. This argument is not new (Davis, 1959; Stinchcombe, 1968; Sztompka, 1974), but it deserves re-statement. Functionalist reasoning tends to be very widespread, even in theorists who are overtly critical of functionalism, and furthermore functionalist explanations can normally be rendered in such a way as to avoid criticism of either their inherent teleogical premises or their static view of social systems (Merton, 1963; Abercrombie, 1980; Cancian, 1960; Moore, 1979). Before launching into this interpretation of critics of Parsons, we have to address a prior question: what is criticism?

## Types of criticism

Criticism is ultimately concerned with what can be said and hence with the coherence, scope and presuppositions of any discourse. To discourse is to move backwards and forwards. To criticise discourse is to ask whether any theoretical movement is valid. The validity of an argument is to do with consistency between primary assumptions and the conclusions drawn from them. A discourse can be criticised on two conditions. We may accept the assumptions of a theory, but argue that the conclusions are incompatible with its assumptions; the argument is thus internally inconsistent and the critique is internalist. We may argue that a theory is perfectly consistent with its presuppositions, but reject the theory because we cannot accept the initial premises; the theory is incompatible with a set of preferred assumptions and the critique is externalist. To criticise is to uncover the crisis (the 'critical situation') which threatens to disrupt the flow of a discourse, in terms of conditions which are either internal or external. The similarities between this categorisation of forms of criticism and the criteria outlined by Stephen Savage (1981) are wholly fortuitous. In addition, the conclusions of this review of Parsonian criticism run counter to Savage's sweeping claim that Parsonian theory 'is not a coherent body of concepts on which to base a social theory' (Savage, 1981, p. 234). If such a criterion of global coherence across an entire corpus of theory were to be uniformly adopted, then 'who would 'scape whipping?' Although coherence is obviously a major goal of any theoretical endeavour, to demand coherence for a theoretical project as extensive and diverse as Parsonianism is too savage.

It is important, however, to distinguish criticism (whether of the internalist or externalist variety) from mere exposition. Although exegesis of difficult texts and exposition of the purpose of an author whose sociology is especially complex may have an educational function with respect to students within a discipline, exposition is either parasitic, unproductive or both. In general, there is an abundance of second-order theory (which is largely expository) and this is especially evident in the case of commentaries on Parsons (Hamilton, 1983; Rocher, 1974; Bourricaud, 1981). The aim of this chapter, and more broadly this book, is not primarily to offer yet another exposition or to debate the issue of continuity in the work of Parsons. The aim is to identify the importance of Parsons' sociology, to offer a defence, where necessary, against criticism which is often spurious and finally to indicate aspects of his sociology which are of enduring importance to the social sciences. The orientation of this chapter is embodied in the following comment on parasitically expository texts:

No serious student of Parsons' work would want – except
for *purely* pedagogic purposes – to spend much time on
summary expositions. The challenge is to *do* the work which
Parsons began. This must mean that Parsons' work has to
be *critically* elaborated – extended and refined analytically
and used with respect to empirical and historical problems
(Robertson, 1982b, p. 284).

It is with the theoretical tasks of refinement and extension as
appropriate objectives that this typology of Parsons' criticism is
elaborated.

It has been argued that criticism starts with an acceptance or
rejection of the basic theoretical and evaluative presuppositions
of a text. Criticism has two further features. It is either largely
negative in that, having discovered the crisis of a theory, no
attempt is made to rescue the theory from its own self-destruction, through external or internal invalidity, or criticism is positive in attempting to provide a cognitive therapy. Critics tend
to regard texts rather like patients – the symptomatology may
be read as pointing to a theoretical crisis which may be termin-
able or interminable. With regard to the assumptions of a
theory, criticism normally implies some principle of convertibility. If we disapprove of the assumptions of a theory, we may
argue that, with some modifications, the theory can be rescued
by making it more compatible with our own assumptions: the
theory can thus be converted. Alternatively, we may assume
that the underlying values and assumptions of a theory are so
far removed from our own ethical and theoretical presuppositions that no amount of evangelical activity can rescue the
theory. Such a theory is regarded as fallen and inconvertible.
The external/internal and convertibility principles provide a
property-space of basic types of criticism:

|   | Internal | External |   |   |
|---|----------|----------|---|---|
| A |          |          | B |   |
|   | Reformation | Reconstruction |   | Convertible |
|   | Resurrection | Rejection |   | Inconvertible |
| D |          |          | C |   |

Such a property-space is a heuristic device for organising a discussion of types of criticism which have been mounted against Parsons. Reformist criticism largely accepts the internal assumptions of a Parsonian model of functionalist explanation, but suggests that some existing defects may be converted by appropriate theoretical work. Reconstructive criticism tends to reject the underlying assumptions or values of the theory, but implicitly or explicitly recommends major translation of the theory into another set of assumptions. The least ambiguous form of criticism is one which both rejects the theory *in toto* and also claims that no exercise of conversion can ever rescue the theory from its fundamental flaws. By contrast, resurrection is the most paradoxical critique. It accepts the internal premises of the theory but regards the extension of the theory as hopelessly confused. At the same time, it provides a critique which reproduces or resurrects many of the internal analytical structures and applications of the allegedly defunct theory. Resurrectional critique is reconstruction from within. In practice, criticism may have elements of all four forms, but I want to argue that in principle this model of criticism embraces a finite range of possibilities; there is no type of criticism which falls outside this range.

## Parsons and his critics

There are various ways by which one could organise and review criticisms of Parsons' sociology. It is possible to examine individuals who have criticised Parsons; for example, reviews of Parsons' sociology and its critics typically provide a simple list of sociologists who offered what, at the time, appeared to be highly damaging assaults on the Parsonian edifice. The list of assailants normally includes Dahrendorf (1968), Gouldner (1971), Wright Mills (1959) and Rex (1961). Any attempt to develop a systematic approach to Parsonian sociology on the basis of a list of critics is not promising as a theoretical strategy, since the results of such an inquiry would be necessarily eclectic and unstable. These critics had little in common, apart from the notion that Parsons' emphasis on value-consensus in society, as the basis of stability, was empirically naive and neglected the obvious importance of coercion. This debate was largely unproductive and its conclusion was the naive assertion that sociology was divided into two traditions, namely conflict and consensus.

It is possible, by contrast to listing critics, to consider Parsons' sociology in terms of phases, distinctive epistemological ruptures and continuities. On close inspection, it is evident that these forms of criticism hinge around the alleged discontinuities between Parsons' early work on the voluntaristic theory of action (Parsons, 1937a) and the later work on systems theory (Parsons, 1951a; 1953a; 1966a). The model for this type of critical exegesis was established by Scott (1963) and the issue of continuity/discontinuity has been followed tirelessly by Bershady (1973), Turner and Beeghley (1974) and Holmwood (1983 a and b). Alongside the issue of a break in Parsons' sociology between an interpretative theory of action and a func-tionalist theory of social systems, there is the related question of Parsons' interpretations of Weber and Durkheim (Pope, 1973; Cohen, Hazelrigg and Pope, 1975). Although this debate raises important epistemological issues, the crucial question in this exchange with Parsons is the accusation that Parsons overstated the importance of normative integration in Durkheim's analysis of social solidarity and understated the centrality of power and coercion in Weber's sociology of domination. The discontinuity between action and order is thus linked to the allegation that Parsons' sociology suppresses the material substratum of action in favour of normative regulation (Lockwood, 1956). In short, Parsons' sociology is a perfect representative of the separation of 'the two sociologies' (Dawe, 1970).

The debate over continuity and discontinuity in Parsons is essentially limited and scholastic in the pejorative sense. The exercise is at best valuable as pure pedagogy (Robertson, 1982b) and at worst, the rattling of dry bones. These second-order interpretations of Parsons rarely attempt to resolve the alleged contradictions between the implied contingency of human action and the implied determinacy of the social system. Their aim is to interpret existing frameworks rather than to develop sociological theory which seeks ultimately to provide expla-nations of social phenomena. Although Parsons was frequently charged with abstrusity and abstract formalism, his theoretical inquiries led decisively to an engagement with social issues; the essays on Germany, social stratification, medicine and the university are perfect illustrations of this point. Parsons' sociology was not, therefore, merely a second-order engagement with theory itself and was not simply a pedagogic inquiry into Weber and Durkheim. Criticisms of Parsons' alleged discontinuities or of his alleged misinterpretations of classical theory produce theoretical results which 'remain mere patchwork' (Münch, 1981, p. 733). Genuine theoretical activity would not address these second-order interpretative difficulties in Parsons, but focus on more fundamental issues, namely whether every sociological theory, if it aspired to generality, would have to contain both a theory of action and a theory of order (Alexander, 1982). One aspect of the importance of Parsons' sociology, was that it aspired to such completeness, by embracing the significance of structured order in social relationships and the 'knowledgeability' of agents (Giddens, 1979).

Another form of criticism of Parsons which also produces a mere patchwork is to grapple with specific 'substantive' issues in Parsons' sociology without relating these to an overall perspective on his work. Examples of what we might term itemised criticism would be discussions of Parsons' analyses of power (Giddens, 1968), professions (Johnson, 1972), the sick-role concept in medical sociology (Gallagher, 1976), religious beliefs (Towler, 1974), motivation (Wrong, 1961) or the structural-functionalist perspective on social stratification (Tumin, 1970). This piece-meal approach to Parsons' sociology typically lacks a general perspective on his work as a whole and, as a result, each substantive area is torn from its location within the Parsonian framework. By contrast, I have in the chapter on Parsons' medical sociology attempted to show that a competent understanding of Parsons' sick-role concept cannot be achieved without an understanding of his work as a whole. It is one odd feature of the interpretation of Parsons that, until recently, there were few systematic attempts to comprehend his work as a whole and that English-speaking sociologists have been especially slow in coming to terms with Parsons. There are two significant contributions from French sociology (Rocher, 1974; Bourricaud, 1981) and one Dutch commentary (Adriaansens, 1980) which have been translated and which join existing overviews of Parsons in English (Hamilton, 1983; Savage, 1981; Menzies, 1976). Although several volumes on Parsons are now forthcoming (Jeffrey Alexander and Herminio Martins), the extent and level of evaluation of Parsonian sociology in English is surprisingly sparse, in view of the impact of Parsons on sociology in the twentieth century. The point of this chapter is to suggest that, before such general evaluations are undertaken, it is important to establish what types of criticism are possible and to undertake this task without adopting the negative approach of Savage (1981). The model proposed in this discussion argues that approaching Parsons via critics, issues or topics is often rather limited and random. A more systematic perspective is to ask what forms of critique are logically feasible and then to consider how Parsons' sociology survives each type (reformist, reconstructive, rejectionist and resurrectional). In this review of critical approaches, the principal focus is on the nature of functionalism and the conclusion is that functionalism is a necessary and proper mode of sociological inquiry. Furthermore, functionalism is one perspective which sociology shares with neo-Marxist thought, especially structuralist Marxism. One consequence of this argument is that it is not the discontinuity between sociology and Marxism which is interesting, but the continuity between them. Finally, we are not forced to choose between a sociology of action and a sociology of order, because there is only one sociology and not two. The importance of Parsons is that he offers a general approach which in many respects transcends what Lukàcs (1971) called 'the antinomies of bourgeois thought'.

## Reformation critique

The most obvious and least problematic form of criticism is reformist, since it does not posit alternative values or assumptions, but attempts rather to systematise an existing theory by an explication of its internal difficulties. One illustration of this reformist critique with respect to Parsonian functionalism would be that of Robert Merton, in his account of so-called 'theories of the middle range'. Merton argued that sociological theory is often couched at such a general level that it is difficult to form any linkage between theoretical propositions and empirical hypotheses; in addition, it is difficult to render low-level empirical findings into any coherent analytical view of society. The solution was to be found in middle-range theory, that is

> theories intermediate to the minor working hypotheses evolved in abundance during the day-by-day routines of research, and the all-inclusive speculations comprising a master conceptual scheme from which it is hoped to derive a very large number of empirically observed uniformities of social behaviour (Merton, 1963, pp. 5–6).

Merton's approach was to reform functionalism by a process of codification. Such a procedure involved: (1) an examination of a range of diverse meanings of such basic terms as 'function' and 'structure'; (2) a criticism of the underdeveloped implications of divergent usage; and, (3) a specification of basic analytical concepts in order to render them appropriate for empirical research. Merton's criticisms of functionalism via the process of codification are well known, especially from his essay in *Social Theory and Social Structure* on 'Manifest and latent functions'. Merton charged functionalism with a number of unwarranted assumptions; he saw existing functionalism as offering timeless, universal statements as to the functional contributions of major institutions (such as religion). Merton argued that, under specified circumstances, some institutions or practices would have a dysfunctional effect on the continuity of a social system. He also attacked the idea of the functional unity of a society and the notion that certain functions or institutions were indispensable, pointing to the importance of the argument that there may be functional alternatives. He also insisted on a crucial distinction between conscious motivations and objective consequences, implying that functionalism was primarily interested in the unintended consequences of behaviour and institutions.

The purpose of Merton's reformist critique was not to undermine or replace functionalism but to convert it into a middle-range theory which was precise, coherent and testable. His codification of the manifest/latent dichotomy was thus an important stage in the development of functionalism, although this distinction has itself been criticised as underdeveloped

(Moore, 1979). Merton's critique was internalist. He rejected, for example, the argument that functionalism was ideologically conservative by drawing attention to the *analytical* parallel between certain forms of Marxism and functionalism generally. Furthermore, Merton's own use of functionalism – as in his contribution to deviancy theory via the theory of anomie – has been criticised as exhibiting a commitment to American values of achievement, affluence and consumption (Taylor, Walton and Young, 1973), a commitment he shares with Parsons (Hacker, 1964). Merton's critique was also, as we have seen, based on an assumption of convertibility, since the point of codification was to transform existing functionalist theories into a coherent, middle-range perspective. It is not surprising therefore that Parsons found Merton's critique largely compatible with his existing framework and it is ironic that Parsons criticised Merton's model of deviance for its 'culture-boundness' (Parsons, 1951a, p. 258), namely that the theory could only work in a society where achievement motivation was a dominant value.

The sociological paradigm which came to dominate much of American sociology in the late 1950s and 1960s was based on Parsons' approach to social systems theory. Sociologists working within this paradigm normally adopted a reformist stance towards Parsonianism. The structural-functionalist perspective within *The Social System* (1951a), *Economy and Society* (1956a) and *Societies* (1966a) was seen to be highly convertible and extendable. This reformist tradition was significant in theories of social change (Etzioni and Etzioni, 1964; Hagen, 1962), the sociology of development (Almond and Coleman, 1960; Hoselitz and Moore, 1960), the analysis of stratification (Barber, 1957), theories of collective behaviour (Smelser, 1962), the theory of complex organisations (Etzioni, 1961) and the analysis of particular societies as social systems (Williams, 1965). Since many of the leading American sociologists of this period were actually Parsons' own students (Hamilton, 1983), these studies were primarily applications of a general theory which was assumed to be relatively coherent and stable.

Reconstructionist critique

A more direct and critical attack on Parsons' sociology came from C. Wright Mills in the essay on 'Grand theory' in *The Sociological Imagination* (Mills, 1959). Mills dismissed Parsons' *The Social System* as 'confused verbiage' and argued that Parsons' complex prose could be translated without loss into direct, everyday English. The result of this translation was an attempt to show that Parsonianism was essentially banal common-sense. As with the majority of mainstream criticism of Parsons, Mills emphasised the coercive and conflictual side of social relations. For Mills, power and coercion were essential features of the coherence of social systems. Mills argued that American society was not organised around a common set of values and in terms of a political system which distributed power and reward between a plurality of institutions. Behind the liberal-democratic façade, there existed an organised 'power elite', which coordinated the new corporate structure of industrial society and this new corporatism was essentially anti-democratic (Mills, 1956). Mills also rejected the professionalisation and positivism of American sociology which produced an uncritical accommodation to the dominant culture and a glib commitment to 'value neutrality' (Horowitz, 1965; Eldridge, 1983). Although Mills had an analytical critique of Parsons which had an intellectual content, the roots of this critique were political and ideological. Critics found it difficult to accept Parsons' argument that American society was the most advanced industrial society in terms of its differentiation of institutions, value-integration, universalism and achievement norms. For Mills, the concentration of power in the corporate elite was the foundation for totalitarianism, whereas Parsons regarded America as a society which had more or less success-fully institutionalised democratic politics. The ideological gap between Parsons and Mills was particularly evident in Parsons' review of *The Power Elite* (Parsons, 1957a). It is, of course, perfectly possible for two sociologists to have profound ideo-logical differences and to share theoretical presuppositions which have a great deal in common. For example, Mills recog-nised (Mills, 1959) that Mosca's political sociology anticipated some of the ideas that went into *The Power Elite*, but clearly Mills and Mosca did not share the same ideological assumptions. Similarly, while Parsons and Mills did not share the same evaluation of American society, I want to suggest that there was a theoretical overlap between them.

   With Gouldner and Dahrendorf, Mills is one of the best known and influential critics of Parsons. However, I want to argue that in four important respects the gap between Parsons and Mills is not unbridgeable. First, the very fact that Mills can translate Parsons into everyday prose suggests directly that Mills regarded Parsonian functionalism as convertible. Convertibility in my argument is a form of translation. Secondly, Mills treated Parsons' emphasis on common values as simply one version of a more general theory of social integration. In fact Mills (1959, p. 49) proposed a continuum of types of integration ranging from pure coercion to pure consensus, arguing that most societies would exhibit mixed forms of coercive and consensual stability. Thirdly, Mills' text book, written with Hans Gerth, was essentially a form of functionalist analysis, being primarily concerned with the linkage between character and the wider institutional orders of society (1954). Fourthly, Mills' major contribution, in my view, to sociology was his analysis of 'vocabularies of motive' (1940) in which Mills argued that 'motive' is to be understood as a feature of social vocabularies of action, not as a biological need or psychological disposition. Questions of motive arise in the context of deviations from norms of action and vocabularies of motive offer accounts of deviance which legitimate and explain behaviour. The answer to a question 'Why did you do that?' is an element of a socially shared discourse. Mills' approach to such problems is to some extent compatible with Parsons' treatment of the 'sick role'. Parsons argued (1951a) that we can regard illness behaviour as a form of deviance and that adoption of a sick role legitimates such behaviour. Occupancy of such a role implies that we have a commitment to get better and thus the sick role provides the linkage between our own behaviour and the medical profession. Although there are differences here between Mills and Parsons, it would be possible to marry these two approaches by suggesting that the sick role involves the adoption of certain appropriate vocabularies of motive by which we can give a socially acceptable account of our behaviour. Vocabularies of motive have certain important social functions in describing, accounting for and legitimating action. One important function is for vocabularies to provide 'excuses' for untoward activities (Austin, 1962). The consequence of these four points of convergence is that, although Mills' criticism was one of external convertibility, there were important areas of convergence at an analytical level between their approaches, especially with respect to the relationship between personality and the social system.

It is, however, important to recognise the differences which remain between Parsons and Mills alongside the theoretical assumptions which they had in common. One clear difference was their respective interpretations of Weber. How we interpret a text is largely a function of the assumptions we bring to it and the problem is, within a relativistic tradition of interpretation, texts are infinitely convertible. From Parsons' convergence thesis in *The Structure of Social Action*, Weber is seen to move progressively away from a Marxist paradigm. From Mills' emphasis on conflicts of interest and organised power groups, Weber was thought to become increasingly Marxist in orientation. According to Parsons, Weber's early work took the form of

> disconnected historical studies with a rather definite
> materialistic bias. A changed orientation came in a rather
> dramatic fashion with Weber's recovery from the nervous
> breakdown which forced his retirement. . . . This new
> orientation . . . took three main directions: first an empirical
> concentration on a particular historical-social phenomenon
> – 'modern capitalism'; second a new anti-Marxian
> interpretation of it and its genesis . . . and third a
> methodological basis for (his analytical sociological theory)
> (Parsons, 1937a, p. 503).

Weber's sociology thus represents, for Parsons, a challenge to both rationalist utilitarian economics and materialist Marxism. In particular, Weber's comparative sociology of religions showed that variations in religious interests (that is, the quest for salvation) explained variations in the direction of socio-economic change. By contrast, Mills interpreted Weber's sociology in terms of a convergence on a Marxist emphasis on interests, class, conflict and power. Thus,

> The more embittered Weber became with German politics, the more he came to appreciate the weight of material interests in the success of ideas, however lofty in content and intention they might be (Gerth and Mills, 1961, p. 63).

This thesis is difficult to sustain since Weber's essay on 'The social causes of the decay of ancient civilization' in 1896 was clearly within a Marxist framework (Weber, 1950). The point is that these contrasted interpretations are consequences of entirely different sets of values and in particular of divergent models of capitalist society. Mills' critique thus remained irreducibly externalist in terms of values and assumptions, but highly convertible at the level of theoretical elaboration.


## Rejectionist critique

The most comprehensive and total critique of Parsonianism has been located in Marxism. Rejectionist critique both argues against the background or domain assumptions of functionalism and asserts that no amount of theoretical repair can resolve the imminent crisis of the theory; functionalism is basically inconvertible. An example would be the critique of Nicos Poulantzas who rejected the whole epistemological and theoretical basis of Parsonianism, especially in the realm of political science. For Poulantzas, the theory is inconvertible because it can never be rescued from its epistemological grounding. Poulantzas criticised Parsons for treating the political as a phenomenon which is diffused throughout the social system and for failing to treat the state as the 'condensation of the contradictions of the social formation' (Poulantzas, 1973; 1978). Parsons was criticised for an inability to grasp the uneven, conflictual and contradictory character of social change. For Poulantzas, the integration of the social system is always unstable because it is punctured by class struggle and, insofar as integration exists, it is brought about by the state and not by common values or socialisation. In this view of the contradictory nature of the levels (political, ideological, economic) of a social formation, Poulantzas followed the structuralist perspective of Louis Althusser (1969), for whom theoretical development is characterised not by its continuity, but by epistemological ruptures. Thus, Parsonian functionalism is always pre-scientific because it is grounded in a common-sense treatment of social data, which have not been transformed by scientific theorisation. The Parsonian problematic cannot be converted into the domain of science.

Mills' game of translation can, however, be played in the opposite direction and the corpus of Althusserian concepts can be rendered back into Parsonian system-theory with very little remainder.

| Parsonian structuralism | Althusserian structuralism |
| --- | --- |
| Society | Social formation |
| Social system | mode of production |
| Cultural system | ideology |
| Socialisation | interpellation |
| Functional imperatives | conditions of existence |
| Dysfunction | contradiction |
| Sub-system | levels |
| Latency/integration | ideological state apparatus |

The parallel has of course been often commented on in recent sociology – for example, by Goran Therborn in a digression on role theory in his *The Ideology of Power and the Power of Ideology* (1980). Similar positions have been taken by Piotr Sztompka (1974) and Jeffrey Alexander (1982). In particular Maurice Godelier (1971) has argued that the points of agreement between Marxism and structural functionalism are: (1) that social relations must be analysed as constituting 'systems'; (2) that elements of a society cannot be explained without reference to their relation to the whole; and (3) that the logic of a social system must be adequately grasped before we can turn to the questions of origins and evolution. My conclusion is that much rejectionist critique, especially in Marxism itself, entails a disguised functionalism and has therefore failed to maintain either externalism or inconvertibility.

Another illustration could be taken from recent debates over 'ideology' in Marxism (Abercrombie, Hill and Turner, 1983).

Following Althusser (1971), contemporary Marxists have argued that we cannot treat ideology as simply a set of false beliefs which incorporate people within a system by 'mystifying' their view of reality. Furthermore, we cannot treat ideology as simply the opposite of science. We have to recognise that ideology, while referring to beliefs, is more interestingly conceptualised as practices which embody human experience of their life-world. If this is the definition of ideology in structural Marxism, it is difficult to see how this could be distinguished from Durkheim's account of religion. Following William Robertson Smith, Durkheim argued that religion is not a collection of false beliefs about spiritual phenomena. Religion was not the opposite of science and would not disappear with the advance of scientific thought. Finally, Durkheim argued that to understand religion we have to start with religious practices, since these embody the actual beliefs of the social group (Turner, 1983). Religion is a language (that is, institution) which, through collective practices, imposes a classification of reality in terms of the sacred/profane dichotomy. Parsons shares this view with Durkheim, in arguing that religion is not simply false belief but a complex of actions, rituals and symbols which structure reality. It is for this reason that there is very little to choose between Althusser's concept of 'ideology' as lived experience of the world, Durkheim's *conscience collective* and Parsons' 'the cultural system'.

## Resurrection critique

The final form of criticism is internalist inconvertibility; to some extent, we may expect this position to be typically an empty box or to converge with other possible types of criticism. It seems difficult to imagine how a critic could accept the general framework of a theory and its domain assumptions, but argue that its inner crisis was inconvertible. What this cell in fact claims is that the problematic of a theory is acceptable but its logic is so faulty that the theory cannot be ultimately redeemed. Two candidates for cell D (that is resurrection) might be symbolic interactionism and ethnomethodology. Both of these traditions offered strong criticisms of prevailing Parsonianism. This criticism involved the following propositions: (1) that

Parsonian functionalism tended to suppress individual agency; (2) to take social order as unproblematic and given; and (3) to accept the overt meaning of symbols as obvious without really examining personal interpretations of meanings. These interpretive perspectives argued that macro-social relations could not be explained without a prior grasp of the dynamics of micro-sociology. They also argued that a micro-sociology approach was more amenable to empirical research problems than so-called 'Grand Theory'. If, however, we take two leading exponents of these traditions – Harold Garfinkel and Erving Goffman – we can see that their position involved internal inconvertibility rather than an externalist critique. Both Garfinkel and Goffman took the 'problem of order' as their focal point, namely how do practical actors ongoing construct order out of the flux of everyday situations; social order becomes imminent in the routine tasks of knowledgeable actors. Parsonian systems theory could not provide an answer to this issue, partly because it was couched at the wrong theoretical level. These approaches accepted the Parsonian question – 'how is order possible?' – but rejected the answer given by Parsons that is in common values, socialisation and internalisation. Their position was thus one of internal inconvertibility. Having accepted the centrality of the problem of order, they argued that Parsonian structural functionalism did not lend itself to the analysis of how in everyday terms interpersonal order is not imposed but negotiated (Denzin, 1969).

It may not be warranted, of course, to combine symbolic interactionism and ethnomethodology under the same rubric as internalist critiques of Parsons' version of the problem of order. For ethnomethodologists, 'social order' does not exist as an entity which can be measured in some neutral or objective fashion. In the ethnomethodological perspective, 'order' is something which is made visible by the practices of societal members, both lay and sociological (Zimmerman and Wieder, 1971). For Parsons, social order is a feature of the social system, not of actors' practical reasonings. In this respect, symbolic interactionism may be perfectly compatible with Parsons' action framework in *The Structure of Social Action* and with Parsons' view of social relationships as involving a dyadic exchange of communications, but far less compatible with his general theory of macro-social systems.

Symbolic interactionism and ethnomethodology were therefore typically regarded as anti-Parsonian in their treatment of sociological issues, their style of presentation, their methodological and ethnographic approaches, and in their focus on everyday social processes. In accepting implicitly the problem of social order as their topic, these criticisms have to be regarded as internalist, but they rejected Parsons' solution by treating social order as fleeting, unstable and imminent in social encounters. However, it is important to realise that Goffman's sociology was in many respects an anthropological treatment of order as the outcome of day-to-day rituals and in this respect Goffman's account of society was in many respects Durkheimian (Gonos, 1977). The ritual order exists, but it is still precarious and subject to ongoing modification and disruption (Strong, 1983). A similar view might be taken of Garfinkel, who sought to show how rules in everyday life are made recognisable, and who demonstrated, for example, the importance of *ad hoc* elaboration of rules in the accomplishment of everyday tasks. In other words, rules in social life can never be sufficiently detailed and precise to achieve an orderly situation without the support of the actor's *ad hoc* rule-making. One implication of this approach is that order is emergent and not imposed by 'the cultural system'. It can be argued that Garfinkel's ethnomethodology is thus an extension rather than replacement of Parsons' interest in the conditions of social order, because Garfinkel indicates the density and complexity of everyday rules and practices which make social life possible. It is important to bear in mind that Garfinkel was a student of Parsons at Harvard and taught a course on Parsons' sociology at the University of California at Los Angeles in 1959. The main criticism of ethnomethodology is that, while micro-social processes are interesting and important, it is difficult to see how one could arrive at, for example, a general explanation of unemployment, demographic transitions or urbanisation from the study of everyday conversations. In short, ethnomethodology is a supplement to rather than alternative of macro-social theories which include reference to 'social systems', 'structure' and 'functions'. These criticisms of Parsons which look like examples of internalist inconvertibility turn out to be more reformist in practice.

Other critics of Parsons and Parsonian sociology also claim to be externalist, but on closer inquiry turn out to be versions of reformism or resurrectional critique. Many strident objections to Parsonian functionalism can be without difficulty translated back into the Parsonian framework. For example, I want to make the controversial claim that Alvin Gouldner's forceful critique of Parsons' world-view and sociology is internalist. Gouldner cannot be regarded in the same reformist tradition as Merton and thus his criticism of Parsons might be initially categorised as internalist inconvertibility, but even this position proves somewhat difficult to sustain, given the distinctively functionalist character of the Gouldner perspective.

On the one hand, Gouldner's critique is often linked with that of Mills' objections to Parsonianism, namely that Parsons' sociology is in fact merely a statement of liberal American ideology which is a thinly disguised apologia for wealth and property. Gouldner's *The Coming Crisis of Western Sociology* (1971) thus converges with Mills' earlier critique of Grand Theory. On the other hand, Gouldner has made some important contributions in his own right to functionalist theory as, for example, in 'Reciprocity and autonomy in functional theory' (1959). Furthermore, many of Gouldner's major contributions to sociology contain clearly functionalist arguments – for example, the analysis of the eufunctions and dysfunctions of the contest system in classical Greece in *Enter Plato* (1965). Some of Gouldner's criticisms of functionalism are therefore more reformist than rejectionist. In part, Gouldner's argument was that elements of a social system may achieve autonomy from the whole and thus generate disequilibrium within a system. Gouldner, like many other critics, emphasised conflict, differences of interest, struggles for power and contradictions within society, but much of his sociology continued to presuppose the general validity of treating society as a system.

The problem for Gouldner was that it is difficult to rescue a system approach from the prevailing assumptions of equilibrium and evolutionism. Gouldner thus in practice assumed the validity of the domain assumptions of structural functionalism, rejected Parsonian liberal values and adopted a position which implied that Parsons' sociology was inconvertible. Yet Gouldner was also able to show how it was possible, through the concept of 'functional autonomy' to develop an analysis of conflicts within a functionalist perspective which did not entail assumptions about functional unity in social systems.

Two conclusions follow from this survey of logically possible criticisms of Parsons' sociology. The first is that, since Parsons outlined what any *general* theory of society would have to consider, most criticisms of Parsons turn out to be extensions or additions to this general theory, rather than alternatives or departures. The second is that objections to Parsons appear to be themselves convertible. Any social theory (whether in economics, psychology or demography) has to have an account of the structure of relations (a theory of 'systemness') and an account of the human agent (a theory of action). This is, so to speak, the grammar of social theory which provides the laws for the distribution of concepts within the *parole* of social sciences. Since the grammar is logically universal, translation (or convertibility) is always highly possible. Criticisms of Parsons often, therefore, turn out to be shifts in theoretical dialect rather than fundamental changes in discourse. Parsonian sociology is the dominant *episteme* and, while externalist inconvertibility held out the promise of new theoretical language, the promise of a new domain of concepts has yet to be realised.


A defence of structural functionalism

'Functionalism' has become a term of abuse by Marxists, Weberians, symbolic interactionists and ethnomethodologists. I have, however, suggested that functionalist analysis is in fact endemic to social science of whatever ideological hue. The principal objections to Parsonian functionalism normally come under two headings: (1) because of its emphasis on normative integration, it cannot explain social change; social change can only be grasped by a theory which has an eye for conflict and contradiction; and (2) it is weak at the level of hermeneutic interpretation because it takes the meaning of action and social phenomena as unproblematic. There are three answers to the first objection: (1) most Marxist or conflict theories in fact typically involve functionalist explanations, for example the function of ideology is to subordinate the working class; (2) functionalism does not in principle rule out reference to conflict and contradiction as the concepts 'dysfunction' and 'functional autonomy' clearly indicate; and (3) the circular character of functionalist explanations can be resolved by positing a cause which sets the circle off. There is one major answer to the second objection: the interpretation of action is the starting point of analysis, not its conclusion. The weakness of interpretive sociology is that in practice it equates interpretation with explanation and it fails to provide an account of 'unintended consequences' of action – this is the essence of the debate between Winch, MacIntyre and Runciman (Wilson, 1970; MacIntyre, 1971).

The positive merit of Parsons was that he saw a problem which needed explanation, namely how is society possible? He gave a systematic answer to this problem which involved a functionalist explanation of the role of values and institutions in creating social order. All explanations of social order involve some appeal to functionalist explanation. While there are ample criticisms of both the problem of order as a topic and of functionalism, functionalism itself is inescapable as an explanatory device and functionalism is a necessary device where questions of social continuity and coherence are foci of sociological inquiry.

The origins of the critique of functionalism in Parsons' sociology are not difficult to uncover. Parsons took the nineteenth-century problem of order in classical sociology as the focus of his analysis of social systems and retained a relatively optimistic view of the prospects of moral integration in western capitalism. In the aftermath of two world wars, struggles for colonial independence, global economic recession and industrial stagnation, Parsons' world-view became distinctly unfashionable. It is unfortunate, however, that this ideological critique of Parsons has obscured the genuine merits of his theoretical contribution. I want to argue that certain modifications of Parsons' functionalism could be undertaken in order to overcome the conventional criticisms that Parsonian functionalism cannot deal with the 'fact' that we live in societies which are characterised by value-pluralism, rapid social change and political instability.

Pluralism

Parsons never fully confronts the problem of value-pluralism in
societies which are highly differentiated, because he stipulates
rather than demonstrates that every process of structural differentiation will require and be accompanied by higher-level value-
integration. At an empirical level, all modern industrial societies
as a matter of fact have diverse value-systems based on class,
gender, region, religion, ethnicity, status groups and so forth.
Parsons wants to argue that behind the apparent pluralism,
there are higher-order values of democracy, individualism,
trust, legitimacy and universalism. Any discord in the system
is merely a temporary hitch in the harmony between differentiation and subsequent re-integration on the way to a new equilibrium. The reason Parsons is able to argue in this way is
that he makes an implicit equation between 'social system' and
'society'. In short, a society can only have *one* social system and
hence only *one* system of shared values. His notion of 'social
system' is complex, partly because it is defined at different
levels with different schemes and with different criteria. One
important distinction is that between 'partial' and complete
systems. Parsons writes that a social system

> which meets all the essential functional prerequisites of long
> term persistence from within its own resources, will be
> called a *society* . . . it should contain all the structural and
> functional fundamentals of an independently subsisting
> system. All other social systems will be called a 'partial'
> social system (Parsons, 1951a, p. 19).

This is an inherently problematic definition, but one faced by
all forms of social science. In the modern world, very few
nation-states could on this definition be regarded as self-
sufficient and so the social system will be in fact global. In
addition we must assume that the nation-state is composed of
an indefinite number of so-called partial systems. It follows that
most nation-states which are constituted by a plurality of social
systems of the partial variety will have more than one cultural
system and hence a diversity of value-systems. In short, there
will not be a single system of common values, but a number of
competing value-systems. Two obvious illustrations come to

mind. First in the transition from feudalism to capitalism, there would be two systems of values competing for dominance and thus it could not be said that the members of such a society in transition enjoyed shared values. Secondly, a society like the United Kingdom after the union of crowns between England and Scotland would have a single political system centred on the united monarchy, but two cultural traditions which were preserved long after the fusion of its divergent political traditions. The problem here is analytically parallel to that faced by structuralist Marxism in the distinction between an abstract mode of production and an empirical social formation. A society in transition can be said to have a dominant and an emergent mode of production, and therefore to possess a dominant and an oppositional system of ideologies. There are both theoretical and empirical reasons for arguing that societies do not have single or unitary cultural systems. The argument in favour of the notion of shared values is thus difficult to sustain. However, to argue that any empirical society could be composed of several partial social systems would be compatible with Parsons' structural functionalism without entailing assumptions about coherent value systems, functional unity and equilibrium.

## The state

It has been suggested that Parsons has found it difficult to establish an appropriate theory of power and that his view of the nature of the state is incomplete (Giddens, 1968). When Parsons responded to his critics by attempting to develop a theory of power and influence, he conceptualised power in terms of an analogy to money, that is power is seen as a resource which facilitates the achievement of common goals (Parsons, 1963f). Power does not have to be repressive or coercive; on the contrary, it is a public facility for achieving desired conditions. Like money, it binds the social system together. Although there are merits to such a perspective, there are some unresolved problems with Parsons' view of the state which need to be considered. It is not clear, for example, why the state should not be analysed as a separate sphere alongside the cultural, social, personality and organic systems. For Parsons, the state is a sub-system within the social system. While most sociologists typically regard politics as simply a component of sociology, there may be more compelling reasons for regarding the state as a separate layer or system within the Parsonian schema. For whatever reasons, the state was a much-neglected aspect of Parsons' general sociology.

The problem of order was a central and persistent theme in Parsons' sociology, and the answer to the problem was the existence of shared values, but one issue for Parsons was to explain the origin of these values. One answer for Parsons was primarily Durkheimian, namely that values emerge out of the actual process of sociation. Social values, while having a secular origin, also enjoy a sacred aura. One interesting feature of contemporary theories of the state is that they tend to regard the state as having a legitimating and cohesive function; it is the state which creates order in a capitalist society. For example, Poulantzas (1973) defined the state in terms of its cohesive function in the formation's unity; Habermas (1976) also emphasised the importance of the state as a basis for social legitimation. Althusser (1971) argued that the state has two dimensions – the repressive and the ideological state apparatus. Althusser is especially interesting in relation to Parsons. Unlike Parsons, he regards the state as essentially repressive, but he also argued that the state had ideological functions which were fulfilled via the agency of churches, the family, trade unions, communications and so on. The latency and integration sub-systems within Parsons' social system are thus in Althusser's Marxism part of the state. However, it is important to know whether it is the state or civil society which is the fountain of those values which cement the society together in a social unity. There are no strong theoretical reasons why Parsons could not regard the state as in principle the carrier of such values as universalism, individual achievement and justice. Parsons associated these values with the professions, but he did not adequately consider the importance of the state for supporting and legitimating professionalism, especially in relation to credentialism. One reason for this lacuna is that Parsons' political sociology is largely a product of mid-twentieth-century conditions which were organised around constitutional democracy. For Parsons, the capitalist state may have a significant role to play in the public sphere, but it cannot be the fountain of general values and it cannot generate values which are essential to the private citizen, namely individualism. Parsons did not entertain the possibility which is important for Marxist theory, namely the union of the family and the polity as the foundation of capitalist stability.

One problem with Parsons' view of values as the source of social stability is that general values may often have contradictory relationships (Mann, 1970). For example, it is difficult to reconcile achievement and individualism with egalitarianism and universalism. The quest for individual success and private wealth typically conflicts with notions about the egalitarian distribution of social wealth. Thus, in Parsons' terms, the economic sub-system of a society tends to generate individual inequality in income and wealth, insofar as private property, market competition and freedom of exchange are unchecked by the state. As Durkheim recognised in *The Division of Labour in Society*, one source of social instability is the inheritance of wealth in a society where egalitarian contracts are expected to characterise exchange relationships. Modern capitalist societies are thus unstable because there is a structural conflict between class relations in the sphere of exchange and norms of citizenship in a society where the state becomes a regulative institution in the contradiction between economic individualism and social rights of citizenship (Marshall, 1950). Although Parsons recognised both the relevance of Marshall to such an analysis of modern societies (Parsons, 1977b) and the importance of the state (or polity) as a regulative institution, he was reluctant to admit that a social system could be organised around a contradictory set of forces. Yet such a view of society as a system constituted by contradictory institutions or as a contradiction between different systems would not be incompatible with a structural-functionalist perspective. Indeed it was precisely this adaptation of Parsons which formed the basis of Habermas' view of the state, society and economy relationship in *Legitimation Crisis*.

Conclusion

Any theory of society will have to attempt to resolve the
relationships between agency and structure, order and change,
conflict and consensus. The majority of social theories are typically partial in that they are addressed to a limited range of
issues; they frequently focus on a narrow slice of issues in
being, for example, theories of conflict or human agency or
normative order. The merit of Parsons' sociology was that it
attempted to be a general theory and the very breadth of
Parsons' sociology means that most one-sided objections to
Parsonian sociology are actually incorporated by his analysis or
can be rendered compatible with it. These criticisms are in fact
reformist, despite their claims to be alternatives, and can be
converted back into Parsons' general theory. I have suggested
certain alterations of Parsons' treatment of value-integration
which would render his system approach less prone to charges
of normative conservativism. However, the primary basis of all
externalist critique of Parsons is moral and ideological in being
essentially an objection to his view of American society. The
debate with Parsons would be more productive if the nature of
these moral and ideological objections was made more explicit.

# 5
# Against nostalgia: Talcott Parsons and a sociology for the modern world

*Robert J. Holton
and Bryan S. Turner*

Classical European sociology, as it developed in the century or so leading up to the First World War, presented a profoundly ambivalent stance towards those processes of industrialisation, democratisation and rationalisation which constituted the modern western world. On the one hand, the erosion of traditional constraints upon economic dynamism and political freedom was celebrated as an enlargement of the capacity of human societies to realise the good life. On the other hand, the challenge to social coherence and stability posed by the decline of religious authority, village life and traditional status hierarchies was deeply unsettling. This tension between 'traditional and modern values' is, as Nisbet (1967) has pointed out, fundamental to the underlying assumptions and conceptual structure of nineteenth-century sociology. It is represented in such familiar dichotomies as community and individualism, the sacred and the secular, status and contract.

It is a quite bizarre mis-reading of this interpretation to claim, as Hawthorn (1976) has done, that the project of sociology being presented is essentially conservative. Nisbet's point is, rather, that the preoccupations of Marx, Weber, Durkheim and Simmel involve a paradoxical combination of modern values such as 'science', 'reason' and 'individual freedom', with a conceptual armoury deeply embedded in the conservative desire for order and the restoration of community. While not joining the conservative opponents of the French and Industrial Revolutions, classical sociology demanded, not release from community and tradition, but alignment with social forces seeking 'new forms of moral and social community'. In this way there remained a strong element of nostalgia in the cultural preoccupations and fundamental categories of classical socio-logical thought.

For Marx this took the form of alignment with the labour movement, in its struggle to build a socialist or communist alternative to the alienation of human potential within capitalist society. The central place of the labour theory of value, and the transcendent properties of class struggle within this framework, specify both a community-like conception of the generative forces involved in wealth-creation and a theory of exploitation and social change, which grounds the claims of producers against their oppressors in a sense of violated community. As R. H. Tawney (1960, p. 36) pointed out, the underlying moral argument behind the labour theory of value is directed against the securing of 'private gain by the exploitation of public necessities denying labour the vocation of serving the common need . . .'. In this sense it represents the true descendant of the doctrines of Aquinas, with Marx as the last of the schoolmen.

Marx's humanism has of course been interpreted as an 'early' pre-scientific stage in his thought, to be differentiated from the 'later' mature, scientific Marx, by a profound epistemological rupture (Althusser, 1969). This kind of distinction is however vulnerable to Gouldner's theory of the Two Marxisms (Gouldner, 1980). Here it is claimed that both 'scientific' and 'moral philosophical' elements are necessarily conjoined within Marx's work. The twin legacies of Marx, represented by positiv-istic scientism and humanistic critical philosophy, are thus equally authentic Marxisms. This argument reinforces Nisbet's notion of an intrinsic tension in nineteenth-century sociology, between modern values such as the appeal to scientific auth-ority, and the more traditional claims of communitarian humanism.

A similar ambivalence toward 'tradition' and 'modernity' is evident in the work of Max Weber. In one sense he is quite clearly aligned with the modernising aims of German liberalism. Such aims involved conflict with German autocratic and folk traditionalism and with illiberal and despotic forces outside the German nation-state, most notably Russia. Within Weber's discussion of rational-legal authority and bureaucracy, there is a clear sense of the enhanced scope for individual freedom and authoritative efficiency that such institutions represent, compared with the traditional order. Occidental rationalism is invested with many positive values compared with the civilisations of the world beyond Europe. In another sense, however, these values are linked with a strongly nostalgic hankering for a stable past. This past is one which is specifically religious and in which the possibilities of charismatic individualism are always possible. Max Weber's concept of rationalisation, which in many ways is the key to his whole sociology (Brubaker, 1984), has a nostalgic character to it. Much of Weber's sociology is based upon a religious metaphor of the tree of knowledge, and aspects of Weber's theme of rationalisation argue that modern society has lost innocence by its exposure to scientific knowledge. We can say that much late nineteenth-century social thought was a reflection on Nietzsche and, in particular, a reflection on Nietzsche's notion of the death of God. The modern world is seen as essentially secular, but a secular reality which offers very little in terms of moral guidance. It was Weber who noted that the dominance of science would in some ways liberate us but also in certain respects enslave us. It is for this reason that Weber's concept of the iron cage was so crucial to his sociological perspective on the dilemmas of contemporary society.

For Nisbet, writing in the mid-1960s, contemporary sociology was still living 'in a late phase of the classical age of sociology' (Nisbet, 1967, p. 5). Stripped of the 'tensions' between the modern and traditional worlds as defined by writers like Marx and Weber, sociology would, he felt, be theoretically impoverished, leaving little but 'lifeless heaps of data and stray hypotheses'. There is much to be said in support of this view. Leaving aside a certain uncreative piety among late twentieth-century sociologists towards the 'founding fathers', it is quite clearly the case that the project of reconciling individualism and secularisation with community and moral order remains fundamental to sociological inquiry. While a certain amount of sociology is still written on the presumption that the working class, or the destiny of particular European nation-states, is strategically bound up with the reconciling of this tension, a number of the substantive features of the classical landscape have changed.

In the first place, the Marxist reliance on the revolutionary potential of the working class is now in a profound state of political exhaustion. Gorz' (1982) cry of 'Farewell to the Working Class' in favour of alternative non-classlike social movements (e.g. feminism, peace, ecology) represents an important step beyond one version of the politics of revolutionary nostalgia. In the second place, the privileged status of a narrow set of European nation-states, as the crucible within which the connections between 'past', 'present' and 'future' are worked out, has been superseded by a number of global trends. These include the emergence of super-politics between the USA and Russia, the economic and political mobilisation of the Third World, and the development of a new Pacific economic and political order, linking Japan, China, South East Asia, Australia and the West Coast of the USA. Within this broad context, theories of social change based exclusively upon endogenous developments within Britain, France and Germany have become outmoded.

There is, nonetheless, a sense in which such developments have not disturbed the underlying tension between traditional and modern values that constituted classical sociology. This is evident in the continuing vitality of appeals to 'community' and a unitary moral order in the midst of social science and 'progressive' politics. The enthusiasm of many western Marxists for a succession of charismatic Third World movements from Marxism to the elan of the Latin American revolutionary is testimony to the search for an alternative community building eschatological force to replace the discredited western proletariat. The spectre of Weber's iron cage of rationalisation has also been challenged, most powerfully perhaps by the claims of environmentalist movements for some kind of ecological harmony between society and nature. Here 'science' and 'reason' have been confronted by a strong communitarian sense of the 'sacred'. This has been counterposed to the anomic characteristics perceived in technocratic management. While the political symbols of community among European radicals may have shifted from 'red' to 'green' (Feher and Heller, 1984), the aim of many contemporary social movements is still some type of communitarian quest.

Within contemporary sociology there is a tension between empirical scepticism about the existence of an underlying normative order, and an underlying normative commitment to community. The depiction of modern values such as 'individualism' and 'privatisation' as in some way 'pathological' or 'anomic' relies as much on ontological assumptions about human nature as upon empirical validation. This communitarian critique of modernity is one of the main elements in the attempt by industrial and urban sociology to reconstruct the social relations of the workplace and the modern city. Within this framework greater attention and sympathy is given to workers' control than to the work ethic, and greater concern shown for public rather than private types of consumption. In general, the 'public' remains preferred at the expense of the 'private', in a manner which looks backward to the civic 'virtues' of the ancient Mediterranean world as an inspiration for a critique of modernity (MacIntyre, 1981; Sennett, 1977). On this basis the private is dismissed as 'fetishised' or 'narcissistic' when judged against the collective ethics of community.

For all these continuities between contemporary and classical sociology, there remain some striking contrasts. The foremost of these is the abandonment of confident nineteenth-century expectations as to the inevitability of 'progress'. There is now a far more pessimistic tone to twentieth-century sociological nostalgia. This is especially evident in the so-called critical theory of Frankfurt School writers, such as Horkheimer, Adorno and Habermas. If nineteenth-century social theory was shaped by the aftermath of the French Revolution and then the industrial transformation of Europe, twentieth-century social thought, particularly in the case of the Frankfurt School, has been shaped by global warfare and by the social consequences of fascism. The problem for German social theory was that, given its grounding in the German rational tradition, it was difficult to see how the irrationality of German Nazi society could be explained. What haunted the imagination of the Frankfurt School theorists was the horror of the concentration camps. It was Adorno after all who said that to write poetry after Auschwitz is barbaric. This expression in many ways captures the sense of bitterness which lies at the centre of critical theory and at the heart of its rejection of the claims of instrumental rationality. Twentieth-century social theory appears, therefore, to be shaped by catastrophic global changes, and in particular, those changes associated with mass warfare, nuclear armaments and the systematic extermination of minority groups, such as the Jews in Europe or the aboriginal peoples of the Third World.

There are strong associations between Weber's notion of a rationally ordered society, Adorno's notion of the administered society and Foucault's concept of the panoptic system. These pessimistic views of bureaucracy tend to imply the moral value of a pre-bureaucratic society, characterised by immediacy, spontaneity and affectual social relations. In other words, bureaucratic society stands in direct opposition to the notion of community, where community is based upon shared common values, interpersonal direct relationships and a notion of historic continuity with the past. The critique of society implicit in the work of Weber, Adorno and Foucault suggests a reluctance, or even an incapacity, to come to terms with a society based upon *Gesellschaft* relations. Modern society, based upon such a notion of *Gesellschaft*, is the very embodiment of that instrumental rationality which these theorists saw as incompatible with human existence, at least a human existence based upon a meaningful notion of life.

By criticising mass society, writers like Adorno often appeared highly elitist and withdrawn from contemporary politics. It is also well known that Marcuse assumed that working-class politics were no longer possible in the modern world, and Marcuse sought alternative outlets for a revolutionary and radical activity. In some respects, therefore, Marcuse shared a cultural elitism with writers like Adorno and Horkheimer.

Cultural pessimism and melancholic elitism are perhaps two indicators of the increasing incoherence of the classical nineteenth-century project, insofar as this involved the rejection of key modern western values like individualism and pluralism. Another such indicator is the fate of the concept of 'community' itself. It is particularly striking that the unit-idea regarded by Nisbet as 'unquestionably the most distinctive development in nineteenth century social thought' should have become so refractory to agreed definition in twentieth-century discourse (Bell and Newby, 1974, p. x(iii)). While still part of the rhetoric of moral philosophy and democratic politics, the notion of community increasingly appears as a residual melange of spatial, structural, cultural and emotional components. This is symptomatic of the value-pluralism of modern western society wherein the nostalgia of nineteenth-century sociology appears increasingly redundant.

The confrontation of modern value-pluralism and individualism, with notions of *Gemeinschaft*, however, presents two intellectual options. On the one side lies the re-affirmation of community founded on deep emotional and moral bonds between human actors conceived in terms of what is called 'wholes'. The primary justification for this stance is the moral disorder and imprecision diagnosed in value-pluralism and individual sovereignty in moral choices. Alasdair MacIntyre (1981), in a powerful and courageous statement of this position, reverses as it were the charges made against the sociological coherence of the notion of community. For him it is 'value-pluralism' that constitutes an 'unharmonious melange of ill-assorted fragments', shored up by 'surface rhetoric'. Community, on the other hand, can be re-discovered as an authentic moral standpoint only by rejecting the Enlightenment, and returning to the classical conception of communal virtues and human teleology systematised by Aristotle. In the confrontation between value-pluralism and community MacIntyre turns his face steadfastly against the Enlightenment rationalism, which claims that there can be no rational basis for morality. MacIntyre is against modernity and its 'moral philosopher', Nietzsche, and for nostalgia.

The confrontation of value-pluralism and *Gemeinschaft* need not, however, be resolved through appeals to a backward-looking moral philosophy. The pursuit of nostalgia is not the only option available by which to face the apparently pessimistic or amoral implications of rationalisation and disenchantment. An alternative option is to consider the possibility that *Gesellschaft* permits authentic expressions of values, rather than the 'false', or 'fetishised' forms of consciousness as diagnosed by exponents of the Frankfurt School. In addition, value-pluralism under *Gesellschaft* need be considered neither as a series of private narcissistic worlds, in retreat from the public domain, nor as an irreducible battle of Nietzschian wills. Rather it can be conceived as generating a normative basis for the orderly resolution of pluralism and diversity. The underlying thesis of this study is that the sociology of Talcott Parsons represents a decisive step, both beyond classical sociology, and beyond the 'Aristotle' and 'Nietzsche' options in moral philosophy, in his elaboration of this essentially modern social order.

Compared with the sociologists of the classical period, Parsons is far less ambivalent about the modern world. The evaluative yardstick of 'community' does not appear in a strong form – whether as utopia or social ontology – as a moral foil to such modern developments as instrumental rationality, or individual achievement-orientation. Parsons is neither equivocal with respect to the operation of the market economy, political democracy and the rule of law, nor tortured by pessimistic doubts as to the possibility of a future world based on humanitarian values.

For some critics, Parsons is thereby dismissed as a commentator on the modern world. This is both for his apparent insensitivity to the casualties of capitalism and for his complacency in the face of the nuclear arms race and ecological crisis. At best Parsons seems complacent, at worst morally blind.

Such impressions are, however, largely misplaced. In the first place, Parsons' twentieth-century optimism reflects a profoundly moral and political identification with liberal democratic values, such as equality of opportunity and personal autonomy. Since a number of his critics seem incapable of distinguishing between 'liberalism' and 'conservatism', it is important to emphasise that Parsons cannot be regarded as a spokesman for the 'New Right'. The political implications of Parsons' liberalism include identification with the New Deal, the championing of negro rights (Parsons and Clark, 1966c), and hostility to McCarthyism and religious fundamentalism.

Some of Parsons' optimism about the future of liberal-democratic politics seems faded and even anachronistic in the face of unease about the military and ecological consequences of superpower conflict. It is nonetheless very striking how far modern social movements for peace, environmental protection and women's rights have drawn, however unwittingly, upon the liberal-democratic legacy. This includes the emphasis on popular sovereignty in decision-making and on the establishment of social conditions which will maximise the personal autonomy of the individual (Feher and Heller, 1984).

A second element in Parsons' sociology is his rejection of the dubious sociological assumptions that lie behind political romanticism. For Parsons the emergent features of modern society, including value pluralism and political democracy, lend no credence to the eschatological view that social problems can be solved through some decisive redemptive structural change, able to release some essential communitarian quality in human nature. For Parsons the critique of existing institutions in terms of some absolutist Utopian morality is founded on some version of the doctrine of an underlying harmony of interests. This flies in the face of the heterogeneous individualism characteristic of modern society. Within Parsons' framework, there is neither room for the patrician assumption that 'non-transcendent' social practices are the work of cultural dupes, nor any place for such elitist categories as 'false consciousness'. In this sense Parsons' normative commitment to modernity is both democratic and plebeian.

Thirdly, Parsons is not an apologist for that kind of crass economic individualism that is often taken to underlie the capitalist economy. Rather, in developing Durkheim's insights into the non-contractual basis of contract, he seeks to elaborate much further the value inputs and normative rules that regulate economic life and prevent the unilateral operation of a utilitarian social order. Such rules are not located in the nostalgic communitarian civic rituals or guild-like occupational corporations that Durkheim emphasised. Instead they are given an individualistic, yet morally-informed, construction within such institutions as the work ethic and the extension of 'trust' in relations between savers, investors and producers. Such normative relations are seen to underlie the impersonality and instrumental character of economic relations.

The point here is not that the modern western economy is presented as a conflict-free mechanism always tending to benign equilibrium. It is rather that the inter-penetration of economic and moral individualism in relations between economy and society renders inadmissible any exclusively instrumental or coercive picture of modern economic life. Power relations are seen as fundamental to such relations, as are political collectivities, wherein goals are promoted and resources made available. Yet power is seen as enabling, rather than as an unchecked coercive force emanating from a single location.

In this way Parsons seeks to deny both the utilitarian Utopia of Robinson Crusoe and the negative critique of capitalist alienation from the viewpoint of the community of free producers that underlies the labour theory of value. In opposition to such nostalgic Utopias he presents the emergent structure of the modern economy, more especially the differentiation between producers and consumers, savers and investors, or employers and workers, as functional both to the normatively regulated achievement of a plurality of projects and to social integration. The increasing socialisation of production and consumption, characteristic of the modern economy, renders notions of the pre-social individual or the holistic free producer equally obsolete as romantic fictions. Parsons emerges from most confrontations with his critics as both morally engaged and politically committed, not as an apologist for capitalism, but as an anti-elitist and anti-Utopian social theorist. This standpoint moves us beyond the ambivalence of the classical sociologists towards modernity, in that Parsons unsentimentally rejects the nostalgic foils of *Gemeinschaft* or social Utopia, on which the various classic critiques of alienated labour, rationalisation and *Gesellschaft* depended. While it is obvious that his social theory emerged through a critical commentary on his classical forebears, he does not share their preoccupation with the transitional problems involved in the emergence of capitalism, industrialism and democratisation. Parsons' sociology is much more a post-classical reflection on the problems of individualism in contemporary western society, the emergence of equal rights in societies dominated by social stratification and the question of bureaucratic efficiency in relation to individual wants and needs. While he retains a sense of the 'social community' as the foundation of normative order, this term is used in a highly pluralistic and diffuse, rather than unitary and absolutist, manner. In all these respects Parsons' social theory announces the end of the classical phase of sociological thought.

The transition from classical to post-classical sociology itself reflects a shift in the cultural and political terrain of sociological thought from Europe to America. Whereas nineteenth-century sociology was shaped by an analysis of the 'great transformation' experienced by European society in the epoch of the Industrial and French Revolutions, this pattern of change was not reproduced in American historical development. Lacking a traditionalistic and feudal background, the development of American society posed rather different questions for American sociology. The historic weakness of Marxism and the continuing vitality of liberal-democratic thought within the United States represent an intellectual context significantly different from that which has prevailed in Europe for much of the last 100 years.

For Parsons, the preoccupation of European sociological thought with questions like the fate of capitalism and the politics of class represents a concern with transitional features of the great transformation, rather than with modern society itself. While capitalism has been supplanted by the differentiation between ownership and management, the continuing emphasis on class relations looks back to the past. Parsons sees the underlying normative basis of working-class and capitalist solidarity as a perpetuation of the traditional *Gemeinschaft* orientations of the European peasantry and aristocracy respectively. American society, by contrast, has emphasised the liberation of individuals, emotionally as well as politically, from communitarian bonds founded on ascriptive and particularistic bases. At the same time a sufficiently generalised set of norms has been developed to produce social order. Parsons' theory of social change is quite unequivocal about the contemporary significance of the USA, as having taken over the role of 'leading sector' in modernisation, a role previously located in seventeenth- and eighteenth-century Europe (Parsons, 1971a).

The belief that the USA rather than Europe holds the key to the future of modern society is clearly not a novel one. Nineteenth-century social theorists such as de Toqueville appreciated the extent to which American democracy represented a qualitative extension of the principles currently underlying revolutionary changes in Europe. At the same time much European scholarship has continued to treat the USA more as a 'deviant' case of western development than as a lead sector in social change. Part of the devaluation of the United States as a developmental model has built on an elitist disdain for domestic American phenomena such as mass consumerism, and the cultivation of the individual personality and body. Although such trends have been evident in European society for many years, they still remain disprivileged within the primarily 'classical' preoccupations of contemporary sociological inquiry.

The European critique of 'Americanism' has depended in large measure on the elevation of various cultural and political traditions within Europe to the status of more universalistic and 'civilised' alternatives. For some the lack of a mass socialist movement or Labour Party in the USA has hitherto been taken as indicative of American 'deviance' from a more general model of social change in the western world. The French uprising of 1968 did more to perpetuate belief in a socialist future achieved through proletarian revolution than any event since the inter-war Depression. This vision is now increasingly discredited, even amongst some of its previous proponents. While the French uprising stands more or less alone in recent European history as a quasi-revolutionary challenge to the existing order, radical French social theorists themselves now speak of the demise of the 'culture of industrialism' and bid 'adieu' to the working class (Touraine, 1981; Gorz, 1982). While Labour governments continue to be elected from time to time, it appears they must capture much of the 'middle-ground' to do so. This involves support for the rule of law above class interest, for parliamentary democracy, a mixed economy and a recognition of the 'private' as well as 'public' interests of citizens. The British Labour Party is probably the most 'conservative' and least 'radical' among western Labour movements in espousing Marxism, at a point in time when most other movements have come to accept the incompatibility of traditional conceptions of socialism with the emergent features of modern society. In such respects Europe appears to be converging (however unevenly) with the political experience of those western societies which lack a feudal status-ridden past, such as the USA and Australia.

Another component of the European critique of Americanism has been the emphasis on certain ascribed characteristics of European national cultures, which are given elevated and privileged status. It is noteworthy that such arguments usually depend on an emotional appeal to nation and national symbols. One component of this is the resistance to what is taken to be national language debasement as a result of imported American culture, which is taken to result in an impoverishment of sensibility and civility.

Nationalism of course remains a profound political force. In this context it is somewhat ironic to find French Marxist intellectuals, such as Debray (1977, p. 41), defending an ascriptive view of the motherland 'la patrie', as a force making in some mystical way for the liberation of all oppressed people. This contrasts, at an ideological level at least, with the rational claim of American liberal-democratic pluralism to represent a universalistic, multicultural, non-ascriptive basis for political freedom.

Parsons' construction of a theory of modernity and social change, based on the universalistic evolutionary advantages located in western, and more especially twentieth-century American institutions, has been criticised as an apologia for American liberalism and the sectional interests of American imperialism. There are several elements to this challenge.

The first is that American liberal values have been overtaken by the development of a coercive military-industrial complex. This guarantees neither real personal autonomy to the American poor and unemployed nor freedom to the Third World. In foreign policy the universalistic logic of liberal-democratic pluralism and respect for the international rule of law has not always been uppermost in relations between nation-states in Europe and elsewhere. At least part of the European critique, of 'Americanism', rests on the perceived threat to national sovereignty posed by the military and economic institutions of the super-power (Servan-Shreiber, 1968). While liberal-democratic theory has always been faced with the dilemma of how far to use illiberal measures in defence of liberalism, the charge is that American imperialism has been structurally organised on an illiberal basis. The plausibility of Parsons' case for the USA as a universalistic lead sector in an international context is therefore seen as far more problematic than he realised.

A second line of criticism is that the alleged advantages of America's universalistic institutions have not been confirmed by the expected convergence of non-Western societies to the American model. The main problem here is the stability of the

USSR. While exhibiting a certain economic dynamic, Parsons' expectation was that the undemocratic Soviet political system would prove 'unstable' (Parsons, 1971a). Without the capacity of democratic societies to institutionalise individual goals and hence obtain political consent and loyalty, Parsons expected social and political instability. In this situation the options for the Soviet Union were either a convergence to the western world, or continuing instability and collapse. While 'national' resistance to Soviet domination has produced massive convulsions in Eastern Europe, the instability Parsons forecast for the Soviet Union has not eventuated.

A third more general challenge to Parsons' America-centred theory of social change is its apparent perpetuation of nine-teenth-century emphases on the endogenous causes of social change within nation-states (Smith, 1973). Such a focus is prob-lematic insofar as it neglects problems of inter-state relations and the impact of exogenous forces on social development. These include war and invasion, as well as less coercive forms of cultural diffusion, all of which have played a significant part in the global politics of the twentieth century.

While it is beyond the scope of this study to evaluate these criticisms in any empirical depth, it is possible to confirm the *prima facie* plausibility of Parsons' emphasis on the USA as a 'lead sector', against most of the charges made against him.

In the first place, there are major difficulties with views which wish to assimilate the American nation-state to the worldwide hegemonic interests of a military-industrial complex. One problem with this argument is the reductionism involved in claiming America to be a unitary political economic entity. For Arato and Cohen (1982), on the other hand, there is not one but 'two Americas'. The first is 'the republican liberal-demo-cratic core', whose commitment to the rule of law and a free public sphere (including a free press), represents a highly legit-imate and sometimes effective check on tendencies towards corruption, intimidation and arbitrary power within domestic politics. This critical public sphere is, however, conjoined to American imperialism – the other America. American imperi-alist involvement in 'totalitarian methods of lawless administrat-ive-military rule' are especially evident outside the United States. Whereas Marxist political economists like Mandel (1970) have analysed relations between Europe and America simply in terms of the relative power of two imperialist blocs, the theory of two 'Americas' permits a more complex analysis of internal as well as international political and cultural characteristics.

Although functionalism has often been criticised for presenting a picture of the social system as a seamless web of interconnected institutions, in his empirical essays and shorter commentaries on American society Parsons showed that he was perfectly aware of the tensions, conflicts and strains within American capitalism. These strains were often treated in a rather conventional way, as the gap between the speed of social development and the adaptive capacity of existing institutions. The problem was thus conceptualised via Durkheim as a strain between economic individualism and moral (or institutionalised) individualism. However, Parsons also drew upon T. H. Marshall to argue that there was in modern industrial society an uneasy tension between the *political* principles of egalitarian democracy and the *economic* inequality of the market place (Parsons, 1965b; Parsons, 1970f). Although Parsons did not develop the theme, the relative institutional separation of economic and political realms in capitalism is crucial for the development of political opposition and social critique. Parsons did not espouse a two-Americas theory, but he was, by borrowing from Marshall, aware of the contradiction between democratic universalism and economic inequality as a necessary feature of free-market economies. Similarly, Parsons did not address the problem of the impact of American economic expansion on peripheral societies within the sphere of American political influence. It may be that the growth of the core economies requires the exploitation and subordination of both external and internal colonies. A reply to critics of US foreign policy and trade is possible through, for example, Barrington Moore's concept of 'predatory democracy', developed in his sensitive and humane study *Reflections on the Causes of Human Misery* (Moore, 1970).

Within this framework Parsons' arguments about American universalism seem far stronger in relation to the 'republican liberal-democratic core', than within the international imperialist domain. US support for totalitarian regimes within the Third World cannot easily be reconciled with pluralistic conceptions of liberal-democratic norms, especially where the regimes in question show no signs of long-term liberalisation. Arato and Cohen (1982), drawing on the analysis of Arendt (1958), have nonetheless argued that the liberal-democratic legacy has, paradoxically, been an important factor in the articulation of anti-imperialist resistance in the Third World. This western legacy, according to Arendt, exerts a countervailing check on western imperialism in a way that is not possible in the far more monolithic political structures of the Soviet empire. Here the core nation is itself dominated by a totalitarianism offering no legitimation for resistance. Accordingly, the dissident movements in Eastern Europe look elsewhere, to indigenous nationalist or religious sources or to the west for alternative bases of legitimacy.

It is also important to emphasise that the logic of Parsons' system of evolutionary universals is in large measure transnational. The emergence of the nation-state distinct from particularistic religious commitments is of course seen as a major element in the universalistic thrust of the modern world. Since the basis for normative order has remained national in scope, for the most part, Parsons conducts his analysis of social change in terms of the characteristics and performance of national units. While there is no absolutist commitment to American values on the basis of ascriptive allegiance, Parsons nonetheless accords utmost significance to the universalistic institutions located within the nation-state. Beyond this, however, Parsons goes on to consider, albeit relatively briefly, the development of an international normative order and its relationship to nation-states. Here he welcomes international organisations like the United Nations, the development of a non-aligned group of nations outside the super-power blocs, and the development of a cross-cutting system of international links which presages the end of a sharply polarised international order (Parsons, 1967c). In this way his commitment to America as the leading sector in modernity is not to be read as an apology for the entire course of recent American history. What is most noticeably lacking in all of this is an adequate explanation of the symbolic resilience of the ascriptive international politics of nation-states.

The problematic standing of Soviet Russia in Parsons' theory of social change also warrants further discussion. As already indicated, the confident assumption that the lack of a political democracy would generate instabilities in the Soviet system has not so far proved accurate. Against Parsons' prognoses of Soviet convergence with the west, or of retrogression, Russia has managed to deny both political pluralism and economic freedom of choice for consumers, and yet to have secured effective compliance with the massive post-war expansion of Russian global military power. Failing the collapse of this edifice, it is unclear whether the liberal-democratic pluralism of the USA represents the only road to modernity, as measured in terms of geo-political super-power status. This in turn raises a more general problem with Parsons' social change theory, namely that 'de-differentiation' may be an authentic route to those kinds of evolutionary advantage over the environment and the organisation of social order that he associates only with differentiation.

The 'success' of the Soviet Union in this respect may at one level pose even greater challenges to Marxist social theory than it does for Parsons' meta-theoretical framework. David Lane (1981), for example, has used a modified version of Parsons' four-function paradigm to analyse those features of the Russian revolutionary experience that are neglected in Marxist accounts of the Soviet Union which seek to define this system as some variant of a mode of production, e.g. state capitalism, bureaucratic workers' state, etc. These neglected features include 'culture and values, patterns of integration, and politics as effective goal-attainment'. Lane defines the system-needs of the Soviet Union, as interpreted by the Bolsheviks and subsequent Party Leaders, not only as an upgrading of the adaptive resources of society (or in Marxist terms the productive forces), through a centralised goal-attainment system (i.e. the dictatorship of the proletariat managed by the party), but also as a high level of integration and value-generalisation. The latter needs were secured by a mixture of terror and penal sanctions, together with ideological legitimation, through the translation of Marxism-Leninism into traditional Russian values.

There has been much debate in post-war Marxism over the role of dominant ideologies in western capitalist societies, where these ideologies are thought either to integrate the society, or to incorporate the working class, or to limit the range of perceived alternatives to capitalism (Abercrombie, Hill and Turner, 1980). This debate can be seen as a feature of the exchange between Daniel Bell and his critics over the relationship between culture, polity and economics in advanced capitalist societies (Bell, 1976). Bell's thesis is that the cultural system has been uncoupled from the economy and polity; the emphasis on self-gratification in modernist cultures is no longer closely related to the requirements of efficiency in economic matters. There is thus a contradiction between the disciplines of work, and the hedonism of cultural expression. By contrast, Parsons typically assumed a much closer and more systematic relationship between culture and the economic system, although there is much debate as to whether he was committed to a theory of dominant cultures, and thus presented a mirror-image to the Marxist notion of dominant ideology (Lechner, 1984). Parsons' views on American social experience become problematic in other case studies, because American pluralism was based on a relative separation of economy and polity.

Lane's conclusion is that Parsons' social theory, while more adequately multi-dimensional than Marxism, is nonetheless founded on an illegitimate extrapolation of a general theory of the reciprocal inter-change between social sub-systems and the relatively pluralistic American experience. The example of the Soviet Union suggests an alternative basis to the integration of the social system. Above all else, modern Russia lacks the differentiated inter-relation between sub-systems found in western society. In the Soviet case the goal-attainment function remains predominant and is intimately linked to the adaptive economic functions. Links between the pattern-maintenance sub-system and the goal-attainment sub-system, involving value-commitment to the 'legality of power of office' are in consequence weak. The same applies to the connection between the pattern-maintenance sub-system and the adaptive sub-system in terms of the articulation and satisfaction of consumer wants. Lane's conclusion is that Parsons' general analytical apparatus may be used to demonstrate the possibility of different solutions to the problem of reconciling social change with social order, than those which have emerged in the West. What is less clear from his argument is the relative importance of what might be called the 'American' and 'Soviet' roads in the global evolution of modern societies.

There are two ways of assessing this problem. The first is to consider whether Western trends lead elsewhere than Parsons expected. Here, as already indicated, Parsons' vision of a pluralistic liberal-democratic *Gesellschaft* tied together by inclusive universalistic citizenship rights seems more plausible than a future based on the recreation of traditional *Gemeinschaft*, whether in socialist or Communist garb. There also appears some reason to doubt that the spectre of a bureaucratic or corporatist iron cage, riven with system-crises, is inexorably present. Against this prospect may be cited the fiscal and electoral limits to state expansionism, the continuing resilience of private consumerism, and the contemporary vitality of associational politics, including the politics of resistance to militarism and bureaucratisation. There has been massive state intervention in the economy and the growing dominance of multinational corporations, but there has also been a remarkable continuity and resilience of small business. Both left- and right-wing political parties in western capitalism have been supporting small business as a sector of the economy which can innovate and reduce unemployment. It is also the case that capitalism requires an entrepreneurial function which cannot be satisfied by efficient bureaucracy and economic planning. Political leadership and economic entrepreneurship are parallel activities; the absence of effective leadership, rather than the dominance of impersonal bureaucracy, is the critical problem in western democracies (Eden, 1983). The iron cage may not be the most appropriate metaphor for the analysis of modern democracies, since there are various conditions and processes which point in the opposite direction.

The moral here is not benign optimism, since as Parsons pointed out modern society remains faced with problems of 'intense alienation' in many groups, by lack of stability in the motivational bases of social solidarity, and the threat of nuclear destruction (Parsons, 1971a). It is rather the striking capacity of liberal-democratic societies to meet a multiplicity of diffuse aspirations, by relatively stable processes of inclusion or incorporation, which maximise efficiency, individual freedom, innovation and integration. In contrast to fashionable Doomsday predictions, Parsons' argument implies that problems such as stagflation or technological change can be managed without abandonment of liberal-democratic pluralism, though not without social conflict. If there is a spectre haunting Europe, it is neither Communism nor the iron cage. The best we can hope for is individual freedom and the politics of reform, but this is in itself no guarantee against nuclear war.

While Parsons' evolutionary universals remain plausible as a statement of the continuing trajectory of social change in the west, the problem of 'American' versus 'Soviet' roads to modernity is more complex when applied to the non-western world.

In the first place the shift from ascriptive and particularistic towards more universalistic liberal-democratic institutions outside Europe and the western world is at best uneven and at worst precarious. Japan is of course important as the first major case of successful modernisation in a large non-western society. While possessing certain internal developmental advantages such as an integrated political system, the dynamic for Japan's development has increasingly come to be dominated by 'borrowed' western elements, involving a shift from patrimonial bureaucratic organisation in government and business toward democratic parliamentary institutions and individual achievement-orientation. Set against Japan, however, are a range of Third World countries that have either borrowed large elements of the centralised Soviet model, such as Cuba and Vietnam, or promoted relatively dynamic processes of social change on an ascribed, relatively undifferentiated basis, as in the resurgent Islamic societies like Pakistan, Malaysia and Iran.

In the face of this complexity, the recent history of post-Maoist China offers some indication that the Soviet route to modernity may be less typical of Third World socialism than has hitherto been thought. Maoism, while hostile to capitalism, individualism and a market economy, undoubtedly deviated from orthodox Soviet development strategies in its hostility to bureaucratisation, its commitment to mass political mobilisation and its conception of revolutionary society as conflictual not harmonious. While Maoism has itself been depicted as 'market socialism', policy changes since the death of Mao and the demise of the Gang of Four have introduced a much less ambiguous shift towards western conceptions of development. These have included the differentiation of economic goals, such as productivity and efficiency, from political and ideological controls, whether these stem from Soviet-like bureaucratic sources or from the mobilised peasant *Gemeinschaft* of Maoism. These changes in planning mechanisms have been associated with a trend towards consumer privatisation and pluralism in the economy, and a commitment to the rule of law and independence of the judiciary (Gray, 1982).

It would certainly be premature on the basis of this evidence to argue for the inexorable convergence of post-Maoist China with Parsons' western 'evolutionary universals'. China still retains a high degree of centralised planning and authority outside a democratic framework. On the other hand, recent developments do lend plausibility to the argument that non-western modes of social change may not, after all, be quite so refractory to Parsons' discussion as certain of his earlier critics believed. Parsons' evolutionary universals remain a fruitful addition to the repertoire of social change theory, even when non-Western developmental patterns are brought into consideration.

The most serious difficulty with Parsons' argument lies not at the level of convergent 'evolutionary universals' within leading nation-states, but at the level of inter-state relations. Parsons shares with his nineteenth-century forebears the tendency to consider change, in most cases as the product of the endogenous history of nation-states, supplemented only residually by diffusionist connections between one national unit and another. The neglect of exogenous influences that this approach entails (Smith, 1973) may be seen as a serious deficiency in the light of international economic and political relationships that transcend national limits. The recent development of Wallerstein's 'world system' theory (Wallerstein, 1974, 1980) and the revival of interest in international geo-politics (Mann, 1984) are in large measure post-Parsonian responses to the inadequacies of endogenous nation-state analysis. While the nation-state and nationalist allegiance remain extremely resilient, phenomena such as international capital movements by multinational companies, or the concentration of international political domination within two inter-locking super-powers, both suggest that the fate of most national units is determined to a large extent exogenously.

Parsons' social change theory may at first sight seem doubly disqualified from intervening in such debates. This is both because of its 'national endogenous' bias, and its tendency to look for a reciprocal basis to inter-changes between different elements within a social system. This logic is somewhat easier to locate in domestic intra-state relations, where 'social order' is deemed functionally necessary, than in international relations between economic or political collectivities, operating outside any 'societal community, yet which possess large measures of coercive power'.

There is of course no logical reason why Parsons' social system framework need be restricted to the internal operation of nation-states. While this may be testimony to the robustness of the formal specifications of the general theory of action and social systems, whatever the setting, it is clear that the problem of international relations and international order is very much 'residual' to the main thrust of his theory of change. However we should also note that a number of sociologists are concerned to develop Parsonian sociology towards a theory of international systems which would focus on the emergence of various forms of inter-societal culture. For example, there is some evidence of a certain 'globalisation' of culture above the system of nation-states (Nettl and Robertson, 1968; Robertson, 1982a). The issue here is to construct a sociological model of global culture which would be analogous to the Wallersteinian concept of 'world-system'. Although Parsonian sociology was initially focussed on the nation-state as a social system, Parsons' sociology can be developed at a more general level as a perspective on modernisation as a supra-national process.

The revival of neo-evolutionary optimism among Parsons and his American colleagues occurred at that somewhat fleeting and atypical historical moment in the late 1950s and early 1960s when the epoch of world war, fascism and capitalist collapse seemed past, and contemporary preoccupations such as the threat of nuclear war, ecological disaster and Third World famine were yet to be widely thematised. In addition, the first round of challenges to Parsonian evolutionary optimism tended to focus on domestic instabilities and conflicts connected with student radicalism and racial violence in the USA, that is on 'internal war', more than upon international disorder. In spite of events like the Cuban missile crisis of 1962, such domestic preoccupations have only subsequently become subsumed in questions of world politics.

While international relations do not feature in his key article 'Evolutionary universals' (Parsons, 1964d), they are addressed at more length in the paper 'Polarisation of the world and international order' (Parsons, 1967c) and more fleetingly in 'On the concept of political power' (Parsons, 1963f) and in 'The system of modern societies' (Parsons, 1971a). Here an attempt is made to cut through the fatalistic assumptions underlying much contemporary comment on world politics by adducing rational arguments in support of the emergent possibility of an international normative order. The problem here is couched in terms of the transcendence of the national territorial boundaries wherein commitments to normative order are generally contained. Having recognised that recourse to coercion has 'almost from time immemorial' been an 'endemic feature of relations between organised political systems', Parsons enumerates a number of possible indicators of an emergent, if rather vulnerable, international normative order. These include the ideological dimension of super-power conflict which presupposes a common frame of reference wherein differences make sense, the relative success of procedural norms for conflict resolution in international trade and international law with respect to persons, and the creation during the twentieth century of institutions like the United Nations for the first time in history. The further extension of these developments is incorporated within his discussion of evolutionary universals, by emphasis on the pluralistic rather than absolutist basis of political values, and on compromise rather than rigid commitment to final goals. While referring to the positive potential of non-aligned or neutral nations in undermining political absolutism, Parsons conceives of change very largely in terms of the triumph of western pluralism over the Soviet monolith. However, he does concede the importance of minimising the self-righteous implication that only we are true to these values, while our opponents are not!

It is not clear from this analysis how often and for what

reasons the west might not have been true to its own values. Parsons evades the paradox at the heart of liberal-democratic theory whereby 'illiberal' measures are justified as means of protecting liberalism from its illiberal opponents. The possibility that the illiberal defence of liberalism may become an apologetic myth for illiberalism itself is not discussed. For all this, Parsons' specification of the social preconditions for international order is symptomatic of what has been seen as the characteristically twentieth-century commitment to simultaneous support for the 'freedom' and continuing 'life' of the human species (Feher and Heller, 1984). Since his death, the development of mass peace movements can be interpreted as manifestations of a new ulti-mate value of novel historical significance. For Roth (1984), support for 'peace' as the precondition for the survival of the human species and society, transcends both the salvation concerns of religious virtuosi and the political Utopias of revol-utionaries. Peace movements may thereby be seen acting, in Parsonian terms, as 'steps in value-generalisation'. They presage a pluralistic international order free from the ascriptive politics of nationalism.

Although the lack of a sociology of the international order represents a major absence in Parsons' social change theory, it is arguable that Parsonian neo-evolutionary optimism represents a decisive advance beyond the two faces of classical sociology. Its modern character is to be seen both in the challenge to the Utopian mode of nineteenth-century evolutionary optimism, seeking to regenerate community around some version of the myth of *Gemeinschaft,* and to twentieth-century cultural pessi-mism in the face of privatised individualistic *Gesellschaft.* In contrast to Marx' eschatalogical stance towards the Communist future, Weber's stoic resignation in the face of the iron cage, and the Frankfurt School's despair at consumer society, Parsons accepts what he takes to be the universalistic thrust of modern society. This notion of universalism is grounded as much in a normative commitment to liberal-democratic pluralism, as in empirical analysis, but such normative elements are a crucial feature of all theories of social change. Pre-suppositionless, normatively irrelevant sociology is neither possible nor worth having.

Parsons' project does not involve subsuming the individual and private life under communitarian virtues akin to those of the ancient city-states, peasant village-life, or medieval guilds. Nor does Parsons expect the withering away of private property, bureaucratic administration or social conflict. Rather his evolutionism accepts the functional significance and integrity of modern social institutions. Here he follows the spirit of Durkheim's axiom that 'No persistent social practice can rest upon a lie'. What such institutions as the market, the rule of law, bureaucracy and political democracy have in common is their attempt to balance public equality of opportunity and reciprocity in exchange with diverse individual and associational 'ends'.

This is not to resurrect those rather crass versions of convergence theory in which free market capitalism is seen as the universal future for humankind. Parsons, in his critique of utilitarian economics, denies that an unregulated free market system devoid of extra-economic normative constraints could produce a stable social order. There is in other words no evolutionary advantage to social systems constructed on the basis of the unilateral domination of the free market. To think in these terms is to sacrifice social integration and distributive justice to productive efficiency. From this viewpoint Parsonian sociology might be utilised as the basis of a critique of the New Right programme of monetarism and the pursuit of welfare through the reconstitution of the traditional family. Parsons' 'evolutionary universals' are more consistent with Keynesian macro-economic planning within a mixed economy and positive legislative programmes to combat ascriptive inequalities, than with Chicago School economics and fundamentalist attempts to privatise welfare and de-secularise education. In this respect his prognoses for the American 'lead sector' in modernisation underestimated the possibility of the emergence of movements like the New Right.

Parsons' evolutionary optimism is muted, in the sense that he offers no utopian projection of social equilibrium in which social strains and conflict can ever be overcome. In this sense he is a more thorough-going conflict theorist than Marx. Although Parsons sometimes writes as if modernity were an endpoint which had actually been reached in the universalistic institutions of the western world, the formal characteristics of his

differentiation-reintegration model of change point rather to
modernity as an open-ended process of ever-enlarged evolutionary capacity. It should also be emphasised that this model
is not unilinear in the sense that there is no expectation that all
societies must inevitably follow one sequence of change. The
presence of a functional advantage within a social institution
gives no guarantee that the institution will always be preferred.

Parsons' sociology is therefore against nostalgia, for the
modern world, and unambiguously post-classical. Unlike
Weber, he did not believe that questions of value and morality
would remain totally refractory to solution, given the value-
conflict basic to secular society. Instead he developed a form of
liberal secular Protestantism geared especially to the needs of
American culture. It was his confidence in the possibility of
moral debate which prevented a premature pessimistic
conclusion to his thought. Parsons' legacy is therefore one
which avoids on the one hand the dilemmas of pessimistic
relativism and on the other avoids the problem of a purely
scientific view of reality, that is a scientific view grounded in a
simple positivism. Parsons provides us with a comprehensive
and general theory of social action and modernity which has
coherence, plausibility and relevance to moral and political
choices and activism. Parsons' sociology picks out for us a range
of critical issues in such fields as economic sociology, education,
sociology of knowledge, modernisation, professions, medical
sociology and social change which need further elaboration and
investigation. He also offers a general framework within which
all of this can be conceptualised. Our evaluation of Parsons
provides ample basis for abandoning the attitude of critical
aloofness which has so often characterised approaches to his
social thought. It also invites sociologists to move beyond
exegesis towards the further extension and critique of the
Parsonian research programme. Parsons' legacy is rich and
immensely stimulating. It is a legacy worth embracing.

# Bibliography of Talcott Parsons

1928    'Capitalism' in Recent German Literature: Sombart and Weber, I. *Journal of Political Economy*, vol. 36: 641–61.

1929    'Capitalism' in Recent German Literature: Sombart and Weber, II. *Journal of Political Economy*, vol. 37: 31–51.

1930    Max Weber, *The Protestant Ethic and the Spirit of Capitalism* (translated by Talcott Parsons), London: Allen & Unwin; New York: Scribner's.

1931    Wants and Activities in Marshall, *Quarterly Journal of Economics*, vol. 46: 101–40.

1932    Economics and Sociology: Marshall in Relation to the Thought of His Time, *Quarterly Journal of Economics*, vol. 46: 316–47.

1933    Malthus, *Encyclopedia of the Social Sciences*, vol. 10: 68–9. Pareto. *Encyclopedia of the Social Sciences*, vol. 11: 576–8.

1934a   Some Reflections on 'The Nature and Significance of Economics', *Quarterly Journal of Economics*, vol. 48: 511–45.

1934b   Society, *Encyclopedia of the Social Sciences*, vol. 14: 225–31.

1934c   Sociological Elements in Economic Thought, I, *Quarterly Journal of Economics*, vol. 49: 414–53.

1935a   Sociological Elements in Economic Thought, II, *Quarterly Journal of Economics*, vol. 49: 645–67.

1935b   The Place of Ultimate Values in Sociological Theory, *International Journal of Ethics*, vol. 45: 282–316.

1935c   H. M. Robertson on Max Weber and His School, *Journal of Political Economy*, vol. 43: 688–969.

1936a   Pareto's Central Analytical Scheme, *Journal of Social Philosophy*, vol. 1: 244–62.

1936b   On Certain Sociological Elements in Professor Taussig's Thought, *Explorations in Economics: Notes and Essays Contributed in Honor of F. W. Taussig*, Jacob Viner (ed.), New York, McGraw-Hill, pp. 352–79.

1937a   *The Structure of Social Action*, New York: McGraw-Hill. Reprint edition, 1949.

1937b   Education and the Professions, *International Journal of Ethics*, vol. 47: 365–9.

1938a   The Role of Theory in Social Research, *American Sociological Review*, vol. 3: 13–20. Address presented to the 1937 annual meeting of the Society for Social Research at the University of Chicago.

1938b   The Role of Ideas in Social Action, *American Sociological Review*, vol. 3: 653–64. Address written for a session on the problem of ideologies at the 1937 annual meeting of the American Sociological Society. Reprinted in *Essays in Sociologial Theory* (1949).

1939a   The Professions and Social Structure, *Social Forces*, vol. 17: 457–67. Address written for the 1938 annual meeting of the American Sociological Society. Reprinted in *Essays in Sociological Theory* (1949).

1939b   Comte, *Journal of Unified Science*, vol. 9: 77–83.

1940a   Analytical Approach to the Theory of Social Stratification, *American Journal of Sociology*, vol. 45: 841–62. Reprinted in *Essays in Sociological Theory* (1949).

1940b   Motivation of Economic Activities, *Canadian Journal of Economics and Political Science*, vol. 6: 187–203. Public lecture at the University of Toronto. Reprinted in *Essays in Sociological Theory* (1949) and in *Human Relations in Administration: The Sociology of Organization*, Robert Dubin (ed.).

1942a   Max Weber and the Contemporary Political Crisis, *Review of Politics*, vol. 4: 61–76, 155–72.

1942b   The Sociology of Modern Anti-Semitism, *Jews in a Gentile World*, J. Graeber and Stuart Henderson Britt (eds), New York, Macmillan, pp. 101–22.

1942c   Age and Sex in the Social Structure of the United States, *American Sociological Review*, vol. 7: 604–16. Address presented to the 1941 annual meeting of the American Sociological Society. Reprinted in *Essays in Sociological Theory* (1949); in *Sociological Analysis*, Logan Wilson and William Kolb (eds), and in *Personality in Nature, Society, and Culture*, Clyde Kluckhohn and Henry A. Murray (eds).

1942d   Propaganda and Social Control, *Psychiatry*, vol. 5 (no. 4): 551–72. Reprinted in *Essays in Sociological Theory* (1949).

1942e   Democracy and the Social Structure in Pre-Nazi Germany,

*Journal of Legal and Political Sociology*, vol. 1: 96–114. Reprinted in *Essays in Sociological Theory*, revised edition (1954).

1942f    Some Sociological Aspects of the Fascist Movements, *Social Forces*, vol. 21 (no. 2): 138–47. Presidential address presented at the 1942 annual meeting of the Eastern Sociological Society. Reprinted in *Essays in Sociological Theory*, revised edition (1954).

1943    The Kinship System of the Contemporary United States, *American Anthropologist*, vol. 45: 22–38. Reprinted in *Essays in Sociological Theory* (1949).

1944    The Theoretical Development of the Sociology of Religion, *Journal of the History of Ideas*, vol. 5: 176–90. Reprinted in *Essays in Sociological Theory* (1949) and in *Ideas in Cultural Perspective*, Philip Wiener and Aaron Noland (eds), New Brunswick, Rutgers University Press, 1962.

1945a    The Present Position and Prospects of Systematic Theory in Sociology, *Twentieth Century Sociology*, Georges Gurvitch and Wilbert E. Moore (eds), New York, Philosophical Library. Reprinted in *Essays in Sociological Theory* (1949).

1945b    The Problem of Controlled Institutional Change: An Essay on Applied Social Science, *Psychiatry*, vol. 8: 79–101. Prepared as an appendix to the *Report on the Conference on Germany after World War II*. Reprinted in *Essays in Sociological Theory* (1949).

1945c    Racial and Religious Differences as Factors in Group Tensions, *Unity and Difference in the Modern World*, Louis Finkelstein et al. (eds), New York, Conference of Science, Philosophy, and Religion in Their Relation to the Democratic Way of Life.

1946a    The Science Legislation and the Role of the Social Sciences, *American Sociological Review*, vol. 11 (no. 6): 653–66.

1946b    Population and Social Structure, *Japan's Prospect*, Douglas G. Haring (ed.), Cambridge, Mass., Harvard University Press, pp. 87–114. (This book was published by the staff of the Harvard School for Overseas Administration.) Reprinted in *Essays in Sociological Theory*, revised edition (1954).

1946c    Certain Primary Sources and Patterns of Aggression in the Social Structure of the Western World, *Psychiatry*, vol. 10: 167–81. Reprinted in *Essays in Sociological Theory* (1949) and as 'The Structure of Group Hostility', in *Crisis and Continuity in World Politics* (2nd ed.), G. Lanyi and W. McWilliams (eds), New York, Random House, 1973, pp. 220–3.

1946d    Some Aspects of the Relations between Social Science and Ethics, *Social Science*, vol. 22: 23–217. Address presented to the 1946 annual meeting of the American Association for the Advancement of Science.

1947a    Science Legislation and the Social Sciences, *Bulletin of Atomic Scientists* (January). Reprinted in *Political Science Quarterly*, vol. 62 (no. 2).

1947b    *Max Weber: The Theory of Social and Economic Organization* (co-edited and translated with A. M. Henderson), Oxford University Press, Introduction by T. Parsons. (The Introduction was reprinted in *Essays in Sociological Theory*, first edition, 1949). Reprinted by the Free Press (1957).

1948a    Sociology, 1941–1946 (co-authored with Bernard Barber), *American Journal of Sociology*, vol. 53: 245–57.

1948b    The Position of Sociological Theory, *American Sociological Review*, vol. 13, 156–71. Address presented to the 1947 annual meeting of the American Sociological Society. Reprinted in *Essays in Sociological Theory* (1949).

1949a    *Essays in Sociological Theory Pure and Applied*, Chicago, Free Press, revised edition 1954.

1949b    The Rise and Decline of Economic Man, *Journal of General Education*, vol. 4: 47–53.

1949c    Social Classes and Class Conflict in the Light of Recent Sociological Theory, *American Economic Review*, vol. 39: 16–26. Address presented to the 1948 annual meeting of the American Economics Association. Reprinted in *Essays in Sociological Theory*, revised edition (1954).

1949d    *The Structure of Social Action* (reprint edition), Chicago, Free Press.

1950a    The Prospects of Sociological Theory, *American Sociological Review*, vol. 15 (no. 1): 3–16. Presidential address presented to the 1949 annual meeting of the American Sociological Society. Reprinted in *Essays in Sociological Theory*, revised edition (1954).

1950b    Psychoanalysis and the Social Structure, *Psychoanalytic Quarterly*, vol. 19: 371–84. Substance of this paper was presented at the 1948 annual meeting of the American Psychoanalytic Association. Reprinted in *Essays in Sociological Theory*, revised edition (1954).

1950c    The Social Environment of the Educational Process, *Centennial*, Washington, D.C.: American Association for the Advancement of Science, pp. 36–40. Address presented to the AAAS Centennial Celebration (September 1948).

1951a    *The Social System*, Chicago, Free Press.

1951b    *Toward a General Theory of Action*, Editor and contributor with Edward A. Shils et al., Cambridge, Mass., Harvard University Press. Reprinted, Harper Torchbooks, 1962.

1951c    Graduate Training in Social Relations at Harvard, *Journal of General Education*, vol. 5: 149–57.

1951d    Illness and the Role of the Physician: A Sociological Perspective. *American Journal of Orthopsychiatry*, vol. 21: 452–60. Address presented to the 1951 annual meeting of the American Orthopsychiatry Association. Reprinted in *Personality in Nature, Society, and Culture* (2nd ed.), Clyde Kluckhohn, Henry A. Murray, and David M. Schneider (eds), New York, Knopf, 1953.

1952a    The Superego and the Theory of Social Systems, *Psychiatry*, vol. 15: 15–25. Substance of this paper was presented at the 1951 meeting of the Psychoanalytic Section of the American Psychiatric Association. Reprinted in *Social Structure and Personality* (1964) and in *Working Papers in the Theory of Action* (2nd ed.), Talcott Parsons, Robert F. Bales, and Edward A. Shils (eds), Chicago, Free Press, 1953 and 1967.

1952b    Religious Perspectives in College Teaching: Sociology and Social Psychology, *Religious Perspectives in College Teaching*, Hoxie N. Fairchild (ed.), New York, Ronald Press, pp. 286–337.

1952c    A Sociologist Looks at the Legal Profession, *Conference on the Profession of Law and Legal Education*. Conference Series Number II, Chicago: Law School, University of Chicago, pp. 49–63. Address presented to the Fiftieth Anniversary Celebration of the University of Chicago Law School (December 1952). Reprinted in *Essays in Sociological Theory* (1954).

1953a    *Working Papers in the Theory of Action* (in collaboration with Robert F. Bales and Edward A. Shils), Chicago, Free Press. Reprint edition 1967.

1953b    Psychoanalysis and Social Science with Special Reference to the Oedipus Problem, *Twenty Years of Psychoanalysis*, Franz Alexander and Helen Ross (eds), New York, Norton, pp. 186–215. Substance of this paper was presented to the Twentieth Anniversary Celebration of the Institute for Psychoanalysis (October 1952).

1953c    A Revised Analytical Approach to the Theory of Social Stratification, *Class, Status, and Power: A Reader in Social Stratification*, Reinhard Bendix and Seymour M. Lipset (eds), Chicago, Free Press, pp. 92–129. Reprinted in *Essays in Sociological Theory* (1954).

1953d    Illness, Therapy, and the Modern Urban American Family (co-authored with Renee C. Fox), *Journal of Social Issues*, vol. 8: 31–44. Reprinted in *Patients, Physicians, and Illness*, E. Gartly Jaco (ed.), Chicago, Free Press, 1958.

1953e  Some Comments on the State of the General Theory of Action, *American Sociological Review*, vol. 18 (no. 6): 618–31.

1954a  The Father Symbol: An Appraisal in the Light of Psychoanalytic and Sociological Theory, *Symbols and Values: An Initial Study*, Bryson, Finkelstein, MacIver, and McKeon (eds), New York, Harper & Row, pp. 523–44. Substance of this paper was presented to the 1952 annual meeting of the American Psychological Association. Reprinted in *Social Structure and Personality* (1964).

1954b  *Essays in Sociological Theory* (rev. ed.), Chicago, Free Press.

1954c  Psychology and Sociology. *For a Science of Social Man*, John P. Gillin (ed.), New York: Macmillan, pp. 67–102.

1954d  The Incest Taboo in Relation to Social Structure and the Socialization of the Child, *British Journal of Sociology*, vol. 5 (no. 2): 101–17.

1955a  *Family, Socialization, and Interaction Process* (co-authored with Robert F. Bales, James Olds, Morris Zelditch, and Philip E. Slater), Chicago, Free Press.

1955b  'McCarthyism' and American Social Tension: A Sociologist's View, *Yale Review*, 226–45. Reprinted as 'Social Strains in America', in *The New American Right*, Daniel Bell (ed.), New York, Criterion Books.

1956a  *Economy and Society* (co-authored with Neil J. Smelser), London, Routledge & Kegan Paul; Chicago, Free Press.

1956b  *Eléments pour une théorie de l'action* (translated, with an introduction, by François Bourricaud), Paris, Plon.

1956c  A Sociological Approach to the Theory of Organizations, I, *Administrative Science Quarterly* (June): 63–85. Reprinted in *Structure and Process in Modern Society* (1960).

1956d  A Sociological Approach to the Theory of Organizations, II, *Administrative Science Quarterly* (September): 225–39. Reprinted in *Structure and Process in Modern Society* (1960).

1957a  The Distribution of Power in American Society, *World Politics*, vol. 10 (October): 123–43. Reprinted in *Structure and Process in Modern Society* (1960).

1957b  Malinowski and the Theory of Social Systems, *Man and Culture*. Raymond Firth (ed.), London, Routledge & Kegan Paul.

1957c  Man in His Social Environment – As Viewed by Modern Social Science, *Centennial Review of Arts and Sciences*, vol. 1 (no. 1): 50–69.

1957d  The Mental Hospital as a Type of Organization, *The Patient and the Mental Hospital*, Milton Greenblatt, Daniel J. Levinson, and Richard H. Williams (eds), Chicago, Free Press.

1957e    Réflexions sur les organisations religieuses aux Etats-Unis, *Archives de la sociologie des religions* (January–June): 21–36.

1957f    *Sociologia di dittatura*, Bologna: Il Molino.

1957g    La teoria de la accion, *Boletin del Instituto de Sociologia*, vol. 10 (no. 1): 1–68.

1958a    Authority, Legitimation, and Political Action, *Authority*, C. J. Friedrich (ed.), Cambridge, Mass., Harvard University Press. Reprinted in *Structure and Process in Modern Society* (1960).

1958b    The Definitions of Health and Illness in the Light of American Values and Social Structure, *Patients, Physicians and Illness*, E. Gartly Jaco (ed.), Chicago, Free Press. Reprinted in *Social Structure and Personality* (1964). Translated into German as 'Definition von Gesundheit und Krankheit im Lichte der Wertbegriffe und der sozialen Struktur Amerikas'.

1958c    Social Structure and the Development of Personality, *Psychiatry* (November): 321–40. Reprinted in *Social Structure and Personality* (1964).

1958d    General Theory in Sociology, *Sociology Today*, Robert K. Merton, Leonard Broom, and Leonard S. Cottrell, Jr (eds), New York, Basic Books.

1958e    Some Ingredients of a General Theory of Formal Organization, *Administrative Theory in Education*, Andrew W. Halpin (ed.), Chicago: Midwest Administration Center, University of Chicago. Reprinted in *Structure and Process in Modern Society* (1960).

1958f    Some Reflections on the Institutional Framework of Economic Development, *The Challenge of Development: A Symposium*. Jerusalem: Hebrew University. Reprinted in *Structure and Process in Modern Society* (1960).

1958g    Some Trends of Change in American Society: Their Bearing on Medical Education, *Journal of the American Medical Association*, vol. 167 (no. 1): 31–6. Reprinted in *Structure and Process in Modern Society* (1960).

1958h    The Pattern of Religious Organization in the United States, *Daedalus* (Summer): 65–85. Reprinted in *Structure and Process in Modern Society* (1960).

1958i    The Concepts of Culture and of Social System (co-authored with A. L. Kroeber), *American Sociological Review* (October): 582. Reprinted in *Ideas of Culture: Sources and Uses*, Frederick Gamst and Edward Norbeck (eds), New York, Holt, Rinehart & Winston, 1976.

1958j    A Short Account of My Intellectual Development, *Alpha Kappa Deltan*, Claremont, Pomona College, pp. 3–12.

1959a    An Approach to Psychological Theory in Terms of the Theory of Action, *Psychology: A Study of a Science*, Sigmund Koch (ed.), New York, McGraw-Hill, vol. 3: 612–711.

1959b    The Principal Structures of Community: A Sociological View, *Community*, C. J. Friedrich (ed.), New York, Liberal Arts Press. Reprinted in *Structure and Process in Modern Society* (1960).

1959c    'Voting' and the Equilibrium of the American Political System, *American Voting Behavior*, Eugene Burdick and Arthur Brodbeck (eds), Chicago, Free Press.

1959d    Comment on 'American Intellectuals: Their Politics and Status', *Daedalus*, vol. 88 (no. 3): 493–5.

1959e    Durkheim's Contribution to the Theory of Integration of Social Systems, *Emile Durkheim, 1858–1917: A Collection of Essays, with Translation and a Bibliography*, Kurt H. Wolff (ed.), Columbus, Ohio State University Press, 1959.

1959f    Implications of the Study ('Book Selection and Retention in California Public and School Libraries', by Marjorie Fiske), *The Climate of Book Selection*, a symposium of the University of California School of Librarianship, Berkeley, University of California Press.

1959g    Some Problems Confronting Sociology as a Profession, *American Sociological Review*, vol. 24 (no. 4): 547–59.

1959h    The School Class as a Social System, *Harvard Educational Review*, (Fall). Reprinted in *Social Structure and Personality* (1964) and in *Education, Economy, and Society*, A. H. Halsey, Jean Floud, and Arnold C. Anderson (eds), New York, Free Press, 1961. Also reprinted in *Socialization and Schools*, Reprint Series No. 1, compiled from the *Harvard Educational Review*, 1972: 69–90.

1959i    An Approach to the Sociology of Knowledge, *Proceedings of the Fourth World Congress of Sociology* (Milan, Italy), vol. 4: 25–49.

1960a    Mental Illness and 'Spiritual Malaise': The Roles of the Psychiatrist and of the Minister of Religion, *The Ministry and Mental Health*, Hans Hofmann (ed.), New York: Association Press. Reprinted in *Social Structure and Personality* (1964).

1960b    *Structure and Process in Modern Society* (A collection of essays), Chicago, Free Press.

1960c    In memoriam: 'Clyde Kluckhohn, 1905–1960', *American Sociological Review* (August).

1960d    Commentary on *The Mass Media and the Structure of American Society* (co-authored with Winston White), *Journal of Social Issues*, vol. 16, (no. 3): 67–77.

1960e    Pattern Variables Revisited: A Response to Professor Dubin's Stimulus, *American Sociological Review* (August).

1960f    Toward a Healthy Maturity, *Journal of Health and Human Behavior*, vol. 1 (Fall): 163–73. Reprinted in *Social Structure and Personality* (1964).

1960g    Social Structure and Political Orientation: A review of *Political Man*, by Seymour M. Lipset, and *The Politics of Mass Society*, by William Kornhauser, *World Politics*, vol. 13 (October): 112–28.

1960h    Review of *Max Weber: An Intellectual Portrait*, by Reinhard Bendix, *American Sociological Review* (October).

1960i    The Physician in a Changing Society, *What's New*, no. 220: 11–12.

1961a    *Theories of Society* (two vols) (co-edited with Edward Shils, Kaspar D. Naegele, and Jesse R. Pitts), New York, Free Press.

1961b    Some Principal Characteristics of Industrial Societies, *The Transformation of Russian Society since 1861*, C. E. Black (ed.), Cambridge, Mass., Harvard University Press. Reprinted in *Structure and Process in Modern Society* (1960).

1961c    The Link between Character and Society (co-authored with Winston White), *Culture and Social Character*, S. M. Lipset and Leo Lowenthal (eds), New York, Free Press. Reprinted in *Social Structure and Personality* (1964).

1961d    The Contribution of Psychoanalysis to the Social Sciences, *Science and Psychoanalysis*, vol. 4.

1961e    The Cultural Background of American Religious Organization, *Proceedings of the Conference on Science, Philosophy and Religion*.

1961f    The Point of View of the Author, *The Social Theories of Talcott Parsons*, Max Black (ed.), Englewood Cliffs, Prentice-Hall.

1961g    The Problem of International Community, *International Politics and Foreign Policy*, James N. Rosenau (ed.), New York, Free Press.

1961h    Polarization of the World and International Order. *Preventing World War III*. Q. Wright, W. M. Evan and M. Deutsch (eds), New York, Simon & Schuster. Also in the *Berkeley Journal of Sociology* (1961).

1961i    Some Considerations on the Theory of Social Change, *Rural Sociology*, vol. 26 (no. 3).

1961j    A Sociologist's View, *Values and Ideals of American Youth*, Eli Ginzberg (ed.), New York, Columbia University Press.

1961k    Comment on 'Preface to a Metatheoretical Framework for Sociology', by Llewellyn Gross, *American Journal of Sociology*, vol. 68 (no. 2): 136–40.

1961l    In memoriam: 'Alfred L. Kroeber, 1876–1960', *American Journal of Sociology*, vol. 67 (no. 6): 616–17.

1961m   Comment on 'Images of Man and the Sociology of Religion', by William Kolb, *Journal for the Scientific Study of Religion* (October).

1961n   Discussion of Trends Revealed by the 1960 Census of Population. *Proceedings of the American Statistical Association Section on Social Statistics*, American Statistical Association.

1961o   Clyde Kluckhohn, Anthropologist, *Science*, vol. 144 (no. 3464): 1584.

1962a   Foreword to *Herbert Spencer. The Study of Sociology*, Ann Arbor, University of Michigan Press (paperback).

1962b   In memoriam: 'Clyde Kluckhohn, 1905–1960' (co-authored with Evon Z. Vogt), *American Anthropologist*, vol. 64 (no. 1), pt. 1: 140–61. Reprinted as the Introduction to a new edition of Clyde Kluckhohn, *Navajo Witchcraft*, Boston, Beacon, 1962.

1962c   Comment on 'The Oversocialized Conception of Man', by Dennis Wrong, *Psychoanalysis and Psychoanalytic Review* (Summer).

1962d   Review of *Law and Social Process*, by Hurst, *Journal of the History of Ideas*, vol. 23 (no. 4): 558–65.

1962e   The Aging in American Society, *Law and Contemporary Problems*, vol. 27 (no. 1): 22–35.

1962f   The Law and Social Control, *Law and Sociology*, William M. Evan (ed.), New York, Free Press.

1962g   In memoriam: 'Richard Henry Tawney, 1880–1961', *American Sociological Review* (December).

1962h   Review of *Reason in Society: Five Types of Decision and Their Social Conditions*, by Paul Diesing, *Industrial and Labor Relations Review*, vol. 16 (no. 4): 630–1.

1962i   *La Struttura dell' azione sociale* (introduction by Gianfranco Poggi), Bologna: Il Molino. Translation of *The Structure of Social Action* (1937).

1962j   Considerazione teoriche intorno alla sociologia della medicina, Estratto dai *Quaderni di sociologia*, vol. 11 (no. 3): 243–79.

1962k   The Cultural Background of American Religious Organization, *Ethics and Bigness: Scientific, Academic, Religious, Political, and Military*, Harlan Cleveland and Harold D. Lasswell (eds), New York, Conference on Science, Philosophy, and Religion in Their Relation to the Democratic Way of Life, pp. 141–67.

1962l   Youth in the Context of American Society, *Daedalus* (Winter): 97–123. Reprinted in *Social Structure and Personality* (1964) and in *Youth: Change and Challenge*, Erik H. Erikson (ed.), New York, Basic Books, 1963.

1963a   Introduction to Max Weber, *The Sociology of Religion* (translated by Ephraim Fischoff from *Wirtschaft and Gesellschaft*), Boston, Beacon.

1963b   Social Strains in America: A Postscript (1962), *The Radical Right*, Daniel Bell (ed.), Garden City, Doubleday.

1963c   Christianity and Modern Industrial Society, *Sociological Theory, Values, and Sociocultural Change: Essays in Honor of Pitirim A. Sorokin*, Edward A. Tiryakian (ed.), New York, Free Press, pp. 33–70.

1963d   Social Change and Medical Organization in the United States: A Sociological Perspective, *Annals of the American Academy of Political and Social Science*, vol. 346: 22–3.

1963e   On the Concept of Influence (with rejoinder to comments), *Public Opinion Quarterly* (Spring). Reprinted in *Sociological Theory and Modern Society* (1967).

1963f   On the Concept of Political Power, *Proceedings of the American Philosophical Society*, vol. 107 (no. 3): 232–62. Reprinted in *Sociological Theory and Modern Society* (1967). Translated into Italian as 'Il concetto di potere politico', I. *Il Politico* (University of Pavia), vol. 28 (no. 3): 614–36. 'Il concetto di potere politico', II. Ibid. (no. 4): 830–955.

1963g   Death in American Society (co-authored with Victor M. Lidz), *American Behavioral Scientist* (May): 1963. Reprinted in *Essays in Self-Destruction*, Edwin Schneidman (ed.), New York, Science House, 1967.

1963h   Old Age as Consummatory Phase, *Gerontologist*, vol. 3 (no. 2): 53–4.

1963i   The Intellectual: a social role category, in P. Rieff (ed.), *On Intellectuals*, Garden City, Anchor, pp. 3–24.

1964a   Some Theoretical Considerations Bearing on the Field of Medical Sociology, Written for a symposium that did not take place. Published in *Social Structure and Personality* (1964).

1964b   *Social Structure and Personality* (A collection of essays), New York, Free Press.

1964c   The Ideas of Systems, Causal Explanation, and Cybernetic Control in Social Science, *Cause and Effect*, Daniel Lerner (ed.), New York, Free Press. Address presented at the Fourth Hayden Colloquium, Massachusetts Institute of Technology (1964).

1964d   Evolutionary Universals in Society, *American Sociological Review*, vol. 29 (no. 3): 339–57. Translated into German as 'Evolutionare Universalien der Gesellschaft'. Reprinted in *Essays on Modernization of Underdeveloped Societies*, A. R. Desai (ed.), Bombay, Thacker, pp. 560–88.

1964e    Max Weber, 1864–1964, *American Sociological Review*, vol. 30 (no. 2): 171–5.

1964f    Sociological Theory, *Encyclopedia Britannica*.

1964g    Some Reflections on the Place of Force in Social Process, *Internal War: Basic Problems and Approaches*, Harry Eckstein (ed.), New York, Free Press.

1964h    Levels of Organization and the Mediation of Social Interaction, *Sociological Inquiry* (Spring): 207–20.

1964i    Die Juengsten Entwicklungen in Der Strukturell-Funksionalem Theorie, *Koeiner Zeitschrift fuer Soziologie and Sozial-psychologie*, pp. 30–49. (English version in Haring *Festschrift*.)

1964j    Youth in the Context of American Society, *Man in a World at Work*, Henry Borow (ed.), Boston: Houghton Mifflin. Modified version of an article previously written for *Daedalus* (1961).

1964k    Unity and Diversity in the Modern Intellectual Disciplines: The Role of the Social Sciences, *Daedalus* (Winter) 1965: 39–65.

1964l    La Théorie de la société, *Les Etudes philosophiques, perspectives sur la philosophie nord-americaine*, vol. 3 (no. 4): 537–47.

1964m    Commentary, *Crane Review*, vol. 7 (no. 2): 92–7. Address presented to the First Crane Conference on the Ministry (October 1963).

1965a    An American's Impression of Sociology in the Soviet Union, *American Sociological Review*, vol. 30 (no. 1): 121–5.

1965b    Full Citizenship for the Negro American? *Daedalus* (November). Reprinted in *The Negro American*, Talcott Parsons and Kenneth Clark (eds), Boston, Houghton Mifflin, 1966.

1965c    Changing Family Patterns in American Society, *The American Family in Crisis*, Forest Hospital, Des Plaines, Ill.: Forest Hospital Publications, vol. 3: 4–10.

1965d    Max Weber, 1864–1964, *American Sociological Review*, vol. 30 (no. 2): 171–5.

1965e    Evaluation and Objectivity in the Social Sciences: An Interpretation of Max Weber's Contributions, *International Journal of the Social Sciences*. Reprinted in *Sociological Theory and Modern Society* and in *Max Weber and Sociology Today*, K. Morris (trans.), New York, Harper & Row, 1971. This address presented to the Weber Centennial (April 1964) was published first in German (*Wertgebundenheit und Objektivitat in den Sozialwissenschaften*: Eine Interpretation der Beitrage Max Webers) in *Max Weber und die Soziologie Heute*, Otto Stammer (ed.), Tubingen, Mohr, pp. 39–64.

1966a    *Societies: Evolutionary and Comparative Perspectives*, Englewood Cliffs, Prentice-Hall.

1966b    The Political Aspect of Social Structure and Process, *Varieties of Political Theory*, David Easton (ed.), Englewood Cliffs, Prentice-Hall.

1966c    *The Negro American* (co-edited with Kenneth Clark), Boston: Houghton Mifflin.

1966d    Die Bedeutung der Polarisierung fur das Sozialsystem: Die Hautfarbe als Polarisierungsproblem, *Militanter Humanismus*, Alphons Silbermann (ed.), Frankfurt, Fischer.

1966e    'Religion in a modern pluralistic society', *Review of Religious Research*, vol. 7, pp. 125–46.

1967a    The Nature of American Pluralism, *Religion and Public Education*, Theodore Sizer (ed.), Boston, Houghton Mifflin.

1967b    Social Science and Theology, *America and the Future of Theology*, William A. Beardslee (ed.), Philadelphia, Westminster.

1967c    *Sociological Theory and Modern Society*, New York, Free Press.

1967d    Death in American Society (co-authored with Victor M. Lidz), *Essays in Self-Destruction*, Edwin Shneidman (ed.), New York, Science House.

1967e    Comment on 'An Economist Looks at the Future of Sociology', by Kenneth Boulding et al., vol. 1 (no. 2).

1967f    *Working Papers in the Theory of Action* (reprint edition) (in collaboration with Robert F. Bales and Edward A. Shils), New York, Free Press.

1967g    'Social science and theology' in W. A. Beardslee (ed.), *America and the Future of Theology*, Philadelphia, Westminster, pp. 136–57.

1968a    Components and Types of Formal Organization, *Comparative Administrative Theory*, Preston P. LeBreton (ed.), Seattle, University of Washington Press.

1968b    Comment on 'The Future of the Nineteenth Century Idea of a University', by Sir Eric Ashby, *Minerva* (Spring).

1968c    *American Sociology* (A collection of essays edited by Talcott Parsons), New York, Basic Books.

1968d    Commentary on 'Religion as a Cultural System', by Clifford Geertz, *The Religious Situation: 1968*, Donald R. Cutler (ed.), Boston, Beacon.

1968e    Christianity. Emile Durkheim. Interaction: Social Interaction. Vilfredo Pareto: Contributions to Economics. Professions. Systems Analysis: Social Systems. Utilitarians: Social Thought, *International Encyclopedia of the Social Sciences*, David L. Sills (ed.), New York, Macmillan and Free Press.

1968f    The Position of Identity in the General Theory of Action, *The*

*Self in Social Interaction,* Chad Gordon and Kenneth J. Gergen (eds), New York, Wiley.

1968g    *The American Academic Profession: A Pilot Study* (co-authored with Gerald M. Platt), Cambridge, Mass., multilith (out of print).

1968h    The Academic System: A Sociologist's View, *Public Interest* (special issue), no. 13 (Fall).

1968i    On the Concept of Value-Commitments, *Sociological Inquiry,* vol. 38 (no. 2). Reprinted in *Politics and Social Structure,* New York, Free Press, 1969.

1968j    Cooley and the Problem of Internalization, *Cooley and Sociological Analysis,* Albert J. Reiss, Jr. (ed.), Ann Arbor, University of Michigan Press.

1968k    Sociocultural Pressures and Expectations (A paper presented to the American Psychiatric Association), *Psychiatric Research Reports* (February).

1968l    Order as a Sociological Problem, *The Concept of Order,* Paul G. Kuntz (ed.), Seattle, University of Washington Press.

1968m    The Problem of Polarization on the Axis of Color, *Color and Race,* John Hope Franklin (ed.), Boston, Houghton Mifflin.

1968n    Considerations on the American Academic System (co-authored with Gerald M. Platt), *Minerva,* vol. 6 (no. 4).

1968o    Law and Sociology: A Promising Courtship? *The Path of the Law from 1967,* Harvard Law School Sesquicentennial Papers, Arthur E. Sutherland (ed.), Cambridge, Mass., Harvard University Press.

1968p    The Disciplines as a Differentiating Force (co-authored with Norman Storer), *The Foundations of Access to Knowledge,* Edward B. Montgomery (ed.), Syracuse, Division of Summer Sessions, Syracuse University.

1969a    Research with Human Subjects and the 'Professional Complex', *Daedalus* (Spring), Chapter 2 of this volume.

1969b    *Politics and Social Structure,* New York, Free Press.

1969c    On Stinchcombe's Conceptualization of Power Phenomena: A Review of *Constructing Social Theories,* by Arthur L. Stinchcombe, *Sociological Inquiry* (May): 226–31.

1969d    '"The intellectual": a social role category' in Philip Rieff (ed.), *On Intellectuals,* New York, Doubleday, 1969, pp. 3–26.

1970a    Some Problems of General Theory in Sociology, *Theoretical Sociology: Perspectives and Developments,* John C. McKinney and Edward A. Tiryakian (eds), New York, Appleton-Century-Crofts.

1970b    Age, Social Structure, and Socialization in Higher Education (co-authored with Gerald M. Platt), *Sociology of Education*, vol. 43 (no. 1).

1970c    Decision-Making in the Academic System: Influence and Power Exchange (co-authored with Gerald M. Platt), *The State of the University: Authority and Change*, Carlos E. Kruythosch and Sheldon I. Messinger (eds), Beverly Hills, Sage Publications.

1970d    Theory in the Humanities and Sociology, *Daedalus*, vol. 99 (no. 2).

1970e    The Impact of Technology on Culture and Emerging New Modes of Behavior, *International Social Science Journal*, vol. 22 (no. 4).

1970f    Equality and Inequality in Modern Society, or Social Stratification Revisited, *Sociological Inquiry*, vol. 40 (Spring): 13–72.

1970g    On Building Social Systems Theory: A Personal History, *Daedalus*, vol. 99 (no. 4). Reprinted in *The 20th Century Sciences: Studies in the Biography of Ideas*, Gerald Holton (ed.), New York, Norton, 1972.

1970h    Some Considerations on the Comparative Sociology of Education, *The Social Sciences and the Comparative Study of Educational Systems*, Joseph Fischer (ed.), Scranton, International Textbook.

1971a    *The System of Modern Societies*, Englewood Cliffs, Prentice-Hall. Companion volume to *Societies: Evolutionary and Comparative Perspectives* (1966).

1971b    Kinship and the Associational Aspects of Social Structure, *Kinship and Culture*, Francis L. K. Hsu (ed.), Chicago, Aldine.

1971c    Comparative Studies and Evolutionary Change, *Comparative Methods in Sociology*, Ivan Vallier (ed.), Berkeley, University of California Press, pp. 97–139.

1971d    The Normal American Family, *Readings on the Sociology of the Family*, Bert N. Adams and Thomas Weirath (eds), Chicago, Markham, pp. 53–66. Reprinted from *Man and Civilization: The Family's Search for Survival*, Farber, Mustacchi, and Wilson, New York, McGraw-Hill, 1965.

1971e    Belief. Unbelief, and Disbelief, *The Culture of Unbelief: Studies and Proceedings from the First International Symposium on Belief*, Rocco Caporale and Antonio Grumelli (ed.), Berkeley, University of California Press, pp. 207–45.

1972a    Higher Education as a Theoretical Focus, *Institutions and Social Exchange: The Sociologies of Talcott Parsons and George C. Homans*. Richard Simpson and Herman Turk (eds), Indianapolis, Bobbs-Merrill.

1972b     Higher Education, Changing Socialization, and Contemporary
          Student Dissent (co-authored with Gerald M. Platt), *Aging and
          Society*, vol. 3: *A Sociology of Age Stratification*, Matilda W. Riley,
          Marilyn E. Johnson, Anne Foner, New York, Russell Sage.
1972c     Commentary on 'Structural-Functionalism, Exchange Theory
          and the New Political Economy: Institutionalization as a
          Theoretical Linkage' by Terry Clark, *Sociological Inquiry*, vol.
          42 (nos 3–4): 299–308.
1972d     *Readings on Premodern Societies* (co-edited with Victor M. Lidz),
          Englewood Cliffs, Prentice-Hall.
1972e     Field Theory and Systems Theory: With Special Reference
          to the Relations Between Psychological and Social Systems,
          *Modern Psychiatry and Clinical Research: Essays in Honor of Roy
          R. Grinker, Sr.*, Daniel Offer and Daniel X. Freedman (eds),
          New York, Basic Books.
1972f     The Action Frame of Reference and the General Theory of
          Action Systems. *Classic Contributions to Social Psychology: Read-
          ings with Commentary*, Edwin P. Hollander and Raymond G.
          Hunt (eds), New York, Oxford University Press, pp. 168–76.
          Slightly abridged from *The Social System*, New York, Free
          Press, 1951, pp. 3–11, 15–19.
1972g     The 'Gift of Life' and Its Reciprocation (co-authored with
          Renee C. Fox and Victor M. Lidz), *Social Research*, vol. 39 (no.
          3): 367–415. Reprinted in *Death in American Experience*, Arien
          Mack (ed.), New York, Schocken, 1973, pp. 1–49.
1972h     Review of *Scholarship and Partisanship*, by Reinhard Bendix and
          Guenther Roth, *Contemporary Sociology*, vol. 1 (no. 3): 200–3.
1972i     Culture and Social System Revisited, *Social Science Quarterly*.
          (September): 253–66. Reprinted in *The Idea of Culture in the
          Social Sciences*, Louis Schneider and Charles Bonjean (eds),
          Cambridge: University Press, 1973, pp. 33–46.
1973a     Durkheim on Religion Revisited: Another Look at *The Elemen-
          tary Forms of the Religious Life, Beyond the Classics? Essays in the
          Scientific Study of Religion*, Charles Y. Glock and Phillip E.
          Hammond (eds), New York, Harper Torchbooks, pp. 156–80.
1973b     *The American University* (co-authored with Gerald M. Platt and
          in collaboration with Neil J. Smelser), Cambridge, Mass.,
          Harvard University Press.
1973c     Clyde Kluckhohn and the Integration of Social Science, *Culture
          and Life: Essays in Memory of Clyde Kluckhohn*, Walter W. Taylor,
          John L. Fischer, and Evon Z. Vogt (eds), Carbondale,
          Southern Illinois University Press, pp. 30–57.
1973d     Review of *A Critique of Max Weber's Philosophy of Social Science*,
          by W. G. Runciman, *Political Science Quarterly*.

1973e    The Bellah Case: Man and God in Princeton, New Jersey, *Commonwealth*, vol. 98 (no. 11): 256–9.

1973f    Religious Symbolization and Death, *Changing Perspectives in the Scientific Study of Religion*, Allan Eister (ed.), New York, Wiley-Interscience.

1973g    Some Reflections on Post-Industrial Society, *Japanese Sociological Review*, vol. 24 (no. 2): 109–13. Address presented to the Japan Sociological Association (September 1973).

1973h    The Problem of Balancing Rational Efficiency with Communal Solidarity in Modern Society, *International Symposium on 'New Problems of Advanced Societies'*, Tokyo, Japan Economic Research Institute, pp. 9–14.

1973i    The Social Concept of the Present Civilization, *Tribuna Medica* (September): 19–20.

1973j    Review of *Sociology and Philosophy*, by L. T. Hobhouse, *Sociological Inquiry*, vol. 43 (no. 1): 85–7.

1973k    Review of *Capitalism and Modern Societal Theory: An Analysis of the Writings of Marx, Durkheim, and Max Weber*, by Anthony Giddens, *American Political Science Review*, vol. 67 (no. 4): 1358–60.

1974a    The University 'Bundle': A Study of the Balance Between Differentiation and Integration, *Public Higher Education in California: Growth, Structural Change, and Conflict*, Neil J. Smelser and Gabriel Almond (eds), Berkeley: University of California Press.

1974b    Review of *A God Within*, by René Dubos, *Commonweal*, vol. 100 (no. 2): 42–4.

1974c    The Institutional Function in Organization Theory, *Organization and Administrative Sciences*, vol. 5 (no. 1): 3–16. Address presented at the Comparative Administrative Research Institute, Kent State University (May 1974).

1974d    Sigmund Freud, *The Interpretation of Dreams, Daedalus* (special issue), vol. 103 (no. 1): 91–6.

1974e    The Life and Work of Emile Durkheim. Emile Durkheim, *Sociology and Philosophy* (reprint ed.), New York, Free Press, pp. xliii–lxx.

1974f    Review of *Ideology and Social Knowledge*, by Harold J. Bershady, *Sociological Inquiry*, vol. 44 (no. 3): 215–21. Reprinted as part of Chapter 6 in *Social Systems and the Evolution of Action Theory* (1977).

1974g    Review of *Social Organization: A General Systems and Role Theory Perspective*, by Alvin L. Bertrand, *Social Forces*, vol. 53 (no. 1): 126–7.

1974h    Comment on 'Current Folklore in the Criticisms of Parsonian Action Theory', by Turner and Beeghley, *Sociological Inquiry*, vol. 44 (no. 1): 55–8.

1974i    'Religion in post industrial America: the problem of secularization', *Social Research*, vol. 41, pp. 193–225.

1975a    Pareto's Approach to the Construction of a Theory of the Social Systems, Rome, Accademia Nazionale dei Lincei. Address presented at the International Conference on Vilfredo Pareto (October 1973).

1975b    The Present Status of 'Structural-Functional' Theory. *The Idea of Social Structure*, Lewis A. Coser (ed.), New York, Harcourt Brace Jovanovich. Reprinted in *Social Systems and the Evolution of Action Theory* (1977), Chapter 4.

1975c    The Sick Role and the Role of the Physician Reconsidered, *Millbank Memorial Fund Quarterly*, vol. 53 (no. 3): 257–78. Reprinted in *Action Theory and the Human Condition* (1978).

1975d    Social Structure and the Symbolic Media of Interchange, *Approaches to the Study of Social Structure*, Peter M. Blau (ed.), New York, Free Press. Reprinted in *Social Systems and the Evolution of Action Theory* (1977), Chapter 9.

1975e    Some Theoretical Considerations on the Nature and Trends of Ethnicity, *Ethnicity: Theory and Experience*, Nathan Glazer and Daniel P. Moynihan (eds), Cambridge, Mass., Harvard University Press. Reprinted in *Social Systems and the Evolution of Action Theory* (1977), Chapter 13.

1975f    Commentary on 'Classic on Classic: Parsons' Interpretation of Durkheim', by Whitney Pope and 'Moral Freedom through Understanding in Durkheim', by Jere Cohen, *American Sociological Review*, vol. 40 (no. 1): 106–10.

1975g    Commentary on 'De-Parsonizing Weber: A Critique of Parsons' Interpretation of Weber's Sociology', by Cohen, Hazelrigg, and Pope, *American Sociological Review*, vol. 40 (no. 5): 666–9.

1975h    Commentary on 'A Radical Analysis of Welfare Economics and Individual Development', by Herbert Gintis, *Quarterly Journal of Economics*, vol. 89: 280–90.

1975i    Comment on 'Parsons as a Symbolic Interactionist', by Jonathan Turner, *Sociological Inquiry*, vol. 45 (no. 1): 62–5.

1976a    Some Considerations on the Growth of the American System of Higher Education and Research, *Culture and Its Creators: Essays in Honor of Edward Shils*, T. N. Clark and J. Ben-David (eds), Chicago: University of Chicago Press. Reprinted in *Action Theory and the Human Condition* (1978).

1976b   The Sociology and Economics of Clarence E. Ayers, *Science and Ceremony: The Institutional Economics of Clarence E. Ayers*, Culbertson and Briet (eds), Austin, University of Texas Press.

1976c   Social Stratification. Professions. *Enciclopedia italiana*, Vincenzo Cappelletti (ed.), Rome.

1976d   Reply to Cohen, Hazelrigg, and Pope, with Special Reference to Their Statement 'On the Divergence of Weber and Durkheim: A Critique of Parsons' Convergence Thesis', *American Sociological Review*, vol. 41 (no. 2): 361–4.

1976e   A Few Considerations on the Place of Rationality in Modern Culture and Society, *Revue européenne des sciences sociales et cahiers Vilfredo Pareto* (special issue), vol. 14 (nos 38–39).

1976f   Vico and History, *Social Research*, vol. 43 (no. 4): 881–5. Social Science: The Public Disenchantment, *American Scholar*. (Autumn): 580–1.

1976g   Faculty Teaching Goals, 1968–1973 (co-authored with Gerald M. Platt and Rita Kirshstein), *Social Problems*, vol. 24 (no. 2): 298–307.

1977a   *The Evolution of Societies* (edited, with an introduction, by Jackson Toby), Englewood Cliffs, Prentice-Hall.

1977b   *Social Systems and the Evolution of Action Theory*, New York, Free Press.

1977c   A 1974 Retrospective Perspective: Alfred Schutz, Talcott Parsons, *Zur Theorie Sozialen Handelns, Ein Briefwechsel*. Herausgegeben und Eingeleitet von Walter M. Sprondel, Frankfurt am Main, Surkamp Verlag.

1977d   Comment on Burger's Critique: A Reply to Thomas Burger, 'Talcott Parsons, the Problem of Order in Society, and the Program of an Analytical Sociology', both in *American Journal of Sociology*, vol. 83, (no. 2): 335–9 and 320–34.

1977e   Two Cases of Social Deviance: Addiction to Heroin, Addiction to Power (co-authored with Dean R. Gerstein), *Deviance and Social Change*, Edwin Sagarin (ed.), Beverly Hills, Calif., Sage Publications.

1978a   Parsons, T., 'Health and disease: a sociological and action perspective', *Encyclopedia of Bioethics*, New York, Free Press.

1978b   Parsons, T., 'Death in the Western World', in T. Parsons, *Action Theory and the Human Condition*, pp. 331–51.

1978c   Parsons, T., *Action Theory and the Human Condition*, New York, Free Press.

1978d   Parsons, T., 'Law as an Intellectual "Stepchild"', *Sociological Enquiry*, vol. 47 (nos 3–4).

1978e    Parsons, T., 'Epilogue' in E. B. Gallagher (ed.), *The Doctor–Patient Relationship*.

1981a    Parsons, T., 'Revisiting the classics throughout a long career' in Buford Rhea (ed.), *The Future of the Sociological Classics*, London, pp. 183–94.

1981b    Parsons, T., 'Letter to Edward Tiryakian', *Sociological Enquiry*, vol. 51, pp. 35–6.

# General Bibliography

Abercrombie, N. (1980), *Class, Structure and Knowledge*, Oxford: O.U.P.

Abercrombie, N., Hill, S. and Turner, B. S. (1980), *The Dominant Ideology Thesis*, London: Allen & Unwin.

Abercrombie, N., Hill, S. and Turner, B. S. (1983), 'Determinacy and Indeterminacy in the Theory of Ideology', *New Left Review*, No. 142, pp. 55–66.

Adriaansens, H. P. M. (1980), *Talcott Parsons and the Conceptual Dilemma*, London: Routledge & Kegan Paul.

Alexander, J. (1982), *Theoretical Logic in Sociology. Positivism, Pre-suppositions and Current Controversies*, vol. 1, London: Routledge & Kegan Paul.

Alexander, J. (1983), *Theoretical Logic in Sociology. The Antimonies of Classical Thought: Marx and Durkheim*, vol. 2, London: Routledge & Kegan Paul.

Alexander, J. (1984), *Theoretical Logic in Sociology, The Modern Reconstruction of Classical Thought: Talcott Parsons*, vol. 4, London: Routledge & Kegan Paul.

Almond, G. A. and Coleman, J. S. (1960), *The Politics of the Developing Areas*, Princeton, New Jersey: Princeton Uni. Press.

Althusser, L. (1969), *For Marx*, Harmondsworth: Penguin Books.

Althusser, L. (1971), *Lenin and Philosophy and Other Essays*, London: New Left Books.

Althusser, L. and Balibar, E. (1970), *Reading Capital*, London: New Left Books.

Arato, A. and Cohen, J. (1982), 'The Peace Movement and Western European Sovereignty', *Telos*, vol. 51, pp. 158–71.

Arendt, H. (1958), *The Origins of Totalitarianism*, London: Allen & Unwin.

Ariès, P. (1981), *The Hour of our Death*, New York: Knopf.

Austin, J. L. (1962), *How To Do Things With Words*, Oxford: O.U.P.

Ayres, C. (1957), Review 'Economy and Society', *American Economic Review*, vol. 41, pp. 686–8.

Bakke, E. W. (1933), *The Unemployed Man*, London: Nisbet.

Baran, P. and Sweezy, P. (1966), *Monopoly Capital*, New York: Monthly Review.

Barber, B. (1957), *Social Stratification, a comparative analysis of structure and process*, New York and Burlingame: Harcourt, Brace & World.

Baum, R. C. (1982), 'A revised interpretive approach to the religious significance of death in western societies', *Sociological Analysis*, vol. 43, pp. 327–50.

Baumol, W. (1964), *Business Behaviour, Value and Growth*, London: Macmillan.

Bell, C. and Newby, H. (eds) (1974), *The Sociology of Community*, London: Cass.

Bell, D. (1976), *The Cultural Contradictions of Capitalism*, London: Heinemann.

Bellah, R. (1970), *Beyond Belief*, New York: Harper & Row.

Bellah, R. (1973), 'Introduction' to *Emile Durkheim on Morality and Society*, Chicago: University of Chicago Press.

Bellah, R. (1975), *The Broken Covenant: American Civil Religion in a Time of Trial*, New York: Seabury Press.

Bellah, R. (1980), 'The Five Civil Religions of Italy' in R. Bellah and P. Hammond, *Varieties of Civil Religion*, New York: Harper & Row.

Bendix, R. (1969), *Max Weber an Intellectual Portrait*, London: Methuen.

Bensusan-Butt, D. (1978), *On Economic Man*, Canberra: ANU Press.

Berger, P. L. (1969), *The Social Reality of Religion*, London: Faber & Faber.

Berger, P. L. and Luckmann, T. (1966), *The Social Construction of Reality*, London: Doubleday.

Bershady, H. J. (1973), *Ideology and Social Knowledge*, Oxford: Basil Blackwell.

Black, M. (ed.) (1971), *The Social Theories of Talcott Parsons*, Englewood Cliffs, N.J.: Prentice-Hall.

Blackburn, R. (1967), 'The Unequal Society' in R. Blackburn and A. Cockburn (eds), *The Incompatibles: Trade Union Militancy and the Consensus*, Harmondsworth: Penguin.

Bleicher, J. (1982), 'System and meaning, comments on the work of Niklas Luhmann', *Theory, Culture and Society*, vol. 1, pp. 49–52.

Bottomore, T. (1984), *The Frankfurt School*, London: Tavistock.

Bourricaud, F. (1981), *The Sociology of Talcott Parsons*, Chicago: University of Chicago Press.

Braverman, H. (1974), *Labour and Monopoly Capital*, New York: Monthly Review Press.

Bronfenbrenner, M. (1966), 'Trends, Cycles and Fads in Economic Writing', *American Economic Review*, Papers and Proceedings, vol. 56, pp. 538–52.

Brubaker, R. (1984), *The Limits of Rationality*, London: Allen & Unwin.

Bryant, C. (1983), 'Who now reads Parsons?', *Sociological Review*, vol. 31, pp. 337–49.

Buchanan, J. and Tulloch, G. (1962), *The Calculus of Consent*, Ann Arbor: University of Michigan Press.

Burger, T. (1977), 'Talcott Parsons, the problem of order in society, and the program of an analytical sociology', *American Journal of Sociology*, vol. 83, pp. 320–34.

Bush, P. D. (1981), 'Radical Individualism vs Institutionalism', *American Journal of Economics and Sociology*, vol. 40, pp. 139–46.

Campbell, J. D. (1978), 'The child in the sick role: contributions of age, sex, parental status and parental values', *Journal of Health and Social Behaviour*, vol. 19, pp. 35–51.

Cancian, F. (1960), 'Functional Analysis of Change', *American Sociological Review*, vol. 25, pp. 818–26.

Caplan, A. L. (1981), 'The "Unnaturalness" of aging – a sickness unto death', in A. L. Caplan, H. T. Engelhardt and J. McCarthy (eds), *Concepts of Health and Disease, interdisciplinary perspectives*, Reading, Mass: Addison-Wesley, pp. 725–37.

Cartwright, A. and O'Brien, M. (1978), 'Social class variations in health care and in the nature of general practice consultations', in D. Tuckett and J. M. Kaufert (eds), *Basic Readings in Medical Sociology*, London: Tavistock, pp. 89–97.

Chamberlain, C. (1983), *Class Consciousness in Australia*, Sydney: Allen & Unwin.

Chinoy, E. (1965), *Automobile Workers and the American Dream*, Boston: Beacon Press.

Chodorow, N. (1978), *The Reproduction of Mothering*, Berkeley, University of California Press.

Clarke, J. N. (1983), 'Sexism, feminism and medicalism: a decade review of literature on gender and illness', *Sociology of Health and Illness*, vol. 5, pp. 62–82.

Coats, A. W. (1976), 'Economics and psychology; the death and resurrection of a research programme', in S. J. Latsis (ed.) *Method and Appraisal in Economics*, Cambridge: Cambridge University Press, pp. 43–64.

Cockerham, W. C. (1982), *Medical Sociology*, Englewood Cliffs, N.J.: Prentice-Hall.

Cohen, G. A. (1978), *Karl Marx's Theory of History*, Oxford: Oxford U.P.

Cohen, J., Hazelrigg, L. and Pope, W. (1975), 'De-Parsonising Weber: a critique of Parsons's interpretation of Weber's sociology', *American Sociological Review*, vol. 40, pp. 229–41.

Dahrendorf, R. (1968), *Essays in the Theory of Society*, London: Routledge & Kegan Paul.

Davis, K. (1959), 'The myth of functional analysis in sociology and anthropology', *American Sociological Review*, vol. 24, pp. 757–72.

Dawe, A. (1970), 'The two sociologies', *British Journal of Sociology*, vol. 21, pp. 207–18.

Debray, R. (1977), 'Marxism and the Nation', *New Left Review*, vol. 105, pp. 25–41.

Demsetz, H. (1967), 'Toward a Theory of Property Rights', *American Economic Review*, Papers and Proceedings, vol. 57, pp. 347–59.

Denzin, N. K. (1969), 'Symbolic interactionism and ethnomethodology: a proposed synthesis', *American Sociological Review*, vol. 34, pp. 922–34.

Dore, R. (1967), *Aspects of Social Change in Modern Japan*, Princeton, N.J.: Princeton University Press.

Dore, R. (1973), *British Factory, Japanese Factory*, London: Allen & Unwin.

Dore, R. (1983), 'Goodwill and the spirit of market capitalism', *British Journal of Sociology*, vol. 34, pp. 459–582.

Douglas, M. (1966), *Purity and Danger*, London: Routledge & Kegan Paul.

Douglas, M. and Isherwood, B. (1979), *The World of Goods*, London: Allen Lane.

Downs, A. (1957), *Economic Theory of Democracy*, New York: Harper.

Doyal, L. (1979), *The Political Economy of Health*, London: Pluto Press.

Dunlop, J. T. (1958) *Industrial Relations Systems*, New York: Holt.

Durkheim, E. (1978), 'Crime and social health' in M. Traugott (ed.), *Emile Durkheim on Institutional Analysis*, Chicago and London: Chicago U.P., pp. 181–90.

Eden, R. (1983), *Political Leadership and Nihilism, A Study of Weber and Nietzsche*, Tampa: University of Florida Press.

Edwards, R. C., Reich, M. and Gordon, D. M. (eds) (1973), *Labour Market Segmentation*, Lexington: Heath.

Eisenstadt, S. N. (1956), *From Generation to Generation*, Chicago: Free Press.

Eldridge, J. (1983), *C. Wright Mills*, London: Tavistock.

Etzioni, A. (1961), *A Comparative Analysis of Complex Organizations*, New York: Free Press.

Etzioni, A. and Etzioni, E. (eds) (1964), *Social Change, Sources, Patterns and Consequences*, New York: Basic Books.

Feher, F. and Heller, A. (1984), 'From red to green', *Telos*, vol. 59, pp. 35–44.

Feldman, W. and Moore, W. (1969), 'Industrialisation and industrialism' in W. A. France and W. H. Form (eds), *Comparative Perspectives on Industrial Society*, New York: Little, Brown.

Fenoaltea (1975), 'Authority, efficiency and agricultural organisation in medieval England and beyond', *Journal of Economic History*, vol. 35, pp. 693–718.

Flanders, A. (1965), *Industrial Relations*, London: Faber & Faber.

Flinn, M. W. (1961), 'Social theory and the industrial revolution' in T. Burns and S. B. Saul (eds), *Social Theory and Economic Change*, London: Tavistock.

Foucault, M. (1973), *The Birth of the Clinic, an Archaeology of Medical Perception*, London: Tavistock.

Fox, R. (1967), *Kinship and Marriage*, Harmondsworth: Penguin.

Friedman, A. L. (1977), *Industry and Labour*, London: Macmillan.

Friedman, M. (1957), *A Theory of the Consumption Function*, Princeton, N.J.: Princeton U.P.

Friedson, E. (1970), *Profession of Medicine*, New York: Harper & Row.

Gallagher, E. B. (1976), 'Lines of reconstruction and extension in the Parsonian sociology of illness', *Social Science and Medicine*, vol. 10, pp. 207–18.

Gay, W. C. (1978), 'Probability in the social sciences: a critique of Weber and Schutz', *Human Studies*, vol. 1, pp. 16–37.

Gerth, H. and Mills, C. Wright (1954), *Character and Social Structure, the Psychology of Social Institutions*, London: Routledge & Kegan Paul.

Gerth, H. H. and Mills, C. Wright (1961), *From Max Weber: Essays in Sociology*, London: Routledge & Kegan Paul.

Giddens, A. (1968), '"Power" in the recent writings of Talcott Parsons', *Sociology*, vol. 2, pp. 257–72.

Giddens, A. (1979), *Central Problems in Sociological Theory*, London: Macmillan.

Godelier, M. (1971), *Rationality and Irrationality in Economics*, New York: Monthly Review Press.

Goffman, E. (1961), *Asylums*, Harmondsworth: Penguin Books.

Goldthorpe, J. H. et. al. (1968), *The Affluent Worker: Industrial Attitudes*, Cambridge: Cambridge University Press.

Goldthorpe, J. H. (1978), 'The current inflation: towards a sociological account' in F. Hirsch and J. H. Goldthorpe (eds), *The Political Economy of Inflation*, London: Martin Robertson, pp. 186–213.

Goldthorpe, J. (1982), 'On the service class, its formation and future' in A. Giddens and G. MacKenzie (eds), *Social Class and the Division of Labour*, Cambridge: Cambridge University Press.

Gonos, G. (1977), '"Situation" versus "frame" – the "interactionist" and the "structuralist" analyses of everyday life', *American Sociological Review*, vol. 42, pp. 854–67.

Gordon, H. S. (1954), 'The economic theory of a common property resource', *Journal of Political Economy*, vol. 62, pp. 124–42.

Gorz, A. (1982), *Farewell to the Working Class*, London: Pluto.

Gould, C. C. (1978), *Marx's Social Ontology*, Cambridge, Mass.: M.I.T. Press.

Gouldner, A. W. (1959), 'Reciprocity and autonomy in functional theory' in L. Gross (ed.), *Symposium on Sociological Theory*, New York: Basic Books, pp. 241–70.

Gouldner, A. W. (1965), *Enter Plato, Classical Greece and the Origins of Social Theory*, London: Routledge & Kegan Paul.

Gouldner, A. W. (1971), *The Coming Crisis of Western Sociology*, London: Heinemann.

Gouldner, A. W. (1980), *The Two Marxisms*, New York: Seabury Press.

Gove, W. R. and Tudor, J. F. (1973), 'Adult sex roles and mental illness', *American Journal of Sociology*, vol. 78, pp. 813–35.

Grathoff, R. (ed.) (1978), *The Theory of Sound Action*, Indiana University Press.

Gray, J. (1982), 'Introduction' and 'Conclusion' in J. Gray and G. White (eds), *China's New Development Strategy*, New York: Academic Press.

Habermas, J. (1971), 'Technology and science as ideology' in *Toward a Rational Society*, London: Heinemann.

Habermas, J. (1976), *Legitimation Crisis*, London: Heinemann.

Hacker, A. (1964), 'Sociology and ideology' in M. Black (ed.), *The Social Theories of Talcott Parsons*, Englewood Cliffs, New Jersey: Prentice-Hall, pp. 289–310.

Hagen, E. E. (1962), *On the Theory of Social Change*, Homewood, Ill: Dorsey Press.

Hagen, E. E. (1967), 'British personality and the industrial revolution: the historical evidence' in T. Burns and S. B. Saul (eds), *Social Theory and Economic Change*, London: Tavistock.

Hall, J. R. (1981), 'Max Weber's methodological strategy and comparative life world phenomenology', *Human Studies*, vol. 4.

Hamilton, P. (1983), *Talcott Parsons*, London and New York: Tavistock.

Hart, N. (1983), 'The sick role' in M. Mann (ed.), *Student Encyclopedia of Sociology*, London: Macmillan, pp. 352–4.

Hawthorn, G. (1976), *Enlightenment and Despair*, Cambridge: Cambridge University Press.

Held, D. (1980), *Introduction to Critical Theory, Horkheimer to Habermas*, London: Hutchinson.

Heller, A. (1976), *The Theory of Need in Marx*, London: Allison & Busby.

Henderson, L. J. (1935), 'Physician and patient as a social system', *New England Journal of Medicine*, vol. 212, pp. 819–23.

Henderson, L. J. (1936), 'The practice of medicine as applied sociology', *Transactions of the Association of American Physicians*, vol. 51, pp. 8–15.

Hepworth, M. and Turner, B. S. (1982), *Confession, Studies in Deviance and Religion*, London: Routledge & Kegan Paul.

Heraud, B. (1979), *Sociology in the Professions*, London: Open Books.

Herzlich, C. (1973), *Health and Illness, a Social Psychological Analysis*, London: Academic Press.

Hicks, J. (1956), *A Revision of Demand Theory*, Oxford: Oxford University Press.

Hilferding, R. (1910), *Das Finanz Kapital*, Vienna; London: Routledge & Kegan Paul, 1981.

Hill, S. (1976), *The Dockers*, London: Heinemann.

Hinkle, R. C. (1980), *Founding Theory of American Sociology 1881–1915*, London: Routledge & Kegan Paul.

Hirschman, A. O. (1970), *Exit, Voice and Loyalty*, Cambridge, Mass.: Harvard University Press.

Hollis, M. (1979), 'Introduction' in F. Hahn and M. Hollis (eds), *Philosophy and Economic Theory*, Oxford: Oxford University Press.

Holmwood, J. (1983a), 'Talcott Parsons and the development of his system', *British Journal of Sociology*, vol. 34, pp. 573–90.

Holmwood, J. (1983b), 'Action, system and norm in the action frame of reference: Talcott Parsons and his critics', *Sociological Review*, vol. 31, pp. 310–36.

Holton, R. J. (1978), 'The crowd in history: some problems of theory and method', *Social History*, vol. 3, pp. 219–33.

Holton, R. J. (1981), 'History and sociology in the work of E. P. Thompson', *Australian and New Zealand Journal of Sociology*, vol. 17, pp. 46–55.

Horowitz, I. L. (ed.) (1965), *The New Sociology, Essays in Social Science and Social Theory in Honour of C. Wright Mills*, New York: Galaxy.

Hoselitz, B. (1952), 'Social structure and economic growth', *Economics Internazionale*, vol. 6, pp. 52–77.

Hoselitz, B. F. and Moore, W. E. (1960), *Industrialization and Society*, The Hague: Martinus Nijhoff.

Hutchison, T. W. (1957), Review 'Economy of Society', *Economica*, vol. 24, pp. 376–7.

Inglis, B. (1979), *Natural Medicine*, London: Fontana.

Inglis, B. (1981), *The Diseases of Civilisation*, London: Hodder & Stoughton.

Jay, M. (1973), *The Dialectical Imagination*, London: Heinemann.

Johnson, E. S. and Williamson, J. B. (1980), *Growing Old: The Social Problems of Aging*, New York: Holt, Rinehart & Winston.

Johnson, T. J. (1972), *Professions and Power*, London: Macmillan

Johnson, T. (1982), 'The professions in the class structure' in R. Scase (ed.), *Industrial Society: Class, Cleavage and Control*, London: Allen & Unwin, pp. 93–110.

Jules-Rosette, B. (1980), 'Talcott Parsons and the phenomenological tradition in sociology: an unresolved debate', *Human Studies*, vol. 3, pp. 311–30.

Kahn, H. (1964), *Repercussions of Redundancy*, London: Allen & Unwin.

Kapferer, B. (1983), *A Celebration of Demons*, Indiana University Press.

Katona, G. (1964), *The Mass Consumption Society*, New York: McGraw-Hill.

Kaysen, C. (1957), 'The social significance of the modern corporation', *American Economic Review*, pp. 311–19.

Kellner, D. (1983), 'Critical theory, commodities and the consumer society', *Theory, Culture and Society*, vol. 1, pp. 66–83.

Kerr, C. et al. (1960), *Industrialism and Industrial Man*, London: Heinemann.

King, L. S. (1982), *Medical Thinking, a Historical Preface*, Princeton University Press.

Kolb, W. L. (1954/5), 'The social structure and function of cities', *Economic Development and Cultural Change*, vol. 3, pp. 30–46.

Kubler-Ross, E. (1969), *On Death and Dying*, London: Tavistock.

Lane, D. (1981), *Leninism: A Sociological Interpretation*, Cambridge: Cambridge University Press.

Lassman, P. (1980), 'Value relations and general theory: Parsons' critique of Weber', *Zeitschrift fur Soziologie*, vol. 9, no. 1.

Latsis, S. J. (1972), 'Situational determinism in economics', *British Journal for the Philosophy of Science*, vol. 23, pp. 207–45.

Lazarsfeld, P. F. (1973), *Main Trends in Sociology*, London: George Allen & Unwin.

Lechner (1984), 'Parsons and the common culture theses', *Theory, Culture and Society*, vol. 2, pp. 71–84.

Leiberstein, H. (1976), *Beyond Economic Man*, Cambridge, Mass.: Harvard University Press.

Lemert, E. M. (1967), *Human Deviance, Social Problems and Social Control*, Englewood Cliffs, N.J.: Prentice Hall.

Lenin, V. (1970), *Imperialism: the Highest Stage of Capitalism*, Moscow: Progress.

Levine, D. (1971), *Georg Simmel: On Individuality and Social Forms*, Chicago: University of Chicago Press.

Levine, S. and Kozloff, M. A. (1978), 'The sick role: assessment and overview', *Annual Review of Sociology*, vol. 4, pp. 317–43.

Lipset, M., Trow, M. A. and Coleman, J. S. (1956), *Union Democracy*, Chicago: Free Press.

Lockwood, D. (1956), 'Some remarks on the social system', *British Journal of Sociology*, vol. 7, pp. 134–45.

Lockwood, D. (1974), 'For T. H. Marshall', *Sociology*, vol. 8, pp. 363–7.

Löwith, K. (1932), *Karl Marx and Max Weber*, George Allen & Unwin, 1982.

Luckmann, T. (1967), *The Invisible Religion*, London: Macmillan.

Lukàcs, G. (1971), *History and Class Consciousness*, London: Merlin Press.

Lukes, S. (1973), *Emile Durkheim*, Harmondsworth: Penguin Books.

Lyman, S. M. (1978), 'The acceptance, rejection and reconstruction of histories' in R. H. Brown and S. M. Lyman (eds), *Structure, Consciousness and History*, Cambridge: Cambridge University Press.

MacAulay, S. (1963), 'Non-contractual relations in business: a preliminary study', *American Sociological Review*, vol. 28, pp. 55–67.

MacIntyre, A. (1971), *Against the Self-Images of the Age*, London: Duckworth.

MacIntyre, A. (1981), *After Virtue. A Study in Moral Theory*, London: Duckworth.

McClelland, D. C. (1961), *The Achieving Society*, Princeton: Van Nostrand.

Mandel, E. (1970), *Europe versus America? Contradictions of Imperialism*, London: New Left Books.

Mandel, E. (1975), *Late Capitalism*, London: New Left Books.

Mann, M. (1970), 'The social cohesion of liberal democracy', *American Sociological Review*, vol. 35, pp. 423–39.

Mann, M. (1984), 'Capitalism and militarism' in M. Shaw (ed.), *War, State and Society*, London: Macmillan, pp. 25–46.

Marcuse, H. (1964), *One Dimensional Man*, London: Routledge & Kegan Paul.

Markus, G. (1978), *Marxism and Anthropology*, Assen: van Gorcum.

Marshall, A. (1885), *The Present Position of Economics*, London: Macmillan.

Marshall, G. (1984), 'On the sociology of women's unemployment, its neglect and significance', *Sociological Review*, vol. 32, pp. 234–59.

Marshall, T. H. (1950), *Citizenship and Social Class*, Cambridge: Cambridge University Press.

Marshall, T. H. (1977), *Class, Citizenship and Social Development*, London: Heinemann.

Marx, K. and Engels, F. (1962), 'Manifesto of the Communist Party' in *Selected Works*, vol. 1, Moscow: Progress Publishers.

Marx, K. (1970), *Capital*, vol. 1, London: Lawrence & Wishart.

Mayr, E. (1974), 'Teleological and teleonomic – a new analysis' in Marx Wartovsky (ed.), *Method and Metaphysics, Methodological and Historical Essays in the Natural and Social Sciences*, Leiden, pp. 78–104.

Mechanic, D. (1977), 'Some social aspects of the medical malpractice dilemma' in *Medical Malpractice*, the Duke Law Journal Symposium, Cambridge, Mass., pp. 1–18.

Menzies, K. (1976), *Talcott Parsons and the Social Imagery of Man*, London: Routledge & Kegan Paul.

Merleau-Ponty, M. (1978), 'The crisis of understanding' in *The Primacy of Perception, Consciousness and History*, Cambridge: Cambridge University Press.

Merton, R. K. (1963), *Social Theory and Social Structure*, Glencoe, Ill.: Free Press.

Mills, C. Wright (1940), 'Situated actions and vocabularies of motive', *American Sociological Review*, vol. 5, pp. 904–13.

Mills, C. W. (1956), *White Collar*, New York: Oxford University Press.

Mills, C. Wright (1959), *The Sociological Imagination*, Harmondsworth: Penguin Books.

Mills, C. Wright (1960), *The Causes of World War III*, New York: Ballantine.

Mitchell, J. (1974), *Psychoanalysis and Feminism*, London: Allen Lane.

Moore, B. (1967), *Social Origins of Dictatorship and Democracy: Lord and Peasant in the Making of the Modern World*, Harmondsworth: Penguin Press.

Moore, B. (1970), *Reflections on the Causes of Human Misery and Upon Certain Proposals to Eliminate them*, London: Allen Lane.

Moore, W. E. (1979), 'Functionalism' in T. Bottomore and R. Nisbet (eds), *A History of Sociological Analysis*, pp. 321–61, London: Heinemann.

Moorhouse, H. F. (1983), 'American automobiles and workers dreams', *Sociological Review*, vol. 31, pp. 403–426.

Mumford, E. and Banks, O. (1967), *The Computer and the Clerk*, London: Routledge & Kegan Paul.

Münch, R. (1981), 'Talcott Parsons and the theory of action, 1. The Structure of the Kantian core', *American Journal of Sociology*, vol. 86, pp. 709–40.

Nakane, C. (1973), *Japanese Society*, Harmondsworth: Penguin Books.

Natanson, M. (1978), Foreward in R. Grathoff (ed.), *The Theory of Social Action*, Indiana University Press.

Navarro, V. (1976), *Medicine under Capitalism*, New York: Prodist.

Nell, E. (1972), 'Economics; the revival of political economy' in R. Blackburn (ed.), *Ideology in Social Science*, Glasgow: Fontana/Collins.

Nettl, R. and Robertson, R. (1968), *International System and the Modernization of Societies*, New York: Basic Books.

Nisbet, R. (1967), *The Sociological Tradition*, London: Heinemann.

Nisbet, R. (1969), *Social Change and History*, New York: Oxford University Press.

North, D. C. and Thomas, R. P. (1973), *The Rise of the Western World*, Cambridge: Cambridge University Press.

O'Dea, T. F. (1976), 'The "Emergence-Construction Process" and the Theory of Action' in J. Loubser et al. (eds), *Explorations in General Theory in Social Science*, vol. 1, New York: Free Press, pp. 277–294.

Parkin, F. (1972), *Class Inequality and the Political Order*, London: Paladin.

Parkin, F. (1979), *Marxism and Class Theory: A Bourgeois Critique*, London: Tavistock.

Pearson, H. W. (1957), 'Parsons and Smelser on the economy' in K. Polanyi et al., *Trade and Market in the Early Empires*, Chicago: Free Press, pp. 307–19.

Phillipson, M. (1974), *Understanding Crime and Delinquency*, Chicago: Aldine.

Piore, M. (1979), *Birds of Passage*, Cambridge: Cambridge University Press.

Polanyi, K. (1957), 'The Economy as Instituted Process' in Polanyi, K., Arensberg, C. M. and Pearson, H. W. (eds), *Trade and Market in the Early Empires*, Chicago: Free Press, pp. 243–70.

Polanyi, K. (1977), *The Livelihood of Man*, New York: Academic Press.

Pope, W. (1973), 'Classic on classic: Parsons's interpretation of Durkheim', *American Sociological Review*, vol. 38, pp. 399–415.

Poulantzas, N. (1973), *Political Power and Social Classes*, London: New Left Books.

Poulantzas, N. (1978), *State, Power, Socialism*, London: New Left Books.

Proctor, I. (1980), 'Voluntarism and structural-functionalism in Parsons' early work', *Human Studies*, vol. 3, pp. 311–12.

Reichenbach, H. (1968), *The Rise of Scientific Philosophy*, Berkeley: University of California Press.

Rex, J. (1961), *Key Problems in Sociological Theory*, London: Routledge & Kegan Paul.

Robertson, R. (1982a), 'Parsons on the evolutionary significance of American religion', *Sociological Analysis*, vol. 43, pp. 307–26.

Robertson, R. (1982b), 'Talcott Parsons on religion: a preface', *Sociological Analysis*, vol. 43, pp. 283–6.

Rocher, G. (1974), *Talcott Parsons and American Sociology*, London: Nelson.

Roth, J. (1962), 'Management bias in social science research', *Human Organization*, vol. 21, pp. 47–50.

Roth, G. (1984), 'Max Weber's Ethics and the Peace Movement Today', *Theory and Society*, vol. 13, pp. 491–511.

Saks, M. (1983), 'Removing the blinkers? A critique of recent contributions to the sociology of professions, *Sociological Review*, vol. 31, pp. 1–21.

Savage, P. (1981), *The Theories of Talcott Parsons; the social relations of action*, London: Macmillan.

Scheff, T. (1966), *Being Mentally Ill*, London: Weidenfeld & Nicolson.

Schmalenbach, H. (1982), *On Society and Experience*, eds. G. Luschen and G. P. Stone, University of Chicago Press.

Schumpeter, J. A. (1961), *Capitalism, Socialism and Democracy*, London: Allen & Unwin.

Schutz, A. (1962), *Collected Papers*, vol. I, ed. Maurice Natanson, The Hague: Martinus Nijhoff.

Schutz, A. (1964), *Collected Papers*, vol. II, *The Problem of Rationality in the Social World*, The Hague: Martinus Nijhoff.

Schutz, A. (1976), *The Phenomenology of the Social World*, translated by George Walsh and Frederick Lehnert, London: Heinemann (originally published in 1932).

Scott, J. F. (1963), 'The changing foundation of the Parsonian action scheme', *American Sociological Review*, vol. 29, pp. 716–35.

Seckler, D. (1975), *Thorstein Veblen and the Institutionalists*, London: Macmillan.

Sen, A. K. (1976), 'Rational fools: a critique of the behavioural foundations of economic theory', *Philosophy and Public Affairs*, vol. 6, pp. 317–44.

Sennett, R. (1977), *The Fall of Public Man*, Cambridge: Cambridge University Press.

Servan-Shreiber, J. J. (1968), *The American Challenge*, London: Hamilton.

Shaw, W. H. (1978), *Marx's Theory of History*, London: Hutchinson.

Shneidman, E. S. (ed.) (1967), *Essays in Self-Destruction*, New York: Science House.

Simon, H. A. (1952), 'A behavioural model of rational choice', *Quarterly Journal of Economics*, vol. 69, pp. 98–118.

Smelser, N. J. (1958/9), 'A comparative view of exchange systems', *Economic Development and Cultural Change*, vol. 7, pp. 173–82.

Smelser, N. J. (1959), *Social Change in the Industrial Revolution*, Chicago: Chicago University Press.

Smelser, N. J. (1962), *Theory of Collective Behaviour*, London: Routledge & Kegan Paul.

Smelser, N. J. (1963), *The Sociology of Economic Life*, Englewood Cliffs, N.J.: Prentice Hall.

Smith, A. D. (1973), *The Concept of Social Change*, London: Routledge & Kegan Paul.

Steedman, I. (1977), *Marx After Sraffa*, London: New Left Books.

Steedman, I. and Sweezy, P. (eds) (1981), *The Value Controversy*, London: New Left Books.

Stinchcombe, A. L. (1968), *Constructing Social Theories*, New York.

Strauss, R. (1957), 'The nature and status of medical sociology', *American Sociological Review*, vol. 22, pp. 200–4.

Strong, P. M. (1983), 'The importance of being Erving. Erving Goffman 1922–1982', *Sociology of Health and Illness*, vol. 5, pp. 345–55.

Sztompka, P. (1974), *System and Function: toward a theory of society*, New York: Academic Press.

Tawney, R. H. (1960), *Religion and the Rise of Capitalism*, London: Murray.

Taylor, I., Walton, P. and Young, J. (1973), *The New Criminology, for a social theory of deviance*, London: Routledge & Kegan Paul.

Therborn, G. (1980), *The Ideology of Power and the Power of Ideology*, London: Verso.

Thomason, C. B. (1982), *Making Sense of Reification*, London: Macmillan.

Thompson, E. P. (1978), *The Poverty of Theory*, London: Merlin.

Tillich, P. (1952), *The Courage to Be*, New Haven: Yale University Press.

Titmuss, R. M. (1971), *The Gift Relationship*, London: Allen & Unwin.

Tiryakian, E. A. (1980), 'The mythologist and the sociologist', *Mankind Quarterly*, vol. 21, no. 1, Fall, pp. 53–70.

Touraine, A. (1981), *The Voice and the Eye: An analysis of Social Movements*, Cambridge: Cambridge University Press.

Towler, R. (1974), *Homo Religiosus, sociological problems in the study of religion*, London: Constable.

Tumin, M. M. (ed.) (1970), *Readings on Social Stratification*, Englewood Cliffs, N.J.: Prentice-Hall.

Turner, B. S. (1977), 'The structuralist critique of Weber's sociology', *British Journal of Sociology*, vol. 28, pp. 1–16.

Turner, B. S. (1981), *For Weber: Essays on the Sociology of Fate*, London: Routledge & Kegan Paul.

Turner, B. S. (1982), 'Nietzsche, Weber and the devaluation of politics: the problem of state legitimacy', *Sociological Review*, vol. 30, pp. 367–91.

Turner, B. S. (1983), *Religion and Social Theory, a materialist perspective*, London: Heinemann.

Turner, J. H. and Beeghley, L. (1974), 'Current folklore in the criticism of Parsonian action theory', *Sociological Inquiry*, vol. 44, pp. 47–55.

Veatch, R. (1973), 'The medical model, its nature and problems', *The Hastings Center Studies*, vol. 1, pp. 59–76.

Wallerstein, I. (1974, 1980), *The Modern World System*, 2 vols, New York: Academic Press.

Wallerstein, I. (1976), 'A world-system perspective on the Social Sciences', *British Journal of Sociology*, vol. 23, pp. 343–52.

Weber, M. (1947), *The Theory of Social and Economic Organization*; edited and translated by Talcott Parsons, New York: Free Press.

Weber, M. (1950), 'The social causes of the decay of ancient civilization', *Journal of General Education*, vol. 5, pp. 75–88.

Weber, M. (1958), *The City*, translated and edited by Don Martindale and G. Neuwirth, Chicago: Free Press.

Weber, M. (1970), 'The Social Psychology of the World Religions' in H. Gerth and C. W. Mills, *From Max Weber: Essays in Sociology*, London: Routledge & Kegan Paul, pp. 267–301.

Weber, M. (1978), *Economy and Society* (2 vols), Berkeley: University of California Press.

Williams, R. M. (1960), *American Society. A Sociological Interpretation*, New York: Alfred A. Knopf.

Williams, R. (1971), 'Change and stability in values and value systems' in B. Barber and A. Inkeles (eds), *Stability and Social Change*, Boston: Little, Brown, pp. 123–59.

Willis, E. (1983), *Medical Dominance*, Sydney: Allen & Unwin.

Wilson, B. (1970) (ed.), *Rationality*, Oxford: Oxford University Press.

Wilson, T. P. (1971), 'Normative and interpretive paradigms', in J. D. Douglas (ed.), *Understanding Everyday Life: Towards the Reconstruction of Sociological Knowledge*, London: Routledge & Kegan Paul, pp. 57–79.

Winch, P. (1958), *The Idea of a Social Science and its Relation to Philosophy*, London: Routledge & Kegan Paul.

Wirth, L. (1931), 'Clinical sociology', *American Journal of Sociology*, vol. 37, pp. 49–66.

Wootton, B. (1962), *The Social Foundations of Wage Policy*, London: Allen & Unwin.

Worswick, G. D. N. (1957), Review 'Economy and Society', *Economic Journal*, 67, pp. 700–2.

Wrong, D. (1961), 'The oversocialized conception of man in modern sociology', *American Sociological Review*, vol. 26, pp. 183–93.

Zaret, D. (1980), 'From Weber to Parsons and Schutz: the eclipse of history in modern social theory', *American Journal of Sociology*, vol. 85, no. 5, March, pp. 1180–1201.

Zaretsky, E. (1976), *Capitalism, The Family and Personal Life*, London: Pluto Press.

Zborowski, M. (1952), 'Cultural components in responses to pain', *Journal of Social Issues*, vol. 8, pp. 16–30.

Zelizer, V. (1978), 'Human Values and the Market: The Case of Life Insurance and Death in 19th Century America', *American Journal of Sociology*, vol. 84, pp. 511–610.

Zelizer, V. (1979), *Morals and Markets*, New York: Columbia University Press.

Zelizer, V. (1981), 'The price and value of children: the case of children's insurance', *American Journal of Sociology*, vol. 86, no. 5, pp. 1036–56.

Zimmerman, D. H. and Wieder, D. L. (1971), 'Ethnomethodology and the problem of order: comment on Denzin', in J. D. Douglas (ed.), *Understanding Everyday Life*, London: Routledge & Kegan Paul, pp. 285–98.

Zola, I. K. (1966), 'Culture and symptoms: an analysis of patients' presenting complaints', *American Sociological Review*, vol. 31, pp. 615–30.

Zola, I. K. (1972), 'Medicine as an institution of social control', *Sociological Review*, vol. 20, pp. 487–504.

# Index

*This index does not contain a specific reference to Talcott Parsons. Since there is a reference to Parsons and his work on virtually every page of this text, a reference in the index would be superfluous.*